Seeing Politics Differently

A Brief Introduction to Political Sociology

Karen Stanbridge

Howard Ramos

OXFORD

UNIVERSITY PRESS

OXFORD
UNIVERSITY PRESS

Oxford University Press is a department of the University of Oxford.
It furthers the University's objective of excellence in research, scholarship,
and education by publishing worldwide. Oxford is a registered trade mark of
Oxford University Press in the UK and in certain other countries.

Published in Canada by
Oxford University Press
8 Sampson Mews, Suite 204,
Don Mills, Ontario M3C 0H5 Canada

www.oupcanada.com

Library and Archives Canada Cataloguing in Publication

Stanbridge, Karen, 1962–
Seeing politics differently : a brief introduction to political sociology /
Karen Stanbridge & Howard Ramos.

(Themes in Canadian sociology)
Includes bibliographical references and index.
ISBN 978-0-19-543785-0

1. Political sociology—Textbooks. I. Ramos, Howard, 1974– II. Title.
III. Series: Themes in Canadian sociology

JA76.S75 2012   306.2   C2011-906911-3

Cover image: ZenShui, Ale Ventura / PhotoAlto / Getty

Oxford University Press is committed to our environment.
This book is printed on paper which has been certified by the Forest Stewardship Council®.

Printed and bound in Canada.

1 2 3 4 — 15 14 13 12

Contents

Figures, Tables, and Boxes

Preface

If you are a teacher, university professor, or graduate student specializing in political sociology, we should warn you: this book was not really written with you in mind. We do not provide an exhaustive overview of the theories and debates in political sociology. Nor do we introduce innovative new approaches, groundbreaking methods, or original data on unexamined cases. We wrote this book for students new to political sociology, especially the ones who might think that they are 'not that into politics'. Indeed, it was hearing that phrase uttered so many times over the years by students entering our courses that convinced us our main task in this book would be to challenge that view. It also inspired the title, Seeing Politics Differently. We wanted to help students accustomed to 'seeing' politics only in the usual way, as the tiresome, seemingly distant goings-on of politicians, government committees, and political parties, to begin to think about politics as we do: as the ongoing negotiation and contestation of power among members of societies. Viewed in this way, politics is something that surrounds all of us and in which we ourselves continually take part, rather than an interest or activity that we can choose to be 'into' or not.

We believe one of the best ways to develop such a 'lens' on the world is to cultivate a political sociological perspective, and we hope this book goes some way toward helping students do that. Our goal was to write in an accessible but intelligent manner about some of the key works that shape the field and to offer starting points from which readers can branch off to learn more detail on their own if they wish. We do this by presenting a wide range of scholarship in chapters that loosely follow Max Weber's distinction between class, status, and party. We use this typology, not because either of us is a stalwart Weberian, but because we find that its categories encompass neatly the main political sociological approaches to how power is structured and challenged. We also look at some emerging trends in political sociology and examine how they extend the more traditional analyses of material (class), social and cultural (status), and institutional (party) approaches to power. Throughout, we provide contemporary and everyday examples as illustrations.

But if one of our goals was to convince readers that political sociology is an interesting and worthwhile area of study, we were just as motivated by the desire to get people, young readers in particular, to think and act more politically. By this we do not only mean that we would like more of them to vote, although it would be great if they did. Voter turnout for the 2008 election was the lowest in Canadian history, around 59 per cent, but among youth aged eighteen to twenty-four it was much lower, only 37 per cent (Barnes 2010). And although at the time of writing we know that slightly more Canadians voted in 2011, about 61 per cent, nothing has come to light so far to suggest that youth voted any more enthusiastically in the last election than in 2008 (see Chapter 5, Fig 5.1). Yet, to engage youth—indeed anyone—in the political process, it takes more than politicians courting their vote by appealing to their 'interests', or cutting taxes, or utilizing new forms of social media, or any of the usual means that are trotted out to address political indifference. It requires that everyone develop the capacity to see the social world politically and to understand their own political positions relative to others. And this, we would argue, means adopting a political sociological perspective on the world. That is, cultivating skills that can help one to recognize that social relationships are inherently power relationships whose progress and outcomes depend on the different kinds and strengths of power possessed by individuals and groups.

Thinking about societies as composed of people continually exercising and challenging each other's power might seem like an overly confrontational way to look at life. But it is no more or less confrontational than the more common view: individualism. Individualism conceives of the individual as autonomous and self-seeking, free to make her own decisions and act in whatever way she chooses, and thus responsible for her own fate. To be an individual in this regard means to exert one's power and to realize one's will despite the resistance of others, irrespective of its impact on others. Think about some of the sayings that are supposed to describe modern societies: 'It's a dog-eat-dog world out there.' 'Survival of the fittest.' 'Eat or be eaten.' Now that's confrontational! A political sociological perspective encourages the individual to look outside himself to notice the context and conditions in which he is making his decisions, and consider how these enable or hinder his capacity to realize his will. Easier said than done, of course, because, as all sociologists know, the 'looking outside oneself' takes practice. And as all political sociologists know, it can be hard to interpret what you observe as representative of ongoing negotiations over who is permitted to hold power and on what bases. To see the world this way, it is helpful to know, and know how to use, the concepts and different lenses on the world that political sociologists have come up with to disassemble these interactions.

Ultimately, this is what we mean by 'thinking and acting politically' and what we hope this book encourages. By introducing readers to key concepts and perspectives in political sociology, by describing how the scholars who formulated them employed them in their own work, and by using them to analyze events and circumstances that readers confront every day, we want to develop their capacity to use these concepts as tools in the task of recognizing power differentials in their own lives. For it is by developing this capacity—to see social relations as power relations—that we cultivate our social literacy, our ability to 'read' and critically assess our social realities and, perhaps, create new ones. And when we become socially literate we become politicized. We become conscious of how power is distributed in societies, how and why some groups enjoy it and others don't, open to the possibilities of alternative arrangements, and maybe ready to challenge existing ones. We also become more aware of the forces pushing back against change and the efforts needed to bring it about. 'Politics' in its usual sense, although crucial because it shapes all power relationships owing to the extensive power of the state, is now only one indication of politics in the broader, political sociological sense: the ongoing negotiation and contestation of power in the wider social milieu. Ideally, you need to be aware of the latter before you can respond effectively to the former.

Again, it takes the right tools and lots of practice using those tools to see politics differently, to see politics as political sociologists do. We hope that this book can help you to get there.

Acknowledgements

We would like to thank Peter Sinclair, who provided us with the initial opportunity to write a political sociology text for the Oxford series, and to the series editors, Susan McDaniel, and Lorne Tepperman, for trusting him. We would also like to thank Nancy Reilly, the acquisitions editor who encouraged us to pursue this project and who was one of our greatest supporters and motivators in getting us excited about the book in the early going. We are also indebted to Lisa Ball, the book's production coordinator, for her eagle eye to detail and her approach to moving the project to its end. We appreciate as well the efforts of the Oxford University Press team and of José Julián López, as well as two anonymous reviewers, for their constructive comments.

Andreas Hoffbauer collected many of the articles we cite and provided valued feedback on an early draft of the book. Critical assessments were solicited and offered by Kregg Hetherington, who rightly took us to task for some of our interpretations in earlier drafts of Chapter 5. Mark Stoddart introduced us to literature we would have otherwise missed—thanks, Mark. And thanks to Kumi Stoddart for offering Howard a couch to sleep on while he was travelling to Newfoundland.

Cheers to Paul F. Armstrong for catching us speaking of the book in the active voice, rather than passive. Had he not pointed this out, we might have stuck to the original working title of Politics Seen Differently, which ultimately doesn't capture our position on political sociology. Many of the examples and ideas for chapters have been developed in exchanges with our students and with friends and colleagues in the 'Network' (Canadian Network for the Study of Identities, Mobilization and Conflict), without whom we likely would have written a much less interesting book. Likewise, we've come to realize that Skype rules! Without it, collaborating would have been much more difficult. And last, our thanks to our families, especially to our own and each other's spouses, for keeping the world turning when 'the book' consumed us.

1 Introduction

Learning Objectives

⊛ To learn how political sociologists 'see' politics
⊛ To understand power as a process rather than a thing
⊛ To see that political processes are negotiated, contested, and maintained by groups of people and not just individuals
⊛ To become familiar with three ways that people engage in political processes — through material, cultural and social, and institutional means

Introduction

'*I'm not that into politics.*' You have no doubt heard this said by friends or members of your family. Maybe you have said it yourself! Usually, what people mean by this is that they don't pay attention to the issues and activities involving politicians or governments and that they don't find them interesting or relevant to their lives. It also means that they see politics as separable from their worlds, something that happens 'out there' that they can choose to be 'into' or not.

Political sociologists see politics differently. Rather than being a separate realm that people can decide to engage with or not, political sociologists see politics as penetrating everyone's lives. This is because politics is about the exercise and contestation of *power*. In this sense, politics cannot be avoided; we can't choose to participate in politics or 'leave it at the door'. All of us are 'into' politics all the time because we are always part of social groups that are involved in negotiating power relations.

If this is the case, then for political sociologists, 'politics' must encompass processes, forces, and factors that most of us do not usually think of as politics. It is true that political sociologists are interested in the conduct of politicians and the goings-on of governments; indeed the state as defined by the officials and institutions that we typically understand as comprising politics is a fundamental concern of political sociologists. Yet, unlike political science, which tends to concentrate on institutional or formal politics and the mechanisms of governance, political sociologists are more concerned with examining and explaining how power is distributed and negotiated in society more generally and on what basis. Of course political sociologists are interested in *who* rules and *how*. They recognize the importance of the state and pay attention to the officials and political parties in the government and the means by which they govern. But political sociologists are more likely to ask how these observations are linked to broader questions about how power is negotiated outside the formal realm of politics.

Consider the issue of child care. Political sociologists are certainly interested in the formal politics around government provisions for child care, the parliamentary debates, the positions of different politicians, and the policies that are formulated. But to understand the ways that the issue of child care is taken up by the state and the manner in which it is resolved, political sociologists will also look to how these activities interrelate with the power relations unfolding in a wider society. For example, how are gender inequalities confirmed or challenged by the policies that government leaders choose to pursue? The answer will have important implications for the power of women relative to men more generally. Do tax credits for child care, for example, compared to affordable subsidized programs, promote or hinder the entrenchment of traditional gender norms? That is, do they make it more or less likely that women will enter the paid labour force or stay at home to care for their children in an economically dependent role vis-à-vis their 'breadwinner' spouses? Do they encourage women to pursue demanding careers outside the private sphere or oblige women to take low-paid, low-status, 'flexible' occupations rather than less flexible ones? As the questions illustrate, it is just as important for political sociologists to analyze power relationships not typically included in understandings of politics—such as between men and women as well as adults and children—as it is to examine how formal politics works. So what most people consider politics is included as one component of what political sociologists look at in the negotiation of power relations, but is not the only one.

Political sociologists thus share a commitment to taking power relationships apart to better understand the underlying factors that influence how power is distributed and redistributed in societies. They pursue this general aim in many ways, taking up a diverse array of subjects and using a number of different theoretical perspectives and methodological approaches to identify the common mechanisms and processes that shape power. This book is designed to introduce you to political sociology in all its variety and to help you begin to see politics through its practitioners' eyes—that is, to *see politics differently*.

Before introducing you to the more specific perspectives in political sociology, however, we should have a more sustained discussion of what political sociologists mean by 'power'.

Power: Exercising It, Resisting It

Political sociologists are concerned with *power*—who has it, how they got it, how they use it, and who challenges it. Max Weber, who is considered one of the founders of sociology and who wrote widely on power and the state, defined power as 'the probability that one actor in a social relationship will be in a position to carry out his [or her] will despite resistance, regardless of the basis on which this probability rests' (Weber 1997: 152).

Notice that, according to Weber's definition, the source of power doesn't matter. In one instance, a powerful person might derive her power from her capacity to inflict physical injury or emotional suffering. Power might flow from personal forces, such as her expertise or charm, or impersonal ones, such as her position in an organization. What matters is that the person, the **social actor,** is able to do what she wants despite resistance or opposition from others. Notice that inherent in this observation is that power is *relational*: the social actor possesses power only in relation to others. She has power because others do not and they defer to her desires.

For example, a CEO of a major corporation exercises considerable power in the boardroom. He is paid well, those around him respect his authority, and even political institutions may be swayed by his views—all evidence of his power. Every day he may make decisions that affect thousands of people's lives. He may lay off employees to cut costs, placing them in precarious economic positions, or he may promote a talented young employee to pursue an expansion of the corporation. However, the tables are quickly turned at home when he is compelled to respond to his crying infant at 2:00 a.m. The baby does not recognize his wealth or influence and demands attention. The CEO is now the caring parent whose greatest concern is to satisfy the needs of the infant. His power is relational.

What the example also illustrates is that, because power is not constant and is subject to changing social relationships, everyone—even people who are not obviously influential—can *resist* power in one or another way. A number of social thinkers have illustrated this. Stuart Hall ([1980] 2006), for example, has shown that even when powerful social actors impose an intended meaning on an action, people can resist it by producing an oppositional understanding that challenges the original intent.

Returning to our example, the CEO may meet resistance to his will at work and at home. The board of the company may dismiss his decision to lay off personnel or to expand the corporation. They may vote to place limits on his salary, and newspapers may criticize his decisions, thereby causing him to lose managerial respect and in turn diminishing his authority in other institutions. Thus, people who disagree with the meanings that the CEO may try to impose on his company and his actions—that layoffs are needed to 'enhance profit' and expansions of the company are required to 'encourage innovation'—can produce oppositional understandings of those same actions to challenge his power. Layoffs might be represented by the board as undermining productivity, and expansion could be seen as overextending the company's mandate. At home, the CEO may try to frame his neglect of his crying child as the outcome of an exhausting day. His partner, however, may characterize it as simply neglectful and refuse to visit the in-laws unless he helps with nighttime child care. The punitive actions of the board or the media are clearly very different from the 'cold shoulder' of a spouse, but they are all forms of resistance to power.

The relational character of power and resistance to it is depicted beautifully by Michel Foucault (2002) in his discussion of Diego Velázquez's painting *Las Meninas* (The Maids of Honour—see Figure 1.1).

The painting is set in the Spanish court during the seventeenth century. At first glance, you notice the maids, the infant Margarita, and Velázquez himself painting the scene. As you track the eyes of the different characters, however, the orientation of the painting changes until you realize that the actual subject of the painting is not in the painting at all. The subjects, who can be seen only in a distant mirror, are the king and queen. They are actually 'the true centre of the composition', on whom the eyes of the painter and most of the other characters are focused, even though they do not really appear in the scene (Foucault 2002: 16). Foucault said *Las Meninas* showed how focus and power are relational. Who imposes his or her will on the scene—the painter, the subjects, or the monarchs—depends on how you look at it. But in 'hiding' the true holders of power, the painting also shows how the interpretation of acts of power can be less than straightforward.

FIGURE 1.1 *Las Meninas*, by Diego Velázquez.
Source: © Museo Nacional del Prado (Spain).

Power as a Process

The preceding discussion establishes that political sociologists view power as a process rather than a thing. Power involves and requires ongoing social interaction and is not just something that an individual or group has or doesn't have. Power is not something you can just go out and get, nor is it something you can carry around with you in your back pocket. This makes sense when you think about it. People who hold a lot of power, like Bill Gates, the Prime Minister, or Bono, for example, would have no clout if they were all alone on an ice floe in the middle of the North Atlantic. Gates's money would be of no use, the Prime Minister's directives would be meaningless, and Bono's celebrity would have no audience. All these people need others to recognize their material wealth, organizational authority, or social fame as valuable in order to exercise power. Furthermore, those things have to remain valued for the powerful to maintain their influence. If people decided one day that being rich was a marker of depravity rather than of success and ingenuity or that they no longer cared what rock stars did or said, Gates and Bono would be reviled or at best ignored. That is what political sociologists mean by power being a process: its bases and its exercise are always up for negotiation.

Yet, as flexible as power processes are, the reality is that some social actors have more power than others. In Weberian terms, some individuals and groups are able to 'carry out their will' more often and in a greater number of situations than others. In these cases, political sociologists are concerned with understanding the bases on which these differences exist, that is, the sources of their power and why some people accept it and others resist it.

Political sociologists have identified and analyzed many sources and processes of power. In this book, we introduce key perspectives in the field and the scholars who have contributed to and employ them. To help organize our presentation, we follow Satzewich and Liodakis (2007) and borrow a typology originally conceived by Max Weber (1946: 180–95), who said that power derives from three fundamental bases: *class*, *status*, and *party*. This typology is helpful because its categories encompass many of the processes that political sociologists have argued are central to shaping people's capacities to exercise and resist power. We start by offering a brief preliminary understanding of how each category operates and then elaborate on how we will use the typology in the rest of the book.

Class

Political sociologists have long recognized that the *class* with which a person or group is affiliated plays a significant role in determining their capacity to exercise or resist power. What is class? We usually identify a person's class with the money and wealth he commands and perhaps the profession he occupies and the goods he consumes. Weber's definition is close to this. He said that people belonging to the same class share a common 'market situation'. That is, they make more or less the same incomes and experience similar lifestyles depending on the property they own or the marketable skills they possess. Classes play an important role in political sociological analysis because their members tend to exercise different degrees of power.

As we shall see in the next chapter, not all political sociologists agree with Weber's definition and depiction of class. Marxists, for example, reject his equating of class with market situation, arguing that the amount of money a person makes or the skills he commands mean little compared to his relationship to the means of production, that is, whether or not he has unhindered access to the means to produce his 'material needs'—food, clothing, and shelter. For now, however, know that political sociologists who are concerned with class understand that power inequalities largely and most consistently stem from the possession of or access to *material resources*, the tangible 'stuff' that is valued in a society, and the way that those resources shape interactions among people.

Status

In Weber's view, possession of or access to material resources does not shape power in all situations. Cultural and social *status* or prestige also factor in. Although people can be grouped according to their material circumstances, they can also form groups around their non-material circumstances, such as their religion or sexual orientation or their gender, culture, or ethnicity. A person might identify very strongly with such a status and even prize the relationships enjoyed through it over money or other material gains. Weber said that because these statuses tend to have different levels of 'social honour' or prestige associated with them, they can confer either more or less power on the individuals holding them, independently of class: the more status, the more power. In fact, many people try to exert their will over others in the name of preserving or establishing the legitimacy of their status group. Weber himself made this point by distinguishing the 'old' from the 'new' money in the rapidly industrializing US at the beginning of the last century (see Box 1.1).

Although both groups belonged to the same class, the superior social status accorded to the old moneyed families allowed them to exercise certain powers over families that had come into their wealth more recently, preventing the latter access to their country clubs, for example, or from marrying into their status group. We can see the same sorts of attempts to create or sustain status power in nationalist struggles or in the claims and counterclaims of groups engaged in identity politics, including the efforts of people and groups to challenge and acquire power on the basis of factors like

---

Box 1.1 ❂ Weber on the Distinctions between Class and Status

Although Weber acknowledged that class and status often overlapped in that people of the same economic class often belonged to the same status group, he insisted that they could—and did—operate as distinct sources of power. This was evident, he said, in the revulsion that many in the most powerful status groups felt for the behaviour necessary to achieve economic success. Here is Weber from *Economy and Society* (1978: 936–7):

> The frequent disqualification of the gainfully employed [from the status group] is the direct result of the principle of status stratification, and of course, of this principle's opposition to a distribution of power which is regulated exclusively through the market. . . .[T]he market and its processes knows no personal distinctions: 'functional' interests dominate it. It knows nothing of honor. The status order means precisely the reverse: stratification in terms of honor and styles of life peculiar to status groups as such. . . . Therefore all groups having interest in the status order react with special sharpness precisely against the pretensions of purely economic acquisition. . . . Precisely because of the rigorous reactions against the claims of property *per se*, the 'parvenu' is never accepted, personally and without reservations, by the privileged status groups, no matter how completely his style of life has been adjusted to theirs . . . [I]n most instances the notion of honor peculiar to status absolutely abhors that which is essential to the market: hard bargaining. Honor abhors hard bargaining among peers and occasionally it taboos it for the members of a status groups in general. Therefore, everywhere some status groups, and usually the most influential, consider almost any kind of overt participation in economic acquisition as absolutely stigmatizing.

---

gender, 'race', sexual orientation, and so forth. Political sociologists who consider the power processes related to the maintenance and recognition of status believe that access to *cultural* and *social* resources, over and above material resources, shape the capacity of individuals and groups to exercise their will in significant ways.

Party

Weber identified one more basis of power: *party*. People exercise party power when they come together in a group to press for some desired goal within an established social order. Party power can be exercised by means of membership in political parties of the state. In Canada, the Bloc Québécois, the Conservatives, the Greens, the Liberals, and the New Democratic Party are each composed of 'party faithful' who work in concert to achieve their objectives according to the rules of government. But party power can be exercised by groups outside the realm of 'official' politics too. Any collection of people who come together and pursue an end in an organized fashion can exercise party power. Thus a gathering of neighbours who hold a rally to oppose their town officials' decision to cut down a favourite tree are exercising party power. So too is a group of employees who lobby their boss to establish a lunchroom at their place of work. In each case, people are engaged in collective action toward realizing a common objective (saving a tree, building a cafeteria) within an existing social order (a municipal admin-istration, a workplace hierarchy).

Weber's notion of party power reminds us that collective action, even among people who may not possess abundant material, social, or cultural resources, can create opportunities for exercising and resisting power. It also highlights how important it is to consider the role of *formal institutions* when analyzing power in a society. Because the reality is that most of the time when people exercise and resist power they do so in ways and through organizations that are well established. Furthermore, the ways of behaving in these organiza-tions are often highly institutionalized; that is, they are known, relatively rou-tine, and more or less accepted (or at least tolerated) by most people. Party power is enhanced by a group's control over and knowledge of the routine procedures they must work with or around to achieve their desired ends.

Certainly some of the most important formal organizations in our contem-porary world are *states*. Indeed, states direct most other institutions within society by setting the official rules about how the other power processes are negotiated. We can see, then, that being the leaders of a political party that is elected into office confers on those individuals the potential to exercise a great deal of power over citizens of a country. This is because, in acquiring authority over the institutions of the state, they have greater power to set the rules of the game that everyone else must follow. Political sociologists concerned with party power ponder the ways that access to institutions affects people's ability to exercise and resist power.

Outline of Book

The three bases of power that Weber identified—class, status, and party—were what he termed **ideal types**; they seldom if ever existed or operated in perfect isolation from one another in the real world. He recognized that in most cases powerful individuals and groups draw upon more than one source of power and in turn use them to mobilize other individuals either to maintain or to change social relations. For example, a wealthy business owner (class power) can refer to or call upon her community involvement (party power) in support of her bid for political office, or a group of parents who have lost a child to violence (status power) can enlist the backing of other victims' groups (party power) to help them gain greater media exposure through which to press for legislative changes. Weber nevertheless believed that his typology could serve as a helpful guide for taking apart and analyzing power relationships. We would add that it also provides an effective means of introducing and discussing the main ways political sociologists have understood power inequalities.

Chapter 2 takes up the concept of class power in a discussion of *materialism* in political sociology. Much of early political sociology was shaped by a materialist orientation, which maintains that possession of and access to material resources ultimately determine the capacity of individuals and groups to exercise and resist power. As we shall see, this focus was shaped to a considerable degree by the reaction of thinkers to the massive social changes that accompanied European industrialization in the eighteenth and nineteenth centuries. Beginning with Karl Marx, the indisputable 'father' of the materialist perspective, we introduce you to some important contributors to this approach, including Barrington Moore and Gøsta Esping-Andersen, who used a Marxist-materialist perspective to explain the different development paths and outcomes that countries have taken; André Gunder Frank, who showed how the unequal distribution of material resources established and continues to maintain the inequality among nations that we observe today; and Ralph Miliband, who documented the many ways the modern state sustains the interests of the dominant class. Along the way, we also introduce some early Canadian materialists, namely, Harold Innis and S.D. Clark. Thanks to their dedication to developing social and economic theories of Canada that were grounded in the geography and economic history of the country, Innis and Clark helped establish materialism in its distinctive Canadian guise, *political economy*. This tradition has seen Canadian political sociologists such as John Porter, Gordon Laxer, and William Carroll, among others, take up themes established by scholars like Frank and Miliband, and use them to develop materialist accounts unique to Canada's class politics and economic progress.

Of course, political sociologists are not interested in just the capacity of individuals and groups to exercise power. They are concerned with how people *resist* power as well. Resource mobilization theory (RMT) looks at how a group's access to (or lack of) material resources can affect how successful it is in challenging existing power relationships and bringing about the changes they seek. The chapter describes the research of key RMT scholars John McCarthy and Mayer Zald, as well as some Canadian political sociologists, who adopt a critical political economy approach to social movements and collective action.

Finally, we explore how materialists understand power inequalities between groups divided by things like ethnicity, 'race', gender, and sexual orientation. We spend some extra time here on gender inequality and examine more closely how a materialist perspective, like that taken by Canadian researchers such as Margaret Benston and Pat and Hugh Armstrong, can inform our understanding of data on the lives and experiences of women in Canada. We end the chapter by touching upon a few of the problems flagged by political sociologists who question taking a strictly materialist approach to gender relations and other forms of identity politics.

As Chapter 2 will show, materialists have done much to enhance our understanding of power relations. But if power were governed strictly by material circumstances, you would think that people would be more aware of or responsive to their class position. Often those in the direst material circumstances are the same people to support state policies or regimes that exploit them. Thomas Frank (2004) shows this in his analysis of the conservative shift in American politics. A lot of working and middle-class Americans who, you would think, would support the Democratic Party because of its greater commitment to helping the poor, investing in schooling, improving access to education, and otherwise ensuring the health and well-being of the materially disadvantaged, have come to support the Republican mandate calling for lower taxes and fewer state-funded social provisions, policies that tend to benefit the wealthy the most. Furthermore, world history is filled with examples of people grouping together under identity-based monikers rather than under the banner of class. You just need to look at the efforts of LGBT (lesbian, gay, bisexual, and transgendered) people, ethnic minorities, or nationalist movements to find people making non-material claims to power.

Chapter 3 engages these issues in more detail by taking a cue from Weber's identification of status as a basis for power and looking at how people can acquire and resist power through *cultural* and *social* means. Here you are introduced to scholars operating in the cultural and social tradition. The discussion begins with Max Weber's critique of Marxist materialism and then moves to the ideas of Antonio Gramsci. Gramsci wrote about cultural and ideological domination and laid the foundation for cultural and social analyses of resistance. From the Second World War era, you are introduced to Max Horkheimer and Theodor Adorno, who theorized how control over mass culture—literally, the culture of 'the masses'—can mould interests and mobilize or pacify people. We also introduce the ideas of Pierre Bourdieu, who observed that people can exercise or resist power through their control of non-material as well as material forms of 'capital'. Bourdieu explained how a person's social relationships and cultural preferences are inherently linked to different positions of power. We go on to examine extensions of the idea of social capital by looking at Robert Putnam's use of the concept and at a number of Canadian thinkers that have responded to this work. The chapter likewise examines how cultural and social power is negotiated, by exploring the writings of Erving Goffman and Stuart Hall, as well as how cultural and social power is used as the basis for resistance. The latter is done by looking at approaches conceived by post-colonial thinkers like Frantz Fanon and Edward Said and pondering the role of collective identity in resistance.

The chapter illustrates key concepts by returning to conditions facing Canadian women and considers the experiences of Québécois and Aboriginal Canadians. We examine how the cultural and social capital of women is often ignored in some social spheres and how this in turn intersects with power differences arising from material processes. The chapter also looks at the politics of recognition, identity, and post-colonialism as they have been manifested in Canada in the Quebec nationalist movement and Aboriginal mobilization.

Drawing on Weber's concept of party and his account of how power flows from group behaviour within and against institutionalized settings, we explore in Chapter 4 how *institutions* shape power relations in political sociology. Here we focus in particular on sociologists who study the role of *state* institutions—the organizations and patterned behaviour of individuals and groups in and around government—in influencing people's capacities to impose their will and to resist the will of others. Sociologists have long noted and explored the interactions of the state and its structures with social actors. This includes Weber, whose analysis of bureaucracy, its benefits, and its deficiencies centred on the development of the modern state. In this chapter, we review Weber's analysis as fundamental to later work pertaining to state institutions, especially by those scholars 'who brought the state back in' to political sociological analysis in the 1970s and 1980s. We introduce you to the work of Theda Skocpol and Michael Mann, scholars who highlight among other things the *inertia* and *path dependence* of state institutions. These contribute to the tendency for the processes and procedures associated with politics to resist change, a tendency that can have implications for who gets to exercise the most power in a given society, whether challenges to that power bear fruit, and if so, how. We also highlight other scholars who explore how state institutions have configured the power contests associated with nationalism and nation building, such as Ernest Gellner and Benedict Anderson. In this regard, we examine the role of violence as an action arising from such power struggles. But of course, violence is not the only means people use to challenge institutional power, so we introduce you to the *political process* approach of Peter Eisinger, Charles Tilly, Doug McAdam, and Sidney Tarrow. These researchers ponder how political institutions and, more broadly speaking, the political climate prevailing at a particular time influence whether people will come together in social movements, the tactics they will employ to achieve their ends, and the successes or failures they may experience. Canada has its own sociologists doing this sort of research, and you will meet some of them, including Daniel Béland, Samuel Clark, Jane Jenson, and Suzanne Staggenborg.

Once again, we turn to Canadian cases, those of the Quebec and Aboriginal nations within Canada, to examine in more detail how paying attention to state institutions can reveal some interesting things about how power is organized, distributed, and challenged in society. Specifically, we consider the role of the *Constitution Act, 1982* and federal policies in recognizing the rights of disenfranchised groups, as well as granting 'special' rights to some groups over others.

As we have said, class, status, and party are ideal types of power. Just as Weber acknowledged that the real power of people and groups usually stems from some combination of the three ideal forms, so too do we recognize that political sociologists can engage with some mixture of materialist, cultural and social, and/or institutionalist perspectives. In fact, the work of many political sociologists, like Ernest Gellner, John Porter, William Carroll, C. Wright Mills, and Charles Tilly, straddles all three. Some scholars, however, argue that none of these traditions and tendencies in the field—used alone or in combination—can help us to understand processes of power in the technologized, globalized, culturally diverse, and rapidly changing societies of today. In Chapter 5 we explore some of these 'new' perspectives and their effects on political sociology.

Political sociology emerged largely as a reaction to the unprecedented social transformations that accompanied the Industrial Revolution in eighteenth and nineteenth-century Europe. This meant, among other things, that political sociological analyses were founded on the assumptions that *humans* shape political processes and do so primarily within *states*. That is, most approaches highlight individuals and states as the key actors in power relationships. However, a number of contemporary scholars argue that these founding assumptions led to an underappreciation of many other sorts of power configurations. On this front we examine the work of Bruno Latour and Donna Haraway, who look at how social relations are affected by *non-humans*, that is, how the environment, animals, or technology plays a part in politics. If you don't think these things can be political, just think about how the Hurricane Katrina disaster in the US in 2005 exposed corrupt politics, racialization of the poor, and the ability of a government, indeed a whole country, to look the other way in the face of human misery. We do not usually think about a natural disaster as something that 'exercises agency', but Katrina was certainly a key contributor to the way power relations in the US unfolded at that time. And what about the ongoing replacement of human labourers with robots and the development of artificial intelligence as one of the growth areas in computer science research? How will these technological processes affect, positively or negatively, the capacity of human workers to influence their working conditions and other areas of life? The same may be asked about social movements that have succeeded in stigmatizing traditional Japanese customs of eating whale meat and the practices of Newfoundland sealers by debating the 'rights' of whales and seals to be protected from harvesting by humans. In all of these cases, political claims and power are shaped by or sought for non-humans. We explore these developments by looking at issues around **automobility**, the environment, and animal rights.

Chapter 5 also explores recent claims that the 'old' models of political sociology that emerged in response to the Industrial Revolution do little to help us understand power in the contemporary era. Many scholars believe that economic, cultural and social, and institutional relationships have changed radically, especially over the last thirty years, and so have the axioms of power that govern them. To grasp these new power relationships, some argue that we need to emulate our forebears and come up with new methods and approaches appropriate to our own 'revolutionary' era. On this front we examine the claims of some political sociologists that globalization is a new process that is reordering economic, cultural and social, institutional, and even activist behaviour. We look at how things have begun to change, and we present data that examine the growing internationalism of the world. In doing so, we introduce world polity models and the notion of 'activism beyond borders' and examine how citizenship and human rights are conceived in this purportedly 'new' social order. We also assess competing interpretations of recent claims that we are witnessing the emergence of a new American or Western Empire, and consider transnationalism as an alternative to globalization.

In Chapter 6 we return to ideas and themes that we discussed in Chapter 1 to clarify further what we mean by 'seeing politics differently'. As we reiterate key insights from the previous chapters, we use them to build a more comprehensive representation of what political sociologists do and what, more generally, a political sociological perspective entails. We go on to urge you to improve your skills as a political sociologist, not only to do better in the course or program that you may be studying, but also to enhance your **social literacy**. By this we mean your capacity to 'read' and navigate the social world and the power relations that characterize it. Political sociology not only offers you the tools for observing and reflecting more critically on your own circumstances and those of others but also gives you the means of changing them and creating new realities.

Summary

By the end of this book, you will have been introduced to a broad, preliminary examination of trends in political sociology. With the help of Weber's *class-status-power* typology, we will have highlighted some of the key observations of political sociologists about how power is distributed and negotiated in society through material, cultural and social, institutional, and other means, and how these observations can help us make sense of a number of power contests in Canada, both past and present. These will equip you with theories, concepts, and methods for assessing how power is negotiated through social relations. You will then be better able to analyze power relationships that you have perhaps until now taken for granted or maybe not even noticed. Most importantly, we hope the book will help you to see politics differently, to think about politics as political sociologists do—so that the next time a friend tells you she's 'not that into politics', you can smile and say, 'Think again!'

Questions for Critical Thought

1. What do political sociologists add to the understanding of politics? Why, from a political sociologist's perspective, can't people 'opt out' of politics?

2. What do political sociologists mean when they say that power is 'relational'?

3. What are some of the ways that you exercise and resist power? Who exercises power over you?

4. What groups exercise and resist power in contemporary North American society? Try to think of groups whose power stems from class (material resources), status (cultural and social sources), and party (institutional and organizational sources), or some combination of these.

5. What relationships shape power, inequality, mobility, and social change in contemporary North American society?

Suggestions for Further Reading

Baer, Douglas (ed.). 2001. *Political Sociology: Canadian Perspectives*. Don Mills: Oxford University Press. An edited volume by key Canadian political sociologists.

Brym, Robert J. 2008. *Sociology as a Life or Death Issue*. Toronto: Pearson Allyn and Bacon. Introduces sociological ideas and applies political sociology to a wide range of cases.

Mills, C. Wright. 1959. *The Sociological Imagination*. New York: Pelican Books. A preeminent sociologist whose appeal to sociologists to link personal troubles to public issues is the definitive statement on political sociology.

Weber, Max. 1946. *From Max Weber: Essays in Sociology*. Translated by H. H. Gerth and C. Wright Mills. New York: Oxford University Press. A collection of the writings of one of the founding figures in sociology and the study of power and politics.

Websites

American Sociological Association: Political Sociology Section
www2.asanet.org/sectionpolitic

Canadian Sociological Association
www.csa-scs.ca

Canadian Network for the Study of Identities, Mobilization and Conflict
www.cnsimc.blogspot.com

2 Materialism

Learning Objectives

- ✸ To understand how material resources shape power
- ✸ To examine the ideas of Karl Marx as a founder of materialist accounts of politics
- ✸ To see how Marx's insights remain relevant today
- ✸ To look at how material resources not only shape individual and group power negotiations but also how they help form institutions.
- ✸ To examine how material resources shape international relations between states
- ✸ To understand how material resources can be used to resist existing power arrangements
- ✸ To learn to apply these concepts to relevant cases, including unionization, global inequality, and gender inequality

Introduction

How can we best interpret the way power is negotiated? What factors are most important in determining how it is exercised and challenged? Many of the first political sociologists to try to answer these questions approached them from the perspective of *materialism*. In everyday language people associate materialism with a person's passion for or fascination with *things*, consumer goods especially. When you say someone is 'materialistic' you might mean the person is fixated on getting and accumulating stuff, especially if it is expensive or frivolous. The label also tends to be pejorative. It suggests that a branded person is overly concerned with owning and showing off possessions and might be foolish or flighty owing to his passion for things over more serious or substantive matters. You might even find yourself saying, 'I am not material-istic' because you do not get caught up with buying the latest smartphone, iTunes single, clothes, or what not.

Materialism in political sociology is understood somewhat differently. It is still associated with things, but not only what they are and who owns them. Instead political sociologists examine the underlying relationships that govern whether or not people can *access* them and *control* them. They do this to meas-ure how people's relationships to things shape their capacity to exercise and resist power. Political sociologists who subscribe to a materialist perspective say that people and groups that are able to impose their will on others the most often and most consistently enjoy that capacity because of their access to, ownership of, and control of material resources. These scholars maintain that possession of material assets ultimately determines how much power an individual or group holds relative to others: the more assets, the greater their capacity to impose their will in a wider array of circumstances.

In this chapter we introduce you to the materialist perspective in political sociology, a perspective that explores how material resources shape the negotiation of power. We begin with a discussion of a concept central to materialism: *class*. You have already heard a bit about class in Chapter 1. But it is especially important that you become sensitized to the existence of classes and how class effects manifest themselves in social relations in order to grasp the materialist perspective. We then review the ideas of arguably the most famous materialist, Karl Marx, and explain how his account of the way power is distributed, exercised, and challenged in societies is still relevant today. The chapter moves on to discuss some leading materialists and class analysts of the twentieth and twenty-first centuries who used Marx's formulations to help explain, among other things, how material resources shape the nature of the modern state, the development of countries, and international relations. We also show how material resources can be used to *resist* existing power arrangements. Along the way, you are introduced to the political economy approach unique to Canadian materialists, as well as materialist and class analyses of cases relevant to the Canadian experience, including unionization and gender inequality.

Materialism and Class

Let us think about power inequalities in North American society. Does it make sense to understand them in material terms? It certainly may look as if people who enjoy superior material circumstances—people who make the most money and who have the best, nicest, and the most things—are able to get their own way more often in business, in politics, and in their personal lives, than those who do not. But does their power come from their assets, or have they acquired their assets because they hold power?

This is an important question because most of us would hope it was the latter. We like to believe that people get into important positions from which they can exercise power by earning privileges through their skills, personal ambition, and hard work. Many believe that our material circumstances are not the reason we end up exercising power. They are the rewards for having acquired a powerful position thanks to our individual efforts. Materialists argue otherwise. Although we like to think that a society is **meritocratic**, that people end up where they do entirely because of their own merit, the reality, say materialists, is that people's **life chances** are shaped by the existing distribution of material resources in society, or the *class system*, to a much greater degree than we usually acknowledge. But how so?

Class affects, on the one hand, the personal circumstances into which you are born; for instance, the kind of neighbourhood you live in, the lifestyle you experience, the schools you attend, the friends you have, and the family relationships you will likely be a part of. You may think these are largely determined by your and your parents' individual actions, the education they received, the jobs they hold, the place they chose to live, and the parenting choices they make. Of course this is true to some extent, but the class to which you and your family belong, that is, the material conditions you share with other families, affects your social circumstances in important ways. If you are born into a life of material advantage, you have a better chance of living in a safe and stable community, going to a good school, having friends and family who have a similar lifestyle, and having access to lots of consumer goods at home. These are very different circumstances from those facing someone who lives a less materially advantaged life, who may live in a troubled community, attend a poorer-quality school, and have friends and a family life that are different from her wealthier peers. The point materialists make here is that we do not all begin from the same place nor do we experience our lives independently. People from more advantaged classes have a head start toward securing a powerful position in society because of the better material circumstances they enjoy.

Materialists say, on the other hand, that class also shapes the larger public configurations that structure life. This is a bit more difficult to grasp, but materialists maintain that social institutions such as the state, the education system, the legal system, and other things, like the way cities are organized, the foreign-policy decisions that are made by government officials, even the wars that countries start or join, all favour the interests of the materially advantaged, regardless of how they are explained or justified. And it certainly appears that way sometimes. In Canada, the vast majority of victims of crime, those who commit crimes, and those who end up in jail are from less advantaged backgrounds. As Gannon et al. (2005: 121) note, 'The economic well-being and the characteristics of our communities and our society as a whole exert an important influence on crime, victimization, and fear and perceptions.' Like earlier writers such as John Hagan and Ruth Peterson (1995), recent data reflect a relationship between low **socio-economic status** (**SES**) and exposure to or participation in criminal acts. Such a pattern can also be seen in the number of people from poor and moderate economic backgrounds who join the armed forces. Many join because they cannot afford to pay for trade school or university, leading some, like Massing (2008), to conclude that 'in today's America, the hunger for a college degree is so great that many young men and women are willing to kill—and risk being killed—to get one.' The effects of material advantage are even seen in how states interact with one another, such as when state leaders intervene in the affairs of oil-rich countries and neglect the plight of many poor nations (Chomsky and Barsamian 2003). Can these outcomes be understood entirely as just a result of poor decisions (on the part of prisoners), personal career preferences (in the case of soldiers), and a sincere desire on the part of our state officials to 'bring democracy' to countries that do not have it? Materialists would say no, these outcomes to a large degree reflect how social institutions systematically operate to the benefit of the materially advantaged and to the detriment of the poor.

All this is not to say a person cannot overcome the disadvantages of a poor upbringing, navigate a system built to sustain the interests of the materially advantaged, and then rise to the pinnacle of economic and political power. Everyone can point to a rags-to-riches story like this. But materialists would say these are relatively rare. Barring revolution, the class system—the way material resources and hence power are distributed among the population, indeed the world—is relatively stable over time. Powerful families, powerful groups, and powerful countries tend to stay powerful thanks to their material advantage. The less powerful tend not to improve their material circumstances to any great degree, and so they remain weak, relatively speaking.

The Original Materialist: Karl Marx (1818–1883)

A materialist orientation was especially prevalent among early sociologists. This is in part because sociology, like a lot of our present-day social sciences, emerged as a reaction to the **Industrial Revolution** of the eighteenth and nineteenth centuries. The Industrial Revolution, broadly speaking, encompassed the era when economies in Europe shifted from primarily agricultural to industrial production. This shift was accompanied by unprecedented social change, including large-scale demographic shifts, transformations in the way the home and work were organized and experienced, the growth in the size and power of new commercial and industrial classes, and the widespread questioning of the social and legal customs on which the previous social order had been based. Early social thinkers sought to explain these massive changes and identify the social forces that brought them about, and they pondered the present and future under these new conditions.

Their focus on the role of material inequalities in these processes is not surprising, given the new social realities that they were observing. This was a time before many of the safeguards that now characterize most modern workplaces—like the minimum wage, employment insurance, pensions, workplace safety regulations, and so forth—had been fought for and secured by the working class. The wealth and privilege of the materially advantaged contrasted starkly with the poverty and misery of the workers, especially in the close quarters of the newly industrializing urban areas, where the very poor lived in squalor and had few if any civic or political rights. It is not that huge divisions between the rich and poor had not existed before industrialization. Rather, the conditions that accompanied the industrialization of the cities in which many social thinkers were writing often threw these inequalities into clear focus (see Box 2.1).

Box 2.1 ☀ Observing Class Inequalities, Past and Present

Charles Dickens, the nineteenth-century English author of such famous works as *Oliver Twist*, *David Copperfield*, and *A Christmas Carol*, was known to wander the streets of London for hours at a time, observing the sights of the city he became renowned for describing in his literary works. And apparently those sights were not always pleasant ones. The following passage from *A Christmas Carol* (Dickens 1971: 113–14) describes a common Dickensian setting:

> They left the busy scene, and went into an obscure part of the town, where Scrooge had never penetrated before, although he recognised its situation, and its bad repute. The ways were foul and narrow; the shops and houses wretched; the people half-naked, drunken, slipshod, ugly. Alleys and archways, like so many cesspools, disgorged their offences of smell, and dirt, and life, upon the straggling streets; and the whole quarter reeked with crime, with filth, and misery.

These conditions existed alongside the tremendous wealth enjoyed by upper classes whose lives were far removed from the areas that Dickens described. Indeed, so extreme were class differences that it became popular in nineteenth-century London for the city's wealthy to go 'slumming'—to enter the poorest and most destitute areas of the city, sometimes in disguise—'to see people of whom they had heard, but of whom they were as ignorant as if they were inhabitants of a strange country' (Langtry 1884). The practice soon spread to New York, where readers of the *New York Times* were advised by a columnist that, if they wished to visit the lowest, vilest, places, 'a ward detective is required whose official presence alone would protect the ladies of the party from insult and the gentlemen from violence'. Slumming was recognized at the time as a form of entertainment, the columnist predicting that it would 'become a form of fashionable dissipation this Winter among our belles,' but was also heralded as 'good work in which we [could] all engage' to bring the desperate conditions of the poor to light and encourage charitable work (Langtry 1884).

But have things really changed? Slumming has again become popular, this time among wealthy tourists visiting less developed countries. You can now lay your eyes on how this 'other half' lives in cities such as Rio de Janeiro, Mumbai, and Johannesburg, where your guide will take you on a tour of the homes, neighbourhoods, and businesses of slum dwellers. Opinions on the practice are divided in the same way as they were over a century ago. Some say such an experience can be life-changing, that witnessing the actual conditions under which these people live fosters greater understanding and respect for the poor. Others argue that it is just another way that the poor are exploited by the wealthy for fun and profit (Weiner 2008). Clearly, class divisions remain as wide—perhaps wider—in the twenty-first century as in the nineteenth.

The person best known for his materialist analysis of the conditions characterizing the 'new' industrializing Europe is Karl Marx. He said that to understand what was going on, indeed to understand human history and existence more generally, we must begin by examining how people interact with nature and each other to satisfy their *material* needs: food, clothing, and shelter. This is because he felt that the acquiring of the things one needs to survive is the most necessary and fundamental human activity and so must be the basis of any investigation of humankind. In *The German Ideology*, Marx and his co-author Friedrich Engels argued that this was self-evident: 'The first premise of all human history is, of course, the existence of living human individuals.... The writing of history must always set out from these natural bases and their modification in the course of history through the action of men [and women]' (Marx and Engels 1970: 42).

Marx observed that although people had produced the things they needed in order to survive in a variety of ways throughout history, control over them and how they were distributed looked quite similar across time. Specifically, he found that throughout human history a minority of individuals often controlled material resources. They could dictate who had access to those resources and who could use them, thus enjoying a privileged position within their society. In contrast, the vast majority of people had only restricted access to these **means of production**, which was mediated by the owning group. This meant that they had limited ability to produce the goods needed to sustain themselves, and even if they could produce them they did not have the power to choose how to use them. That was concentrated in the hands of the minority.

Marx found that this was true during the **feudal period**, roughly speaking, 1100–1500 CE in the West, when a minority, consisting of **nobles**, had control over the means of agricultural production. This minority controlled the land needed to grow food and restricted access to it by the majority **peasant** class, thus limiting their ability to produce and consume the materials they required for their very survival.

It is also true, said Marx, of the modern period, in which he identified the minority as **bourgeoisie** or *capitalists*, who owned and exercised control over the means of capitalist production. Instead of land, this meant factories, machines, and techniques of industry, which helped produce the things that were bought and sold during this period. Again the majority of people, the labourers, whom he called the **proletariat**, had limited access to these means of production and the goods they made.

The condition of ownership and non-ownership of the means of production was crucial to Marx because he argued that it dictated the circumstances by which the minority exercised power over the majority. Because in order to survive, the masses needed access to the means of production, to land on which to grow food in the feudal period, or to mechanized processes in the modern capitalist period to produce consumer goods, they were naturally beholden, and hence **subordinate**, to the elite minority, which was **dominant**. As a result, because the bourgeoisie possessed the means required by everyone to produce the necessities of life, they literally held the power of life and death over the majority. This power allowed them to exploit the majority in almost any fashion they wished, forcing them to work long hours, for example, under conditions over which they had no control, and for minimal compensation.

So for Marx, dominant and subordinate relationships depend on a person's **class**, her *relationship to the means of production*. That is, whether she owns the means of production or only seeks access to it. This in turn shapes her life conditions to a considerable degree. If she owns the means of production, she holds power and can exercise that power by influencing who has access to those means, for example, and how and for what purposes they can be used. If she does not own the means of production, she is effectively powerless, compelled to submit to the owning class to gain access to the means she needs in order to survive (see Box 2.2).

But the power of the owning class, the dominant minority, went much beyond the manor estate or the factory, said Marx. The other institutions that make up a society—structures like the state, religion, the family, and the educational and legal systems, the collection of which Marx called the **super-structure**—reflects and sustains the power of the dominant class. Thus religion, according to Marx, served the interests of the powerful by operating as an 'opiate of the people'. Religion was 'the sigh of the oppressed creature' that lulled the majority into accepting that their subordination was divinely determined rather than purposefully structured. Their salvation came at death after a life of obedient toil rather than through real struggles against the own-ing group (Marx 1977: 131). As a result, material conditions also influenced the very ideas that people had, the beliefs they held about how the world works and on which they based their actions. These also sustained the domin-ance of the owning class.

Simplifying somewhat, the system Marx described was one in which the majority subordinate class did not engage and challenge the underlying material inequalities that existed; rather they were deceived by the dominant class into thinking the power inequalities that were manifested in social institutions and the ideologies that sustained them were natural, common-sensical, or at best unchangeable. The subordinate class thus operated under a **false consciousness** because these phenomena masked the true reasons why the elites held power, which were that they controlled or owned the means of production.

Although Marx expressed these ideas over 150 years ago, they still have relevance today. We hear constantly how important education is to future success. Education—especially post-secondary education—is upheld by educators, by state officials, by almost everyone, as a key determinant of

BOX 2.2 ⁙ CLASS AS A LIFE AND DEATH STRUGGLE

Although Marx wrote at the end of the nineteenth century, his insights can still be applied today. Did you know that in less developed countries in Asia and Latin America thousands of people grow the food eaten by North Americans on plantations owned by agribusinesses such as Dole, Chiquita, and Del Monte, but many do not earn enough money to feed their own families? In Marxist terms, the agri-corporations own the means of production in these countries and so can exercise power over the workers, who do not. And they do, paying them poor wages and compelling them to labour in less-than-satisfactory, often dangerous, working conditions, in order to keep down the prices we pay for fruit and vegetables. You may not have thought about it before, but the fact that you can buy a tropical banana for a few cents at a grocery store in Canada is a manifestation of the imbalance of material power relations between workers and owners in developing countries, and between poor and rich countries more generally.

Have you ever complained about how much the TV or smartphone or computer that you 'just have to have' costs? Well, it would probably cost a lot more if the people who assembled it enjoyed wages and working conditions comparable to those of most North American workers. Many of the electronics we use are assembled in export-processing zones (EPZs) like the *maquiladoras* of Northern Mexico running along the US border. Local people are brought into these duty- or tariff-free zones to work as cheap labour in factories that export their products, primarily to richer countries. These workers often suffer a low standard of living and have difficulty paying for the necessities of life, let alone the products they have assembled. But again, they are compelled to work under these conditions to, in Marxist terms, acquire access to the means of production.

And if you think such exploitation occurs only among unskilled labour in poor countries, think again. A recent article in *Fortune* reported that companies in desirable sectors such as marketing and public relations in the US are starting to 'hire' university graduates wishing to enter these highly competitive industries— *without pay* (Reynolds 2011). Workers take these unpaid 'jobs' in the hope that the company will eventually hire them to work for a regular salary; employers use them like paid employees, even complaining when the workers fail to demonstrate their commitment to the task or have the audacity to 'moonlight' in a paid job to make ends meet. These situations differ from those faced by plantation and *maquiladora* workers in that university-educated North Americans still have many more employment choices available to them. But just like Dole and Del Monte, Sony and Toshiba, these US companies own the means of production to which workers must have access and so have the power to set the conditions under which their employees labour.

gaining a well-paying job, an investment that pays off when we enter the workforce and acquire that position of wealth and power. But is this the way it really works? The statistics are not so clear. Data from the 2006 Canadian census indicate that fully 60 per cent of Canadians between the ages of 25 and 64 have at least some post-secondary education; the number who reported a completed university degree increased by almost 24 per cent between 2001 and 2006 (see Tables 2.1 and 2.2). So, you might wonder are up to 24 per cent more people doing much better in Canada than ten years ago? Sadly, recent data, shown in Figure 2.1, indicate that **income distribution** in Canada has changed very little over the past thirty years. In other words, people in Canada are making more or less the same money relative to others than they did in the 1970s. The increase in the proportion of Canadians

TABLE 2.1 Total Population Aged 25 to 64 by Level of University Attainment, Canada, 2001 and 2006

Level of University Attainment	2001	2006	% increase
Total	16,288,310	17,382,115	7
No university degree	13,080,875	13,396,370	2
Subtotal—University degree	3,207,440	3,985,745	24
Bachelor's degree	2,079,650	2,538,355	22
University certificate or diploma above bachelor level	331,285	416,815	26
Degree in medicine, dentistry, veterinary medicine or optometry	102,340	113,740	11
Master's degree	584,745	774,655	32
Earned doctorate	109,420	142,180	30

Source: Statistics Canada, Educational Portrait of Canada, 2006 Census, 97-560-XIE2006001, March 2008; http://www.statcan.gc.ca/bsolc/olc-cel/olc-cel?catno=97-560-XIE&lang=eng#formatdisp

TABLE 2.2 Number and Proportion of Persons Aged 25 to 64 by Level of Educational Attainment and Age Groups, Canada, 2006

Level of Educational Attainment	25–34 years	35–44 years	45–54 years	55–64 years	Total	%
Less than high school	433,940	603,605	811,240	834,725	2,683,510	15
High school diploma	897,835	1,091,465	1,294,505	872,930	4,156,740	24
Post-secondary qualification	2,655,300	3,099,025	2,845,665	1,941,870	10,541,865	61
Trade certificate	416,045	609,270	651,920	478,770	2,156,010	12
College diploma	906,155	1,064,810	972,500	589,910	3,533,375	20
University certificate or diploma below bachelor level	181,350	235,965	245,230	204,185	866,735	5
University degree	1,151,750	1,188,975	976,015	669,005	3,985,745	23
Total	3,987,075	4,794,100	4,951,410	3,649,530	17,382,115	100

Source: Statistics Canada, Educational Portrait of Canada, 2006 Census, 97-560-XIE2006001, March 2008; http://www.statcan.gc.ca/bsolc/olc-cel/olc-cel?catno=97-560-XIE&lang=eng#formatdisp

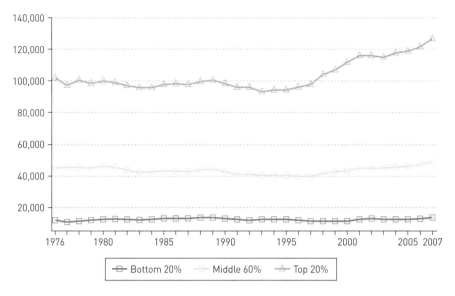

FIGURE 2.1 Average after-tax income, by income group, Canada, 1976–2007
          (2007 Constant Dollars)

Source: HRSDC. Accessed from: http://www4.hrsdc.gc.ca/.3ndic.1t.4r@-eng.jsp?iid=22[19/03/2011 14:33:36]

with post-secondary degrees has not been accompanied by an increase in the proportion of people doing better materially. But maybe the improvements do not appear at this general level. Maybe the payoffs from all those post-secondary degrees are evident in the data that track people's **social mobility**, that is, changes in their socio-economic status during their lives or across generations. If education enhances your chances of landing in a well-paid and powerful position in society, then your occupational status should improve as you acquire more credentials. It should certainly improve in comparison with that of your parents if, as is still the case in many Canadian families, you are better educated than your mother or father. But for decades now, scholars who study the correlation between educational and occupational attainment and other factors have found that your father's income and occupation are still a consistent predictor of whether you pursue more education and end up in a powerful job or not (Nakhaie 2000; Nakhaie and Curtis 1998; Wanner 2005). In other words, your socio-economic success depends on your *class background*—on whether you come from a materially advantaged family or from less privileged circumstances.

It is not that education is irrelevant. These same studies show that educational level is very closely related to one's occupational status. It is just not as strong a determinant as we are often led to believe. This of course would come as no surprise to Marxists, who maintain that the education system, as part of the superstructure, operates to sustain the power of the dominant class. They would say our strong belief that the world operates as a meritocracy in which success is determined entirely by individual effort is merely dominant ideology masquerading as common sense.

We have gone into some detail here about Karl Marx because he laid the foundations for the materialist understanding of human history and society that many political sociologists after him embraced and expanded upon. We turn now to the work of some of these thinkers to explore how the perspective has shaped the field.

Materialism after Marx

In this section we introduce you to some key materialists, including several Canadian ones, who followed Marx and elaborated on his theories to apply them to a modernizing world. Marx may have based his theories on his observations of the conditions characterizing industrialization in Western Europe, but as we have seen, his views appear to still hold true today. Materialists would say this is possible because, although the Industrial Revolution occurred over a century ago, there is considerable continuity between the *class conditions* that accompanied industrialization and the way material resources—and hence power—are negotiated today. But how can that be?

References to the industrializing of Europe raise images of bleak brick factories with huge chimneys belching out black clouds of smoke; men, women, and children working long hours on dangerous machines; city slums filled with poor and miserable people, disease-ridden and hungry, with few if any rights or public supports to help them if they fail. These conditions are very different from the sleek office buildings and clean and comparatively safe office jobs that so many people hold in most major cities these days. Certainly the manufacturing jobs that many people work at in North America today are much more acceptable than factory work 100 years ago. Until recently, unionized blue-collar workers, like those in the auto industry, have been some of the best-paid Canadians earning an average of about $35 an hour (Stanford 2009: 7). The harsh exploitation of workers that was common in Europe in the nineteenth century doesn't happen any more, at least in Western countries. Class may have been an important way to interpret power inequalities in Marx's day, but it seems increasingly irrelevant to contemporary societies.

However, before we write class off, materialists would like us to reflect on the fact that the benefits that many modern Western workers enjoy did not come about in spite of the class inequalities that characterized early industrialization but because of them. Universal suffrage, the 'one person, one vote' democratic system that we take for granted today, was not something that was extended to the working class willingly by Western state officials or by wealthy elites who had held, unchallenged, all the positions of power in societies for generations. Neither were working conditions improved because of a sudden attack of conscience on the part of employers. These changes were gradual and hard won, achieved chiefly by the coming together or **mobilization** of working-class people in Europe, North America, and elsewhere, especially in *union movements*. The late nineteenth and early twentieth centuries were witness to the rising consciousness and militancy of the Western working classes.

You see throughout Europe and North America during this period the creation of working-class unions, protests, general strikes, and confrontations between workers and employers. That period is likewise characterized by strong, often violent, attempts by employers and the state through its police forces to suppress these conflicts (see Box 2.3). Little by little, however, decisions were made to improve wages and counter the worst employment abuses. The vote was extended to working-class men, and then later (in many cases much later) to women, mass education and health care became major government initiatives, and a growing slate of welfare provisions, such as pensions, unemployment insurance, workers' compensation and the like, were adopted. We need to be reminded of the role unions played in helping to secure the wages and employment benefits that we may feel entitled to as citizens, in light of the 'union bashing' that is commonplace among pundits and business and political leaders, even perhaps among family and friends, these days. As in earlier economic downturns (Baer, Grabb, and Johnston 1991), unions are often accused today of being inflexible and greedy in poor economic times and of struggling to retain or improve the already above-average wages and benefits of their members. Union members, it is often claimed, should be satisfied and should feel lucky that they even have a job, rather than make more demands of their bosses. But it is the historical tenacity of unions that helped to bring about, and helps maintain, better working conditions for the working class as a whole.

And if the legacy of class struggle is not enough to persuade us that class still matters, materialists would remind us that looks can be deceiving. Western societies may look very different from industrializing Europe, but the class—and hence power—relations that structure them remain much the same because they are still built by and dependent upon the differential ownership of material assets. If we look at who is working and the kind of working conditions they are exposed to, materialists would say the oppressed and exploited factory labourers of Marx's time and of the early twentieth century have in many respects been replaced by exploited white-collar and service workers who now dominate the ranks of the employed in Western countries. Harry Braverman (1974) drew parallels between service work and factory work more than thirty years ago, and they have become only more apparent. We are not talking here of upper and middle managers, professionals, or CEOs. We are talking about people who work in places like the clerical, cleaning, caring, restaurant, and retail industries. Together, these industries employ some of the most marginalized people in society: youth, retirees, and

Box 2.3 ❋ THE WINNIPEG GENERAL STRIKE

Perhaps there is no greater Canadian example of class mobilization than the Winnipeg General Strike. On 15 May 1919 some 24,000 workers walked off the job and were joined by another 6,000 soon after, launching a six-week strike that shut down the city. Roughly 94 unions participated, representing factory workers and a wide range of public-sector workers like the police and firefighters. The main demands of strikers were the right to collective bargaining, decent wages, and an eight-hour workday (CBC 2010a), all of which are working conditions taken for granted by many workers today.

But the collective efforts by Winnipeg labourers were not to go unchallenged. Local business people and politicians joined forces to crush the massive labour action. Regular police officers were fired and replaced with 1,800 'special' officers, at whose hands the strikers encountered harsh repression and violence (Manitobia 2011). Declaring, with little evidence, that the agitation had been spearheaded by 'foreigners' enflamed by the recent (1917) Russian Revolution, the federal government adopted a number of anti-immigration policies and threatened many Eastern European workers with deportation (see Camfield 2008; Avery 1975). These and other aggressive strike-breaking tactics proved effective: the Winnipeg workers backed down, and the event discouraged Canadian workers from engaging in job action for years. It wasn't until after the Second World War that they began to unionize in large numbers (Bowden 1989).

The Winnipeg General Strike, however, left a legacy that contributed to working-class defiance in Canada's west and to the place of labour in Canadian politics more generally. In 1932, for example, the **Co-operative Commonwealth Federation (CCF)** was founded in Alberta; it was a political party dedicated to representing the interests of labour and other groups committed to socialist ideals. The CCF was the precursor of Canada's current party of the left, the New Democratic Party (or NDP), whose members continue to support the same broad principles. As CCF premier of Saskatchewan, Tommy Douglas overcame stiff opposition to establish universal hospital care in Saskatchewan in the 1940s. Later, as leader of the federal NDP, he was instrumental in the establishment of public health care in the rest of Canada in the 1960s.

Today, when unions are continually being pressed by employers and governments to make wage and other concessions, and many among us complain that unions are outdated or too demanding, it is important to recall the lessons learned from the Winnipeg General Strike and to remember that the labour and social conditions enjoyed by Canadians today are a legacy left by unionism.

recent immigrants. Most of these jobs are not very stable or well-paid. Often they are **part-time**, so that they are exempt from federal and provincial labour laws, with the result that workers are more likely to be over- or under-worked, and subject to inconsistent, haphazard scheduling of their hours and sudden layoffs. Furthermore, people in these types of jobs are often paid only **minimum wage**, which is only $8.75 to $11.00 per hour depending on where in the country they live (Munroe 2011); as a result, some have to work at more than one minimum-wage job just to make ends meet. Many of these people are among the **working poor** of Canada, people who are working but still fall under the official poverty line, and there are more of them than you might think. According to Fleury and Fortin (2006: 17), 'in 2001, there were 653,300 working poor persons in Canada, accounting for 5.6% of all workers, but for about 40% of low-income adults. Including dependants, 1.5 million Canadians lived in a working poor family, of which about one third (531,000 individuals) were children under 18. These 1.5 million persons accounted for almost 40% of all low-income Canadians.' So although a good portion of today's working class may look different from their counterparts of times past and may be dressed in suits and skirts or the uniforms of hamburger chains or dry-cleaning franchises rather than dirty coveralls, materialists would say they still face similar class conditions and vulnerabilities and similar positions of powerlessness, owing to the unequal capacity of people to mobilize material assets on their own behalf.

And like the factory workers of 100 years ago, the low-level service workers of today face resistance to their mobilization and unionization from their employers (Featherstone 1999; Reiter and Stam 2002). In 1998, Canada became the first country to host a unionized McDonald's, when two sixteen-year-old workers in Squamish, British Columbia organized their fellow employees to try to improve wages and working conditions in their restaurant. Attempts to organize have been made elsewhere too, by McDonald's employees in Orangeville, Ontario, in 1993 and St Hubert, Quebec, in 1997, for example, and by workers at a Wal-Mart in Jonquière, Quebec, in 2004. But in all those cases, the workers ultimately failed to secure improvements in their working conditions. In British Columbia, after strong and concerted efforts by McDonald's to 'bust' the Squamish union, employees voted to abandon it (Featherstone 1999; Reiter and Stam 2002). Similar sorts of intimidation were directed by McDonald's at the Orangeville workers, who eventually voted against union certification. And in St Hubert, the company simply shut down the outlet shortly after the workers unionized, throwing everyone out of work (Featherstone 1999; Reiter and Stam 2002). The same thing happened years later when Wal-Mart closed its doors in Jonquière (Bianco 2006). These results show that today's 'proletariat' face the same resistance to their unionizing as their nineteenth-century counterparts did, as well as some tough new challenges. As contemporary materialists like Lowe and Rastin (2000) point out, economic **transnationalization** has fostered conditions that significantly undermine modern workers' attempts to unionize. Thanks to advances in communication technology and transport, large corporations are now able to produce and deliver their goods and services without concerning themselves as much with national laws and boundaries as previously. Assisted by treaties facilitating economic co-operation between countries, like the **North American Free Trade Agreement (NAFTA)**, corporations can now locate or relocate their businesses to places where, for example, they can take advantage of lower labour costs in poorer regions. So when people mobilize to gain better treatment and higher payment for their labour today, the owners of large firms and multinational corporations often threaten, not only to shut down their operations in a particular location, but also to move them out of the country entirely. In this environment, many of the tactics that were successful for the labour movement in the past have become less effective. Whereas a general strike, such as the one that shut down Winnipeg in 1919, forced employers to heed the voices and demands of their workers, present-day unions face the threat of plant and office closures, capital flight, and demands by employers and governments for unions to acquiesce. In recent years the **Canadian Auto Workers** union, one of the largest and most powerful unions in Canada, has been forced to accept cuts to wages and benefits for some of its members. If even the most powerful of unionized workers have suffered a loss of power relative to business elites, imagine the tenuous positions of part-time service workers who have few protections and benefits to begin with and can easily be replaced or have their hours cut if they attempt to unionize. Clearly, the risk of losing their livelihoods as a result of transnationalization can discourage workers from organizing unions these days.

The continued existence of an exploited working class whose attempts to mobilize are often blocked by vastly more powerful capitalist elites is just one reason why some political sociologists say that materialism is still a useful lens through which to view power inequalities in contemporary societies. Although we may not think about or analyze our own lives from a class perspective, materialists say the unequal access to material resources among people, groups, and even countries, still continues to play a fundamental role in determining who will dominate contests over power.

Materialism and Development

Some of the most significant studies undertaken from a materialist perspective have been concerned with the economic and political development of countries. Just as control over material resources shapes power negotiations between individuals and groups, those exchanges also shape the very institutions and structures of countries. That in turn affects how states negotiate power among themselves.

Why did the US develop into such a manufacturing powerhouse in the twentieth century, while its close neighbour Canada remained largely an extractor and exporter of staples (fish, fur, lumber, and minerals), and how were class relations implicated in these developments? Why did the Nordic countries, Sweden, Norway, Finland, and Denmark, develop as **social democracies**, that is, countries that combine high productivity with high taxes and expansive social programs to reduce material inequality, whereas Britain, Canada, and the US develop as **liberal democracies**, countries that favour incentives to business over welfare provisions that lessen disparities in the material conditions of its population? And why has development happened so *unevenly*, with so many people around the world suffering from low standards of living when the West has been relatively well-off for generations?

Political sociologists seeking more refined explanations of development came up with accounts of how class formation and interactions shaped economic and political development in different places and vice versa. A number of the best-known of such accounts are **comparative historical** works that compare the histories of several countries to see how classes have formed and interacted, and how those developments have manifested themselves in different development outcomes. Thus, Barrington Moore (1966) studied and compared the class histories of England, France, the United States, China, Japan, and India to establish how power relations between landed, agrarian, peasant, and other classes unfolded to result in the economies and polities characterizing these places today. His main conclusion, 'no bourgeoisie, no democracy', sounds simple enough, but it could only be stated with confidence after more than five hundred pages of careful class analysis. A more recent example in this tradition is the **power resources theory (PRT)** associated with Walter Korpi and Gøsta Esping-Andersen (Korpi 1983, 1985, 1989; Esping-Andersen 1989, 1990). These scholars looked at differences in **welfare state** regimes, that is, variations in the kinds of economic and political systems countries have. They examined whether those systems favoured workers, through interventionist governments that regulate business and deliver generous benefits to its citizens, or business owners, with little state interference in the economy and comparatively few welfare provisions for its citizens. They said that the differences could be explained by the relative strength of labour and capital as measured by their capacity to muster and employ power resources. These included, most importantly, control over material assets, including the means of production. But they also included **human capital** (education and skills) and the ability to coordinate and organize for collective action, including forming political parties. In countries where the working classes had historically been able to assemble such resources, as was the case in the Nordic countries and to a lesser extent in Canada, welfare provisions were more extensive and material assets—and hence power—

were distributed more equitably. Other works in this tradition include Lipset and Bendix (1959) and Hartz (1964).

If materialism has informed analyses of the economic development of particular countries, it has also influenced studies on the development of the international system of states. **Dependency theory**, which was an approach to global inequality that emerged in the 1950s and 1960s, examined the material conditions of whole countries. It emerged in part as a critical response to post–Second World War approaches that held that underdevelopment derived from factors within a country, such as the failure of its citizens to have the proper attitudes toward achievement (McClelland 1961), or the fact that it was further back on the development trajectory by which all countries became 'modernized' (Kerr et al. 1960; Inkeles 1960, 1975). Dependency theorists said supporters of these approaches seemed to have forgotten that most of the countries that were experiencing 'underdevelopment' were former **colonies** of the US and European powers. For generations, in some cases for centuries, the political and economic development of these regions had been purposely and forcefully restricted by their colonial rulers. This was done in order that they would remain suppliers and producers of raw materials for the 'mother country' and a guaranteed market for its commodities.

Dependency theorists like Andre Gunder Frank (1967) said that, even though most of the former colonies had been **decolonized** by this time and were officially independent countries, colonialism had a strong and lasting effect on how power came to be distributed across countries in the international system after the Second World War. Economic and political interests based in the richer, more developed, countries continued to exercise power over their economies and states in important ways. This included exploiting their natural resources, discouraging economic development and diversification, and cultivating their dependence on Western money and consumer goods. They did this, not through direct rule, as in the colonial era, but by means of their domination of the world economy through multinational corporations and power over international organizations of finance, all backed by massive armies. Dependency theorists challenged the modernists' claim that global inequality was a temporary condition that would eventually go away when poorer nations 'caught up' to the richer ones. They instead described a system that was actively and purposefully orchestrated and maintained by countries that held a material advantage. The **World-Systems Theory** advanced by Immanuel Wallerstein (1974) built upon dependency theory, arguing that the development and economic performance of countries depended on their status in the *world system* or economy as countries of the **core**, **semi-periphery**, or **periphery**. Wallerstein's model was considered an advance over dependency theory since it conceptualized development as an outcome of global rather than just national economic forces. It also acknowledged a place for the semi-developed **newly industrializing countries** like Korea, Singapore, Taiwan, Mexico, and Brazil whose development such scholars as Frank had failed to predict.

We would be remiss if we did not discuss the important influence that materialism has had on Canadian understandings of this country's economic and political development, as well as the significant contributions of Canadian scholars to materialist analyses of development. Indeed, one of the earliest and best-known materialist interpretations of economic development anywhere was in fact theorized by a Canadian economic historian, Harold Innis, who drew upon the Canadian development experience. Innis was no Marxist, but his **staples thesis** reflected the materialist tradition insofar as it focused on material resources. He was less interested in accounting for different classes of people per se than in explaining how the harvesting of actual things like fur, fish, and wheat can shape political relationships (see Box 2.4). Innis argued that countries like Canada, whose economies had been built on and were dependent upon the export of staples, or raw materials and resources, to more advanced countries, would develop in ways that reflected the type of resource in which it specialized. Different regions of the country would develop in different ways depending on which resource was dominant there.

So the nature of the fur trade established what were to become the territorial bounds of the country (Innis [1930] 1956); the early cod fishery in Newfoundland shaped settlement patterns and economic and political development in Atlantic Canada (Innis 1940); and wheat farming shaped development in Canada's prairies (Innis 1954). Ultimately, however, a country dependent on a staples economy, Innis said, would always remain underdeveloped because it would be slow to industrialize and overly dependent on the more technologically advanced countries to which it exported its resources.

Innis's staple thesis has had extraordinary staying power, and it continues to be debated and discussed among economists and political thinkers today. (For a recent defence of its continued relevance, see Watkins 2007.) His thesis also contributed to a materialist tradition in Canadian political sociology in important ways. S.D. Clark, considered a founder of Canadian sociology and one of Innis's students, took up many of the themes Innis identified around *economic* development, especially those related to the material geography of Canada, to explore Canadian **social** development in more detail. Clark (1942, 1948) argued that the harsh conditions facing people engaged in establishing the new staples economy on Canada's remote frontiers often clashed with known or traditional forms of social organization. Settlers had to forge new sorts of social groups and institutions that resonated better with the pioneer experience. So evangelicalism emerged in Canada's West as a frontier response to traditional religious practices that were not compatible with pioneer life (Clark 1948); frontier reform movements arose around leaders who could

BOX 2.4 ❋ INNIS AND HIS 'DIRT RESEARCH'

Harold Innis was a Canadian intellectual who wasn't afraid to get his hands dirty—literally. Innis believed that if scholars were to develop a proper understanding of Canada's political economy, they had to know the facts of Canada. And to do that they had to engage in what he called 'dirt research': leaving their desks in the ivory towers of academe and travelling around the country. But these were no first-class excursions that Innis advocated. Rather, he believed that scholars should traverse the country on foot, by canoe, snowshoe, or dogsled, or by whatever means could best convey the material landscape that faced its inhabitants, and should talk to as many people as possible who made their living from that landscape. This was the only way researchers could really understand why and how people in various areas of the country had established and developed their regional economies. Thus, to grasp better the nature of the Canadian fur trade (Innis [1930] 1956), Innis jumped into a canoe and paddled many of the hundreds of kilometres of waterways the French *coureurs de bois* and traders of the Hudson's Bay Company had negotiated centuries earlier. And he did this in the 1920s, well before any of our modern canoeing and camping conveniences had been invented. The same kind of hands-on experience underlies *The Cod Fisheries* (Innis 1940), which is based on field research Innis conducted in isolated fishing outports in Newfoundland and the Maritimes in the 1920s and 1930s. By the 1940s, Innis had travelled to and experienced most places in Canada and had collected a wealth of first-hand knowledge of the country's geography and its people.

Innis's 'monk-like devotion' (Watson 2006: 398) to dirt research epitomizes the materialist attitude toward understanding human societies and in some ways surpasses even Marx's dedication to grounding social theory in real human activity—by getting up close and personal with the ground itself. Innis's materialism did not make him sympathetic to Marxism, or for that matter, to any other theory of political economy grafted onto the Canadian experience. His approach was nevertheless consistent with Marx's and other materialists' belief that the ways that people use and transform their material surroundings to meet their needs form the foundation of any society and shape its subsequent development.

best articulate how and why the pioneer experience was irreconcilable with traditional institutions (Clark 1959). These early innovations then shaped subsequent development in these areas, said Clark, providing a legacy of Western protest that contributed to the rise of the CCF, for example. Clark thus strengthened the links between material, economic development and the emergence of social groups in Canada that were first conceived by Innis.

Innis and Clark, along with their contemporaries and early followers (Ryerson 1960; Watkins 1963), laid the foundations for a unique brand of materialism—Canadian **political economy**—that shaped how many Canadian political sociologists came to look at contemporary power relations. The central role played by material in these first economic, political, and social histories of Canada helped establish a *critical* tradition in Canadian sociology that is not as well established in the US (Brym and Fox 1989; Brym and St Pierre 1997; McLaughlin 2005; McLaughlin and Puddephat 2008; Helmes-Hayes and McLaughlin 2009). Along with this, the significance of geography in these early histories sensitized Canadian political economy to space and region in ways that continue to be reflected in Canadian political sociology (Clement 2001). These tendencies were most evident in the so-called 'new political economy' (Clement and Williams 1989) of the 1970s into the 1980s, when many of the concerns of materialists outside of Canada were taken up and applied to the Canadian context. The new political economists explored Canadian labour and development from a class perspective, while engaging with Canada's regional diversity and status as a staples producer. Regional studies, works concerned with development on the Prairies and in the Maritime provinces especially (see Brym and Neis 1978; Sacouman 1979, 1980, 1981; Matthews 1981, 1983; Sinclair 1975) were common, as was research that pondered Canada's reliance on industrialized powers as markets for its staples. Here, the overlap with dependency theory came naturally. Some such as Gordon Laxer (1985, 1989) produced innovative analyses combining a traditional Innisian concern with staples production with the dependency approach to explain phenomena like the high rate of foreign corporate ownership in Canada. Others, like William Carroll (1986), offered a different view, of Canadian corporate interests intertwined with foreign capital rather than overly dependent upon them.

Like other political sociologists elsewhere who were operating in the materialist tradition, many of Canada's new political economists favoured a historical or historical comparative approach to Canadian development. Thus appeared works contrasting the development, composition, and power of classes in Canada with the experiences of other countries such as Sweden or the United States (see Black and Myles 1986; Baer, Grabb, and Johnston 1993). The United States, as in Innis's and Clark's day, was often and perhaps unavoidably included in these comparisons, especially in the years following the influential works on political and attitudinal differences between the US and Canada by the American sociologist Seymour M. Lipset (1963, 1964, 1986, 1990). Lipset's claims, including that Canadians were more likely than Americans to join unions and otherwise act collectively along material or class lines because they were less individualistic, were taken up and ultimately challenged by Canadian political sociologists. James Curtis, William Johnston, Douglas Baer, and Edward Grabb, each an experienced class analyst on his own, combined forces in a number of articles to confront Lipset's thesis, showing that Canadians and Canadian development were imbued as much with individualism as were their American counterparts (Baer, Grabb, and Johnston 1990; see also Bowden 1989, 1990). These scholars showed that the stronger position of labour in Canada and the more socialist character of its government did not derive from a formative event comparable to the American Revolution, which Lipset claimed planted the seeds for the strong individualist sentiment in the US. Although their research was perhaps more concerned with countering Lipset's claims than offering alternative material-based explanations of Canada-US differences, it nevertheless demonstrated a continuity with a Canadian political economy perspective traditionally concerned with histories of economic development, geography, and class.

Materialists represented the 'first wave' of political sociologists in many places, including Canada, and questions of development were some of the first that these early scholars tackled. But political sociologists have taken a materialist approach to other social phenomena as well, and it is to some of these we now turn.

Materialism and the State

Anyone can become Prime Minister of Canada. At least that is what we are told or led to believe. All you need are some good ideas, some relevant educational and experiential skills, and the will to succeed, and you can make it into the upper echelons of government. So why is it that so many of Canada's prime ministers have come from wealthy backgrounds? Why have almost all of them been successful business people or lawyers? Why have we not seen former cab drivers or social workers or librarians in the top offices of the Canadian state? Are they less able, less ambitious, less skilled than business people and lawyers? Of course not, say political sociologists who adhere to the materialist tradition. Your *class background*—the material circumstances from which you come and the material conditions that you enjoy—determines your chances of becoming Prime Minister to a much greater degree than your ambition. This is because the state, say materialists, exists primarily to benefit the materially advantaged. And business people and lawyers represent those interests much better than elementary school teachers or nurses.

The state occupies a privileged place in the research of most political sociologists and has, since Marx's day, been understood by materialists to be largely a vehicle of class power. But the state was relatively neglected as a primary focus of study among materialists until the 1970s. It was Ralph Miliband (1969) who changed that. Building upon Marx's ([1888] 1985: 82) treatment of the state as 'but a committee for managing the common affairs of the whole bourgeoisie', Miliband carefully documented the real-life connections between state officials and business interests in countries like Britain and the US to show that the state acted always and directly in the interests of the dominant class. This happened, said Miliband, not because the bourgeoisie forced them to do so, but because the politicians and other high-placed servants of the state were naturally sympathetic to and supportive of capitalist interests. Most of them came from wealthy backgrounds themselves and moved in the same professional and social circles as the corporate elite, places where capitalist goals and ideals were accepted as self-evident truths. Miliband said that politicians and state officials consistently acted in the interests of the bourgeoisie because many shared the same class position and understood the world in the same way as the bourgeoisie.

Miliband's study was significant because it came out at a time when many people thought that class analyses of state power were no longer useful or relevant. After the Second World War, the massive expansion of state-sponsored welfare provisions had convinced many that material inequality would no longer serve as important a basis for political power as it had in the past. Miliband argued otherwise, reminding us of the strong links that continued to exist between material advantage and political power.

Miliband's work inspired a number of political sociologists to take up the study of the state from a Marxist or materialist perspective. Nicos Poulantzas (1973), a contemporary of Miliband's, proposed that the capitalist state was not so much **instrumental** but *relatively autonomous*, in that its officials were capable of occasionally acting independently of the bourgeoisie—provided their policies ensured the continued viability of the capitalist system as a whole. That the state often takes decisions that are contrary to the interests of the capitalist class has concerned other political sociologists too. They have wondered about the positive and negative implications for labour and capital of a state like the welfare state, which appears to be trying to serve both. Ian Gough (1979) said such 'contradictions' in action meant that the state cannot be seen strictly as functioning in the interests of capital. Claus Offe (1984) explored how attempts by state officials to offset economic and legitimacy crises that arise with the progress of capitalism can create new crises (fiscal or administrative, or crises of legitimacy) in their place. These approaches were accompanied by works like that of Piven and Cloward (1971), which rejected the notion that the capitalist state ever operated in the interests of labour but instead passed social welfare policies strictly as a means of pacifying and controlling the working class. Other key critical materialist interpretations of the state include C. Wright Mills's (1955) study. Mills argued that in the post–Second World War period, the US was ruled by a higher circle of corporate, military, and political leaders who controlled the massive and interlocking hierarchies of the economy, army, and state. Mills was not a Marxist but instead subscribed to a broader understanding of where power resided in society, namely, not only in the ownership of the means of production, but also in the capacity to mobilize other sorts of material or material-related assets.

Canada has produced its own stock of works taking a materialist perspective on the state. Miliband's and Mills's commitment to illuminating the links between the corporate elite and the state has been shared by Canadian political sociologists such as John Porter (1965), Wallace Clement (1975, 1977), and Dennis Olsen (1977, 1980). Of these three, Clement's and Olsen's analyses of the Canadian state fall closest to the Miliband tradition, in that they document the close ties between corporate and state interests in Canada. Porter's work was different, being more along the lines of Mills in that it was concerned not only with the owners of the means of production, but with elites more generally. Porter (1965) described a Canadian society that was not the cheerful jumble of different ethnic groups as it had often been portrayed (Gibbon 1938), but a **vertical mosaic** dominated by political, economic, and cultural elites from what he termed the **charter groups**. These were composed of individuals whose heritage was linked to the first groups to dominate the state. In Canada's case, this meant either Anglo or French elites, but especially those with British ancestry. Though not strictly in the political economy tradition, Porter nevertheless inspired the new political economists we discussed above because he contemplated many of the field's traditional concerns, including class, from a historical comparative and macro perspective (Helmes-Hayes and Curtis 1998; Helmes-Hayes 2002; 2009; Clement 2001).

Materialism and Resistance

Marx predicted that the capitalist mode of production, as it approached its zenith, would produce a worldwide and revolutionary proletariat who would overthrow capitalism and institute **communism**. He and Engels assured readers of *The Communist Manifesto* that all this would come to pass, declaring that the "fall [of the bourgeoisie] and the victory of the proletariat are equally inevitable" (Marx and Engels [1888] 1985: 94). Well, the revolution has yet to happen, and the question why the working class has so far failed to rise up against their oppressors has plagued many a political sociologist. To address it, some scholars have attempted to measure whether some of the processes that Marx said would precede the revolution are happening, whether the classes are or are not becoming more polarized, for instance, or whether members of the working class are developing *class consciousness*. This is an awareness of their common class position that Marx said was necessary if they were to recognize and resist the power of the bourgeoisie.

The political sociologist who took up these questions most vigorously is Erik Olin Wright (1985, 1990). He spearheaded the Comparative Project on Class Structure and Class Consciousness (Wright 1989) that sought to assess empirically whether capitalist societies were moving to a strictly two-class (bourgeoisie and proletariat) system and to gauge how strongly people identified with their class position. Surveys undertaken in ten countries produced some interesting findings. In the US, for example, Wright (1989) found a large and persistent middle class, a finding that cast some doubt on whether class polarization was occurring there. Nevertheless, class attitudes were consistent with class position, with working class respondents decidedly more anti-capitalist than their bourgeois counterparts (Wright 1989). While Wright's surveys may not have provided all the answers that Marxists awaiting revolution desired, his efforts to operationalize Marxist concepts and processes that had hitherto never been quantified continue to be debated in Marxist circles.

Not all materialists have been as interested as Wright in finding a strictly Marxist basis for potential resistance in the modern world. Political sociologists have also elaborated on the influence of a broader array of material resources on resistance to power in a wider range of circumstances. **Resource mobilization theory (RMT)** emerged in the 1970s in response to the ways scholars had traditionally understood collective action. **Collective behaviour** theory had until that point said that it was largely psychology or emotions that compelled people to come together in groups to demonstrate or to lobby for change. Thus, Gustave LeBon ([1895] 1995) said that people fall victim to irrational psychological **contagion** when in group situations that can lead to riots or collective action. Proponents of **relative deprivation theory** (Searles and Williams 1962; Gusfield 1963) hypothesized that people come together in social movements because they are angry and feel they have been unjustly treated by someone or some organization or institution. But RMT theorists (McCarthy and Zald 1977) noted that crowds or feelings of anger and injustice, while important, were not sufficient to motivate people enough to start or join in collective activity. They said that in order to sustain mobilization and generate change, groups also have to draw upon and rely on various resources. These include money, of course, which is needed to pay for media campaigns, legal advisors, and so on. But resources also include things like places to meet, connections with important people who can forward the cause publicly or politically, and associations with other established organizations with similar mandates. These can provide the new movement with members and the administrative means to get things done.

Canadian political sociologists have also been interested in the influence of material resources on people's capacity to resist power. Indeed, Canada was one of the countries included in Wright's Comparative Project (John Myles served as principal investigator in 1982 and 1983), the data from which were used to measure Canadian class consciousness (Johnston, Grabb, and Baer 1993). Resource mobilization theory has also been widely used by Canadian researchers analyzing collective and political action (see Nakhaie 1992; Harrison and Krahn 1995; Tindall 2002; Ramos 2006). But the materialist perspective in the resistance literature in Canada has been dominated by political economy, thanks in large part to the work and influence of sociologists like William Carroll. Carroll's on-going critical analysis of Canadian and global corporate capital (1986, 2004, 2007, 2008) has inevitably been part-nered with a close study of the workers' (and now transnational and anti-globalization) movements that have accompanied and resisted the rise of capitalism (Carroll 2006). His sustained focus on the material foundations of power and the resistance to it reflects not only the Canadian tradition in pol-itical economy but also the continued relevance of class to understanding how power is both exercised and opposed in modern societies.

Materialism and Contemporary Inequalities

Political sociologists with a materialist orientation have made important con-tributions to the way we analyze how social actors employ material resources in their exercise of and opposition to power. But, you might ask, what about power imbalances between men and women? Between different racial and ethnic groups? Between people of different sexualities? At first sight these do not look as if they are determined by material relations. It is true that women, people with darker skin, people whose countries of origin lie outside the Western world, and non-heterosexuals are, on balance, not as able to exercise their will as men, people with lighter skin, Westerners, and heterosexuals. But usually we attribute these sorts of power differences to **prejudice** rather than material circumstances, and thus we often understand the **discrimination** that the less powerful groups experience to be due to unjust negative stereo-typing of its members. Can power inequalities among these groups be under-stood in material terms?

Marx gave only the barest indication in his writing of his thoughts on ethnicity, nation, race, family, and women. But later writers used his brief insights to engage with each of these issues. For instance, Edna Bonacich's (1972) **split labour market theory** proposed that ethnic animosities arose not from prejudice, but from the competition fostered by employers among ethnically distinct groups to reduce labour costs; John Porter (1965) said inequality among racial and ethnic groups was not merely the outcome of intolerance or bigotry, but was also a consequence of their positions relative to the charter groups in Canada's vertical mosaic; and Milton Gordon (1978), Raymond Breton (1998), and Grace-Edward Galabuzi (2006) all wrote about how ethnicity, nation, or race are largely intersected with eco-nomic and material conditions. Marxist **feminists** and scholars who employ a political economy approach to the study of women have also found that questions of gender are embedded within material relations. The rest of the chapter will briefly look at how a materialist approach can help account for gender inequality.

It was not until after Marx's death in 1883 that his friend and long-time collaborator, Friedrich Engels ([1884] 1972), articulated the Marxist view of women and the family. Engels said that the domination of women by men, and women's relegation to the private sphere, were modern developments that had emerged to help protect and perpetuate the accumulation of wealth by the bourgeoisie. Monogamy and the subordination of women to men helped to ensure that all children of the bourgeois marriage were legitimate heirs. They guaranteed that the accumulated assets of bourgeois males could be passed down intact to the next generation, thus perpetuating the family's material advantage and in turn the material power of an entire class.

Engels' work served as an important foundation for feminist theorizing in the twentieth century. Marxist feminists of the 1960s and 1970s took up Engels' work most directly. Canadian scholar Margaret Benston (1969) articulated one of the first and most influential Marxist feminist analyses of gender inequality. She explained how the subordination of women was an outcome of an economic system that considered the socially necessary labour performed overwhelmingly by women—cooking, cleaning, child-bearing, and the care of family members to be 'unproductive' because it was work that took place outside the money economy. Women held a lower status than men in modern societies because their work was 'valueless' in a capitalist economy that privileged paid work (Smith 1973; Waring 1990). Marxist feminists also argued that the perception that women's work *in* the home was unproductive extended to perceptions of women's work *outside* the home. The low value placed on women's work in the home undermined the **market worth** of women's labour or what employers were willing to pay women. Women's paid labour, especially in the caring industries such as teaching, nursing, cleaning, and other support services, which are dominated by women, was devalued, in part because it was understood to replicate those 'unproductive' tasks for which women are 'naturally' suited (Luxton 1980; MacDougall 1997).

As a result, say Armstrong and Armstrong (2010), women face a **double ghetto**: they are 'ghettoized,' restricted to spaces where their work is unrecognized and poorly rewarded, in the home and in the workplace. The devaluing of women's work relative to men's even extends to other professions, such as medicine, law, business, and university teaching. In these professions a **wage gap** persists among women and men with the same education and experience, and women moving up in an organization encounter a **glass ceiling** above which they are not promoted. Generally speaking then, a materialist approach to gender inequality says the domination of women by men in and outside the home reflects and sustains the class system by ensuring that (proletariat) labour is 'reproduced' (born and cared for) at no cost to employers; that accumulated (bourgeois) wealth is maintained across generations; and that employers have access to a cheap supply of labour that can be paid less without much justification.

You may be saying to yourself, 'That might have happened in the past, but not today!' But recent Canadian statistics suggest otherwise. As in most developed countries, the proportion of women in the Canadian workforce has risen steadily since the Second World War. In fact, in 2010 approximately

TABLE 2.3 Labour Force and Participation Rates by Sex and Age Group

	2006	2007	2008	2009	2010
			thousand		
Labour force	17,516.7	17,884.2	18,203.9	18,329.0	18,525.1
Men	9,308.3	9,472.3	9,644.4	9,671.3	9,763.3
Women	8,208.4	8,411.9	8,559.5	8,657.8	8,761.8
Participation rates			percentages		
15 years and over	67.0	67.4	67.7	67.1	67.0
Men	72.3	72.5	72.8	71.9	71.7
Women	61.8	62.5	62.7	62.5	62.4
15–24 years	66.2	66.9	67.5	65.5	64.5
Men	66.2	67.4	68.0	65.7	64.4
Women	66.2	66.5	67.0	65.2	64.6
25–44 years	86.9	87.3	87.2	86.9	86.8
Men	92.1	92.1	92.4	91.4	91.3
Women	81.7	82.5	82.1	82.3	82.3
45 years and over	52.8	53.6	54.3	54.5	54.8
Men	59.6	60.0	60.5	60.5	60.7
Women	46.6	47.7	48.5	48.9	49.3
65 years and over	8.3	8.9	10.1	10.5	11.4
Men	12.1	13.0	14.2	15.1	16.2
Women	5.2	5.6	6.8	6.7	7.5

Source: Statistics Canada Summary Tables, http://www40.statcan.gc.ca/l01/cst01/labor05-eng.htm

62 per cent of Canadian women (see Table 2.3) were in the paid labour force, up from about 42 per cent in 1976 (Statistics Canada 2006; 2011).

However the economy still largely advantages men. It appears women continue to be 'ghettoized' in the workforce. As we show in the next chapter, about 67 per cent of all women employed in Canada in 2006 worked in teaching, nursing and health-related occupations, clerical or other administrative positions, or sales and service occupations. These are by far some of the poorest-paid positions in the labour market. Indeed, as of 2003, 'women working on a full-time, full-year basis had average earnings of $36,500, or 71% [of] what their male counterparts made', (Statistics Canada 2006a) indicating the average economic disadvantage faced by women. Furthermore, women, both those who work in and outside the home, continue to shoulder the responsibilities of reproducing labour in the modern economy, performing the lion's share of child and elder care and housework (Statistics Canada 2006b). It is true that, as women have entered the workforce in greater numbers, some of these tasks have been redistributed to others—spouses, cleaners, and child care workers. But it is still largely women, not men, who face a double or triple workday, coming home after a full day's work to another several hours of household duties.

Given the income disadvantage that women face in the labour market, and the continued expectation that they will take the lead in household tasks, it is perhaps not surprising that it is women who are most likely to experience **work disruptions** because of family needs. When a woman gives birth to a child, she usually leaves the paid labour force for a period of time. Women in part-time or less secure jobs must deal with the inevitable loss of income, plus the fact that her job may not be there when she is ready to return. Even full-time workers, who are protected by federal law that compels employers to reserve their jobs, can experience negative economic repercussions. A recent report by TD Economics showed that 'absences related to childcare were found to generate a persistent 3% wage penalty per year of absence' (Caranci and Gauthier 2010). Finally, because of the absence of reliable, universal child care in Canada and various tax incentives, middle-class families often find women choosing to take a leave from work during the early years of their children's lives to avoid exorbitant costs of child care. Yet, a mother's wages will take the inevitable hit when she returns to work.

So according to recent statistics, Canadian women as a group continue to experience material conditions that are inferior to men's. That this disadvantage occurs to a greater or lesser extent among all women regardless of their family circumstances or profession would hardly come as a surprise to materialists. The weak position of women relative to men in society—at home and in the labour market—derives from the capitalist class system itself. The subordination of women and the devaluing of their work are built into the bourgeois mode of production because they serve necessary functions for the maintenance of the existing class system and the continued operation of capitalism more generally. This is why, even with all the advances the women's movement has achieved over last century, women still have less power in most areas of life because of obstacles to their control of material resources.

In the classic Marxist treatment of **patriarchy**, the subordination of women by men would cease upon the revolutionary overthrow of capitalist society. Patriarchy is useful to the bourgeois mode of production; get rid of the latter and the former will disappear. But is it that easy? Not that reconstitution of the entire system would be easy, but is gender inequality really only an outgrowth of class inequality? Some feminist researchers doubt it. Socialist feminists may agree that women's subordination has an 'elective affinity' with the operation of capitalist society, that is, gender inequality conveniently serves certain purposes in the system. But it is not generated by the system. It is a form of oppression that working women experience *over* and *above* class oppression. Women are thus doubly oppressed in contemporary societies: once by the bourgeoisie and once by men (Barrett 1980; Ursel 1986). Materialist analyses of gender inequality have also come under scrutiny by scholars affiliated with various branches of **third-wave feminism**. Earlier feminist accounts are thought to have neglected the experiences of women who are not middle- or upper-class and white. Non-white women, working class women, immigrant women, and women in post-colonial societies face a complex and interacting array of oppressions that cannot be reduced to questions of material ownership alone (see Bannerji 1995, 2000, 2005; Hooks 1981, 1984; Ng 1984, 1988; Spivak 1988). Post-structuralist feminists offer another critique, which charges that traditional approaches to the subjugation of women treat gender as essential and unproblematic rather than socially constituted (see Butler 1990).

Summary

In this chapter we introduced you to some of the ways that political sociologists have understood how access to and control over material resources can shape power relations. You met the founder of materialist accounts of politics, Karl Marx, whose insights continue to frame materialist perspectives today. We showed you, with an emphasis on the Canadian experience, not only how material resources shape individual and group power negotiations, but also how they influence the formation of institutions like the state and international relations. In all of these cases material bases of power sustain political relations but can also be used to challenge them. We looked to RMT and political economy approaches to show how those who are disadvantaged can employ money, organizations, and social networks to mobilize for change. Throughout we made reference to unionization, global inequality, and gender relations to show how political sociologists understand how these play out in the real world.

As we have seen, however, third-wave and post-structuralist feminists challenge pure materialist interpretations, suggesting that power inequalities are more than just class interests in disguise. As we will see in the next chapter, many feminist researchers, and activists too, see inequality as a type of power imbalance that derives from *cultural* and *social* factors.

Questions for Critical Thought

1. What are some of the advantages and, hence, life chances you have experienced because of your access to or control of various material resources?

2. Why is it difficult for non-unionized workers and women to attain material power?

3. Do perspectives on material resources offer better accounts of power inequalities than individual explanations?

4. How do relationships with those around you affect unequal access to and control over material resources and your ability to achieve the goals you wish to pursue?

Suggestions for Further Reading ···

Clement, Wallace, and Glen Williams (eds). 1989. *The New Canadian Political Economy*. Montreal: McGill-Queens University Press. An edited collection that encompasses some of the works of key scholars of the new Canadian political economy approach.

Marx, Karl, and Friedrich Engels. [1888] 1985. *The Communist Manifesto*. London: Penguin Classics. One of the most influential political works to have been produced in modern history. It outlines a course of political action based on materialist grounds.

McMichael, Philip. 2011. *Development and Social Change: A Global Perspective, 5th edition*. Sage/Pine Forge Press. A historical account of the international system of states and how material resources have produced global inequality.

Waring, Marilyn. 1990. *What If Women Counted: A New Feminist Economics*. San Franciso: Harper Collins. A materialist analysis that challenges how researchers value women's work and how they measure it.

Websites ···

Gøsta Esping-Andersen's website
www.esping-andersen.com

Marxists.org
www.marxists.org

Progressive economics
www.progressive-economics.ca

Immanuel Wallerstein's website
www.iwallerstein.com

3   Cultural and Social Status

Learning Objectives

- To become familiar with Weber's critique of Marx's materialist perspective on power
- To understand how social markers can be employed to acquire status power
- To examine the ideas of Antonio Gramsci and others who elaborated on how culture acts in concert with material resources to enhance the power of elites
- To explain Pierre Bourdieu's notions of cultural and social capital and how these concepts have been employed in the analysis of power
- To see how politics in the workplace, LGBT activism, and ethnic nationalism can be understood in terms of the ways cultural and social resources are distributed among social actors
- To examine conceptualizations of collective identity as a foundation for mobilization and contesting power
- To explore how both nationalist and post-colonial scholarship understand and promote the efforts of marginalized groups seeking recognition to enhance their power

Introduction

As we showed in Chapter 2, access to and control over material resources clearly shape the way that power contests unfold. However, as useful as the materialist perspective has proved to be, some political sociologists are dissatisfied with its apparent inability to explain particular sorts of power inequalities. These scholars say that, these days, people seem more likely to see and experience power through what sociologists call *markers of status*. These are signs that communicate *social prestige* to other people and confirm their standing to those who use them. Such markers come in many forms. Signs and symbols, whether they are chosen, like style of dress, or **ascribed**, like physical characteristics, or something in between, like dialect, are of interest to sociologists because any and all of them can affect how people react to one another in different social settings. They can influence whether or not a person is seen as belonging to or excluded from certain social groups or organizations or even from citizenship. This is because markers are valued differently. Some markers, such as expert knowledge or the ability to speak English, are prized by most people. Others, like face tattoos or skimpy clothing, are usually disparaged. People who display undesirable markers tend to hold lower status or social prestige because those markers are perceived to be less valuable in the power negotiations they engage in (see Box 3.1).

BOX 3.1 ❖ EBONICS AND SYMBOLIC POWER

A person's material possessions, like clothes or jewellery, might show how much wealth she has, but they can also indicate that she belongs to a certain social group or **culture**. Wearing a sari, for instance, could identify a person as making *claims* to, or asserting, her membership in Indian or South Asian culture. A person's physical characteristics, such as his sex, skin colour, or physique, can also serve as markers of status, as can traits that are less apparent, for instance, the type of vocabulary he uses in his everyday speech or his accent. Using North American slang or speaking English with a British accent each offers a very different picture of the person speaking and is imbued with very different assumptions of who the person is and hence the power he holds in relation to others.

With respect to the latter, consider the debate in the US about whether **Ebonics** should be taught in schools. Ebonics is a dialect of American English that is associated with African-American culture and status and some say it is distinct enough to be considered a language. In the 1990s, advocates of the dialect urged educators in Oakland, California, to adopt Ebonics in school curricula to make the material taught in schools more relevant to the predominately African-American students. The Oakland board agreed, declaring that many of its 28,000 Black students did not speak 'English' and that schools should do their best to incorporate Ebonics into lesson plans (Applebom 1996). However, other people, such as parents, teachers, and representatives of African-American communities worried that students from these schools would ultimately be disadvantaged because the dominant, non-**racialized** population did not place the same value on the dialect as on 'standard' English. The Rev. Jesse Jackson, a civil-rights leader, lamented, 'This is an unacceptable, surrender, borderlining on disgrace. . . . It's teaching down to our children' (Lewis 1996). Jackson and other critics of the move recognized that Ebonics acted as a marker of status in the US that could limit students' **life chances**, or opportunities to succeed in pursuing their goals, and hence reduce their ability to exert their will in relation to others.

Why shouldn't Ebonics or Spanish or Mandarin Chinese or any other language spoken by a sizable minority have the same social standing as that enjoyed by the dominant language? The answer, say political sociologists, should be sought in the underlying political processes that shape the status—and hence the power—associated with different social and cultural markers.

Like material forms of power, cultural and social markers are not just bound to individual **claims making**. It is not just about how each of us possesses or chooses to use different markers that tell the world 'who we are', although this is part of it. It is also about whether or not other people *recognize* these markers as legitimate and in turn recognize and confer status. This is because status power can derive from markers only if others accept that they should be rewarded in some way.

Thus, like material forms of power, markers of status are *negotiated*. People make claims and others evaluate whether they will be accepted. The ability to obtain and control different markers and the ability to resist them are all central to how power is negotiated. Political sociologists who study how markers are employed in power contests over status are essentially looking at how cultural and social factors shape power relations. These are experienced in everyday life through a myriad of interactions. Because of this, many would argue that, unlike other manifestations of power, such as material or institutional power, the power that flows from cultural and social markers is more malleable, constructed, accessible, and perhaps even more democratic.

In this chapter we look at these ideas in more detail and introduce you to some well-known cultural and social thinkers to help clarify this perspective. We begin by looking at Weber's critique and extension of Marx's work and then at others who have theorized cultural and social power. In doing so, we explore the works of Antonio Gramsci, introduce Pierre Bourdieu's notions of cultural and social capital and Robert Putnam's notions of bridging and bonding social capital. We then also illustrate the importance of collective identity in post-colonial, nationalist, and New Social Movements research by looking at the insights of Frantz Fanon and Alberto Melucci. To understand how these ideas can be applied, we look at examples from Canadian and North American politics, the situation of women in the labour force, LGBT activism, Quebec nationalism, and Canadian Aboriginal mobilization.

Weber—The Original Critic of Marx

One of the first and most influential critics of a purely materialist perspective on power and, more specifically of Marx, was Max Weber. As we noted in the introduction, he not only recognized the importance of material resources in the shaping of power, but also saw that social and institutional resources matter. Weber (1968) criticized Marx for failing to consider non-economic forms of power. He realized that, although the working class could be identified by their common material circumstances, there existed among them a number of divisions based on culture, ethnicity, religion, and so forth. Weber considered these to be forms of different **status groups**, which had varying degrees of recognized prestige or social honour associated with them.

Why did this matter? For Weber, prestige or social honour are key factors in shaping struggles over power. He found that often the individuals that constituted different status groups shared a sense of dignity for which they sought recognition to enhance their reputation, worth, and value. This even happened among members of the same class. As we noted in Chapter 1, Weber

(1946: 192) observed that among wealthy families, people with 'old money' had a sense of dignity that distinguished them from people with 'new money'. Although all the families enjoyed the same material conditions, the 'parvenus', or **nouveaux riches**, were rarely acceptable to the traditional moneyed families as guests, as members of their social clubs, or as marriage partners. The older families distinguished themselves as more cultured, 'in sharp opposition to the pretensions of sheer property', and used various means to distinguish themselves from the brash newcomers (Weber 1946: 187). These types of divisions still exist today among the wealthy, as do examples of ambitious people, not satisfied with their economic or material power, who seek greater social recognition. Conrad Black, a very wealthy Canadian businessman renounced his Canadian citizenship in order to become a (largely symbolic) British peer, and thus able to sit in the House of Lords. If money and material possessions were all that ambitious people like Black needed to acquire the power they desired, why would they sacrifice so much? They do so for social prestige, recognition, or the status those markers confer and in turn the power that comes with them.

Status groups, Weber noted, were identified by common lifestyles. He noticed that people with similar status lived in the same neighbourhoods and often shared common attitudes toward work and culture. These maintained the boundaries of the group, regulated their membership, and distinguished them from other groups within a given society. Shaughnessy in Vancouver, the Bridle Path in Toronto, Westmount in Montreal, and the South End of Halifax are all examples of wealthy and exclusive neighbourhoods, where people share similar values and statuses. In them, people often drive expensive cars and have manicured lawns—sharing similar tastes in consumer goods and aesthetics. They may shop at exclusive stores, send their children to private schools, and engage in exotic leisure activities, and they expect others who subscribe to their culture to do the same. We can also see a similar sharing of lifestyles in ethnic and racial neighbourhoods like Little Italy, Greektown, or Chinatown, which can be found in most large cities. Again, those spaces are shaped by social groups sharing similar statuses, which are expressed through markers, such as where and how members of those groups live. You may not have thought about it before, but where you live or eat your dinner can be understood as an expression of your political power.

Although lifestyle choices may be the most obvious expressions of status, being able to identify the markers of those differences is not the only interest of political sociologists. They are also concerned with how and why markers are attached to different levels of status. They observe that status is usually not chosen, but instead is governed by social forces external to individuals. As Weber recognized, embedded within certain markers and lifestyles are underlying privileges that accrue to those who possess and live them. For instance, individuals with 'old money' held higher status than 'new money' in Weber's day, and members of the latter sought acceptance by the former; since being a British lord bestowed greater honour as far as Conrad Black was concerned than being a plain old Canadian citizen, he was compelled to renounce the latter. Thus, Weber said, contemporary societies are not only materially **stratified**, but they are also socially stratified. Status groups are hierarchically ordered; their members possess different degrees of social honour and hence different capacities to exercise power, and upward **mobility** between status groups is difficult. So like other forms of power, the power derived from status is associated with the ability to gain access to and control something of social value—in this case markers of status. But the negotiation of status power also reveals how important it is that those markers be recognized by others to offer the legitimacy that is an essential ingredient in holding and exercising power.

How people consciously employ markers to enhance their status relative to others may be obvious to you. But often those who have high levels of status fail to see how it contributes to their advantage. Political sociologists are especially interested in revealing the 'hidden', unspoken, or **latent** values placed on social markers in different times and places. They wish to show how access to and control over these markers enhances or detracts from the power of an individual or group. For example, someone whose native language is English and who is a crack squash player or golfer may not spend much time thinking about how these markers benefit her. But the reality is that these traits grant her higher status and hence provide her with more potent sources of power to improve her chances for mobility, than is the case with someone whose mother tongue is Cree and who is skilled in goose hunting. Now it is true that these skills could open doors for both women. Cree and goose hunting would likely allow for greater ease and confidence when participating in Cree culture; English and golf facilitate participation in Anglo-Western culture. But given that the former is a small, subordinate population that has been colonized by the latter, dominant culture, the woman who has easier access to Anglo-Western culture will invariably have more power and enhanced life chances than her Cree-speaking counterpart, whether she realizes it or not.

Although Weber was one of the first critics of the strictly materialist perspective, he was far from the last. Others have taken up his observations of how markers are linked to status and power and in doing so have more explicitly examined the roles of culture and society in their development. It is a rich and varied field of scholarship that has manifested itself in some very complex forms. To help you grasp this approach we will introduce you to some key scholars, like Antonio Gramsci, Pierre Bourdieu, Robert Putnam, and Frantz Fanon, and we will examine how they have dealt with the most crucial questions pertaining to cultural and social sources of power, namely: how does the negotiation of cultural and social power compare with material accounts? How are cultural and social power exercised, and by whom?

Hegemony and the Culture Industry

Many of the first theorizations of cultural and social forms of power were, like Weber's work, responses to Marx and materialist analyses. Others were extensions of it. Although Marx partially dealt with these issues through his notions of superstructure and **utopia**, he did not fully conceptualize them, and they were only fully developed by later scholars that built upon Marxist ideas by elaborating the connection between material advantage and culture. Even though a number of scholars, like Marx, reacted to the Industrial Revolution by looking at the unprecedented reordering of material relations that it caused, other thinkers also considered how those same forces moved societies towards a more centralized, mechanistic, and unified cultural and social history. Antonio Gramsci (1971), a Marxist of the early twentieth century, was one of the many that pondered these forces. Gramsci was troubled by the apparent indifference of the working class to the appeals of Marxist revolutionaries in countries with oppressive and **fascist** states. He theorized that their lack of concern was cultivated by bourgeois-led state officials who exercised power through *cultural* as well as political institutions. The leaders of the **hegemonic** state, Gramsci said, 'manufactured' the consent of the masses by ensuring that the ideologies and values communicated through the schools, the religious institutions, and the media confirmed the status quo. In this sense cultural hegemony determines which markers are granted legitimate status. If the masses were to be mobilized for the purpose of social change, then leaders had to do more than just call attention to their material deprivation. They had to produce **counter-hegemonic** positions by laying claim to alternative cultural and social markers that reconfigured and challenged the hegemony of elites. He thus observed that laying claim to cultural and social markers as well as challenging them is essential for mobilizing people and gaining power.

The problem, said Gramsci, was that the intellectuals, who were positioned to critique and challenge cultural and social hegemony, were **alienated** from the majority of people. As a result, existing markers of culture and social practices largely went unchallenged. Since, as the common expression goes, academics live and work in 'ivory towers', Gramsci feared that the ideas they produced had little salience among everyday people. He thus advocated for **organic intellectuals** who would be able to make arguments that were embedded within mass culture to challenge the hegemonic power of dominant groups. Another way of understanding this is that he encouraged the elite 'brokers of knowledge' to make populist appeals against the dominant culture and initiate social change. He thus recognized that power is found in the control of which markers of culture and social relations are seen as legitimate.

Present-day political sociologists, such as Michael Burawoy (2004), have called on scholars to practise **public sociology**, which is morally bound and self-aware, and which extends outside the realm of academe to affect people's daily lives. Although this idea is not directly linked to Gramsci, it nevertheless encourages the production of counter-hegemonic claims that everyday people can use. While there are political sociologists who agree with Burawoy's position, it is far from uncontentious. Some say that the discipline, especially in Canada, has been too focused on counter-hegemonic values at the cost of solid social science (Goldberg and van den Berg 2009), and yet others worry that the concept is too ambiguous (Creese, McLaren, and Pulkingham 2009; McLaughlin and Turcotte 2007; McLaughlin, Kowalchuck, and Turcotte 2005). Regardless of such concerns, Gramsci's take-home message was that power was exercised, and could only be challenged through cultural as well as material means. Power is not only about class, it is also about shaping and controlling the culture in which class operates.

The roles of cultural and social factors in relation to power were also taken up by a number of writers contemplating the rise of North American consumer culture. Max Horkheimer and Theodor Adorno's (2006) theorization of the **culture industry** is especially enlightening. Both were key figures in the **Frankfurt School** of critical social theory. They argued that the production of culture had become a **total power** in the modern age. Horkheimer and Adorno observed that whereas cultures had once been fragmented and varied, American culture had become an increasingly uniform, holistic, dominant, and hegemonic tool in the hands of a small number of elites—particularly those who wielded material power. Horkheimer and Adorno argued that such homogenization and monopolization of the control of culture has serious consequences for its content and the effects of popular culture on people.

They lamented that, although modern culture may be sold as something that is multi-faceted and that liberalizes individual interests, in reality people have little incentive to or lack the ability to engage culture or, for that matter, to resist the interests of dominant elites. For instance, although contemporary Western culture is presented as diverse, it has actually become very standardized. Any discussion about the differentiation of products is not about what they are but rather who sells them. For example, Horkheimer and Adorno would say that, although we can choose between GM and Toyota, Coke and Pepsi, and Wii and PS3, these differences are purely cosmetic. There is actually little real difference between cars, soft drinks, or gaming platforms. North Americans rarely choose electric bicycles over cars as a means of transportation, chimarrão over pop as something to drink, or writing a play for their community theatre group over playing video games. As can be seen in each of these examples, people choose among different brands and perhaps prices, but they do not imagine alternatives to what the elites provide them as choices. Horkheimer and Adorno (2006: 56) thus concluded that uniformity and standardization in the culture industry diminished consumers' ability to think creatively. It discouraged them from producing ideas that could offer resistance to the cultural homogenization and hegemony fostered by the dominant cultural producers. As a result, people were left with choices but not the freedom to imagine something completely different. If you think about it, the difference between the two is very important. Choice is limited to what is available. Freedom is the ability to do what one wants!

Manufacturing Consent

Later writers, such as Edward Herman and Noam Chomsky (1988), show that the domination of cultural and information production by a few can lead to the '**manufacturing of consent**'. They use a political economy approach, influenced by earlier Marxist analysis, to look at news media in the US. They find that the information provided by media sources, and in turn the views of the audiences that consume it, are shaped by various information 'filters' that together act as a **propaganda model**. The result is that the messages of the powerful are heard at the expense of others, thereby creating misleading information. Such filters include monopoly or concentration of ownership of media among a small number of corporations, the primacy of profit as the driving motivation of the news business, the media's reliance on 'experts' of their choosing as news sources and to frame and explain news events, the use of flak, or negative information, to delegitimize alternative voices, and the propagation of a national ideology as a means of social control. These filters influence what types of issues are covered by dominant news media and ensure that the perspectives of the most powerful are hegemonic.

One of Herman and Chomsky's key observations is that most of the media outlets in the US are controlled by **oligopolies**. This results in people often getting the same messages across different forms of media and limits the number and variation of stories and perspectives to which they could potentially be exposed. It also reduces the amount and kind of information they have for making sense of their worlds. The situation is much the same in Canada today, where the federal government and three to four corporations control the vast majority of media: the CBC, which is a government-funded Crown corporation; and the pillars of privately owned media: BCE, which recently bought part of CTVglobemedia; Shaw Media, which recently bought CanWest; and Vidéotron. On some fronts, for example, BCE and CTVglobemedia operated separately; however, since they had a partial overlap in other media sectors and ownership ties in many media businesses, they shared much content across their various cable, cellular, Internet, news, radio, telephone, and television holdings. The blurriness of this relationship is illustrated in Figure 3.1, which shows the ownership structure of their holdings.

The industry is changing so quickly that after the acquisition of CTV outright by BCE, the chart looks different—as seen in Figure 3.2. Because of continued mergers and acquisitions, even this chart will likely be out of date by the time this book is published. Both charts and Box 3.2 illustrate the current

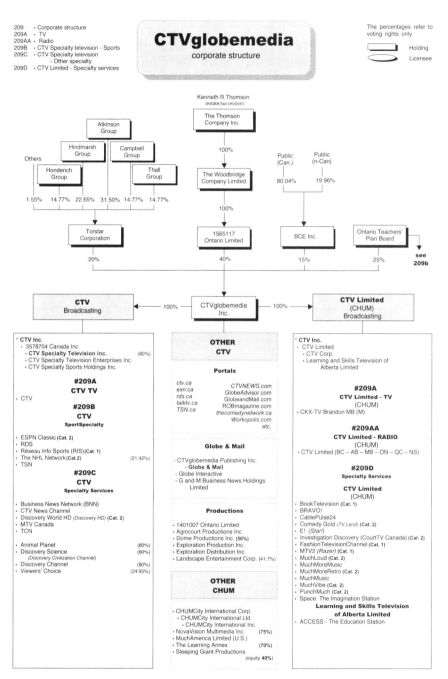

FIGURE 3.1 CTVglobemedia Ownership Chart

Source: CRTC.

Box 3.2 ⁑ How Synergy of Media Led BCE to Buy CTV

With the rise of the Internet during the 1990s, many people declared that *media synergy*, or what others call convergence, would intensify. Media synergy happens when content from one form of media is used in other forms to reduce the cost of content development and increase audience exposure to advertising messages. It is most likely to occur if ownership of different media is concentrated in the hands of a single owner or corporation.

During CTVglobemedia's coverage of the 2010 Vancouver Winter Olympics, for instance, similar and even the *same* reports were available on TSN and CTV News cable channels. The same information could also be found on the Bell cellular network in mobile form and on TSN and CTV's respective websites, with cross postings to the *Globe and Mail* online and its print newspaper. As well, identical stories and event schedules were reported on CHUM radio stations and on local CTV television affiliates across the country. So successful was CTV's synergy of Olympics coverage that Bell Canada Enterprises (BCE), the largest telecommunications company in Canada, was encouraged to acquire CTV, the country's biggest broadcaster, outright—as it ultimately did in 2011. As BCE Chief Executive Officer, George Cope, recalled, 'We say with all sincerity the Olympics was a real important moment because it was really the first time we started to see these new technologies, the impact it had on TV, the impact it had on the Internet and the impact it had on wireless' (LaSalle 2010). He went on to note that BCE wanted to take advantage of broadcasting across multiple 'screens'—smartphone, computer, and television— that was so ably demonstrated by CTV during the Olympics.

'Great,' you might say. Now if you miss your favourite news or sports show on TV, you can pick it up later on another channel, or read about it online or in your local paper, or watch it on your smartphone. But as Horkheimer and Adorno, Gramsci, and Herman and Chomsky would remind us, such convenience comes at a cost. What would they say are the consequences of one company controlling the content of so many different media platforms in Canada, especially to people and groups seeking to express alternative views? And what impact might they say it will have on your ability to distinguish between information broadcast to increase the profits of BCE and enhance your exposure to the messages of advertisers versus the 'facts'?

---

media ownership landscape and show that Canadian media are controlled by a small number of businesses and elites. But so what? Well, Herman and Chomsky feared that concentrated ownership and editorship of media would lead to people receiving skewed information. They recognized that if media refuse to cover the views of people and groups that challenge existing power

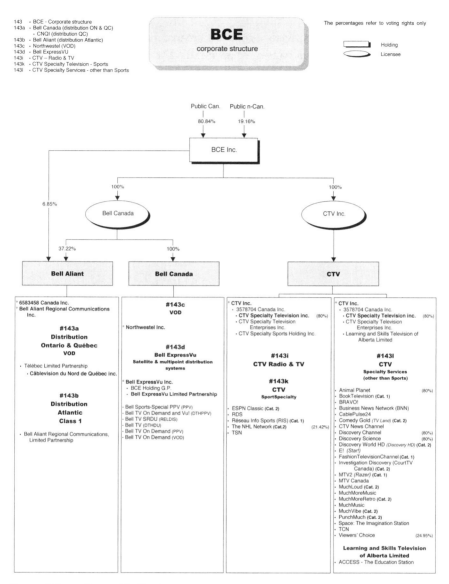

FIGURE 3.2 BCE Ownership Chart
Source: CRTC.

arrangements, or if they repress alternative ways of seeing and understanding the world, then voices of dissent would be silenced, to the detriment of democratic exchange.

You might say, 'Sure, but not in Canada.' Yet, pause for a moment and consider—what information do we get? A number of alternative news media, for instance, noted that there was limited coverage of protesters critical of the Vancouver Olympics in 2010. Many people objected to and rallied against the vast amount of government money spent on the games at the cost of social programs. Indigenous activists protested against the games being held on contested land. Few Canadians were aware that the games cost between $2.5 and $6 billion to run and that provinces across the country contributed between $1.5 and $5 million to support the events (*Huffington Post* 2010; Bramham 2009). If you think about it, that is very high price for a two-week sporting event that largely benefits the most well-to-do Canadians. It is money that could have easily been spent on other more durable things, that would benefit the less privileged, like revitalizing the impoverished Downtown Eastside of Vancouver. A similar lack of news coverage can be seen with respect to issues pertaining to Aboriginal rights and land claims in British Columbia. As Arthur Manuel (2010) noted, 'The Vancouver 2010 Winter Olympics will happen, and very little attention has been given to Canada's dismal human rights record on indigenous peoples. This has to be contrasted with how Tibet human rights issues were raised during the 2008 Summer Olympics in China. Canada decided to do its torch relay inside Canada and used the Four Host First Nations to divide and rule over indigenous peoples in Canada.' Few Canadians were aware either that protesters against the Olympics faced heavily armed police wearing body armour and carrying what reporters believed to be M4 carbine guns, which are similar to the M-16s used during the Vietnam War (Pablo 2010). Regardless of whether they were loaded with plastic bullets or live ammunition, the imagery was one of intimidation used to mute dissent and disempower critics.

Clearly, as the examples illustrate, some stories gain widespread attention while others do not. Horkheimer and Adorno would not have been surprised. The instances of dissent just noted contradicted the 'feel-good' message about the Olympics that the powerful members of Canadian society wished to communicate. As a result, any frank discussion of the social consequences of the 2010 Games for the disadvantaged or even for the average person was pushed off the public radar.

Herman and Chomsky also found that media content is determined by the compulsion to make a profit. Rather than covering a wide range of stories, privately owned media tailor their content to commercial interests. That is, they report on events and issues that they anticipate will attract the largest audience possible to boost their viewership and appeal to advertisers. Informing the public becomes secondary to tantalizing their audiences, which leads to a disproportionate coverage of sensational events and a 'dumbing down' (or a complete disregard) of more complex or contentious issues. As the old news adage goes 'if it bleeds, it leads', but the impact of such coverage is twofold; it leads to an oversimplification of issues and, for those who lack exposure to alternative sources of information, a skewed view of the world (Gerbner 1998). Thus, the claim by some conservative media that the 2008 collapse of the US housing market was caused by irresponsible home buyers cut short any reasoned discussion of the complicated financial mechanisms that contributed to the event. And media researchers continue to show that, fed a constant diet of news stories featuring violent deaths and murders, viewers come to think their communities are much more crime-ridden than they actually are (Roberts, Cook, Roche, and Desai 2001). Ken Dowler (2004) notes that media coverage is influenced by *who* the victims and criminals are. This too influences broader public perceptions. As has been shown by Augie Fleras and Jean Lock Kunz (2001), as well as Frances Henry and Carol Tator (2002) and Rima Wilkes and Danielle Ricard (2005), media coverage of crime is very much racialized, which in turn fosters negative and skewed perceptions of visible-minority and Aboriginal Canadians. As a result, such coverage affects how their 'race' is seen as a marker of their status in relation to other Canadians. The link between news media and crime in Canada has been extensively examined by Ericson, Baraneck, and Chan (1987; 1991) and if you are interested in exploring this further, Dowler, Fleming, and Muzatti (2006) offer a very good overview of the literature dealing with these issues.

Perhaps even more alarming, Herman and Chomsky found that the dominant media rely on a relatively small pool of 'experts' as news sources and to legitimatize stories and to gain access to information. Often such experts, who are used to comment on issues of concern to journalists, are politicians, professionals such as doctors or lawyers, celebrities, or other people with high social status. Herman and Chomsky feared that such reliance on selected experts biased the coverage of news because it tended to make access to the production of information difficult for ordinary people. Only experts have the opportunity to share their views. They also show that powerful people decide who is and is not knowledgeable. Herman and Chomsky also found that when dissenting voices reached different media, the experts would use flak to spin the issues away from dissenting ideas. In other words, negative information is used to discredit the authority and legitimacy of experts that stray from the dominant ideology. For example, after the September 11, 2001 attacks on the World Trade Center and the Pentagon, few voices in the media were critical of the US invasion of Afghanistan and later Iraq. In fact, early commentators that questioned the actions of, or made critical comments about, the US Bush administration often faced harsh repercussions (see Box 3.3).

The last filter of information in US media, said Herman and Chomsky, was 'anti-communism'. By this they actually meant national ideology and how it is often used against those labelled as enemies that challenge the legitimacy of the national ideology. Herman and Chomsky wrote during the **Cold War**, when the biggest challenge to capitalism and North America was understood to be communism. Thus, anything that smacked of communism was likely to be presented in the media in a negative light, whereas Western capitalism and free enterprise were celebrated. The ideas represented as 'national ideology' clearly benefited privileged groups over the less advantaged, and the

BOX 3.3 ✳ THE FATE OF POLITICALLY INCORRECT

When you hear about dissenting voices being suppressed, you might think of far-off, brutal dictators cracking down on protesters, or leaders of distant autocratic states imposing media 'blackouts'. However, you don't have to look too hard to find instances of voices being muted because they express views counter to power holders right here in North America.

After September 11th, 2001, for instance, a number of political commentators critical of the Bush regime faced harsh criticism that in some cases cost them their jobs or their status and legitimacy. Political commentator Bill Maher, for example, paid a heavy price for publicly disagreeing with President Bush's characterization of the terrorists as 'cowardly'. On his late-night national television show *Politically Incorrect* six days after the attack, Maher agreed with his guest, Dinesh D'Souza, a conservative from the American Enterprise Institute, that there was nothing cowardly about '[s]taying in the airplane when it hits the building'. It was the US, Maher said, that was cowardly, 'lobbing cruise missiles from 2,000 miles away.' In response, as *New York Times* reporter Celestine Bohlen (2001) noted, Federal Express and Sears withdrew their sponsorship of his show, and Maher received a warning from the then White House press secretary, Ari Fleischer, that 'people have to watch what they say and watch what they do.' After the incident, advertisers were hard to come by, and the show was eventually cancelled in the spring of 2002.

Around the same time, philosopher Susan Sontag and filmmaker Michael Moore also faced condemnation for their dissenting views. After writing an article for *The New Yorker* that was critical of the ensuing 'war on terror', Sontag was attacked in columns by Charles Krauthammer of the *Washington Post* and by John Podhoretz of the *New York Post*. *The New Yorker* received more than a hundred letters in response to her comments (Bohlen 2001). And when Michael Moore began making *Fahrenheit 9/11*, a film critical of the Bush government, he had difficulty securing production funding (Fleming 2003). Once it was shot, the Walt Disney Company blocked its Mirimax subsidiary company from releasing it (Rutenberg 2004). It was only when the film was released in foreign markets and began to generate interest abroad that a distributor was found and it was finally projected on American screens. Moore continues to be labelled a leftist propagandist and is accused of manipulating the 'facts' around September 11th, even though much of the information in the film has since been proven to be accurate. So can the suppression of dissent happen in North America? Obviously, it can.

media thus acted as tool for maintaining their dominance. Since the fall of the Soviet Union and the declaration of a War on Terror in 2001, 'Islamic fundamentalism' has replaced communism as the West's bugbear. That said, the threat of communism can still evoke a public reaction in the US. President Barack Obama's attempts to introduce public health care were labelled 'socialist medicine' by some conservative media sources. This alarmed many Americans who, along with a number of conservative media pundits, fervently protested the course of action pursued by their 'communist' president, even though it was clearly in their interests to support it.

Like Horkheimer and Adorno, Herman and Chomsky conclude that the people who produce culture, information, and knowledge hold more power than the people who consume it. While consumers may be able to choose from among a number of cultural products, producers determine what the products are themselves. Consumer 'choice' is thus an illusion created by powerful elites and the implication is that most people are largely duped and controlled by dominant power holders, especially the most materially advantaged.

Cultural and Social Capital

As we have seen, many of the earliest observations of how culture and society affect power relations saw culture production as an activity that supported material power and which served to further enhance and sustain the power of the most materially advantaged. The notion that most of us go about our lives unaware that our actions and thoughts are manipulated by powerful elites is both disturbing and compelling. These observations have spawned many valuable critiques of the status quo. But as later scholars began to point out, this treatment does not provide a very nuanced representation of *everyday* power relations. It may be true that the world in which we live is shaped largely by wealthy power holders. Nevertheless, people and groups who do not control the wider mechanisms of culture production and who are not very materially advantaged use cultural and social markers to exercise and hold power over others all the time. Think about the times when people exercise power over you. It is not always because they are rich, is it? If we return to the example of the CEO used in Chapter 1, his crying baby wielded much power over him at 2 o'clock in the morning. The same can be said when your friend pressures you into joining him on a blind date. In both cases obligation and influence are not because of the material power held over others. How can we make sense of this?

Scholars interested in how cultural and social markers work to bestow more power on some people than on others begin with the observation that people assign different value to different markers. Some markers, they say, hold more prestige, status, and perhaps legitimacy than others. Remember the debate that we mentioned in Box 3.1 about teaching Ebonics in US schools?

Objections flowed from the reality that Ebonics does not hold the same status as 'standard' English. Take as another example the distinction between **high** or posh culture versus **popular** or mass culture. More than thirty years ago, Herbert J. Gans (1974: 19) noted that objects, ideas, symbols, and activities associated with high culture, such as hand-crafted furniture, opera, and classical literature and philosophy, are seen as authentic, specialized, organic, experiential, and active. Popular culture, by contrast, held many negative connotations. Even today things connected with pop culture, such as Harlequin romances, fast-food restaurants, and clothes from discount stores are often perceived to have less character and value because they are mass-produced, sterile, interchangeable, mechanical, and predictable, and have a pacifying effect on people. Such distinctions are obviously evaluative, communicating legitimacy on the one hand and illegitimacy on the other. Having access to, control over, or familiarity with high culture will help a person to achieve higher status—and hence greater power—than she could achieve if she were knowledgeable only about pop culture.

Implicit in Gans's observations and the example we offer in Box 3.4 is the fact that ordinary people can enhance their status and in turn their power through their command of different cultural and social markers. Granted, they may not be able to exercise that power in all circumstances. Your ability to deconstruct Romantic poetry would likely not hold much sway at a conference of mechanical engineers. But the point is that because people assign value, not only to material markers, but also to cultural and social markers, everyone holds *some* power *sometimes*.

The sociologist who has gone the farthest in articulating how cultural markers act as a resource in the everyday acquisition and exercise of power is Pierre Bourdieu. He coined what have become key terms in the field, **cultural capital** and **social capital**. These terms have proved so useful to so many interests that they have even made the jump from academe to everyday parlance.

What do these terms mean? Well, when economists use the word 'capital' they are usually referring to money. But strictly speaking, capital is not the equivalent of money. It is, rather, the unseen *value* we place on the different currencies or symbolic markers that we call money. Really, money is just pieces of paper and metal if it is not recognized by the people who use it as exchangeable for some agreed-upon value. Bourdieu argues that something similar goes on in the cultural and social spheres. Again, strictly speaking, the movies one watches, or the clothes one wears, or the dialect one speaks, are just means of entertaining, dressing, and communicating. These things only become indications of one's cultural or social status when others agree that they hold meanings and significance beyond their more obvious or immediate purpose. Just as someone can acquire, employ, and exercise power through capital in the economic realm, she can acquire, employ and exercise power though cultural and or social capital in different spheres.

Box 3.4 ❀ FILM OR MOVIES?

Is there a difference between a 'film' and a 'movie?' Well, it depends on who you ask. Film (imagine someone saying it with an 'e'—*filme*) often refers to foreign or artistic productions that show in repertory or art-house theatres and aim for critical acclaim and recognition by cultural elites rather than broad appeal and financial reward. Often they are viewed and appreciated by connoisseurs but rarely seen or enjoyed by the general public. One such film is Deny Arcand's *Les Invasions Barbares*, which gained widespread international acclaim. Arcand is perhaps one of Canada's most influential film directors, yet most Canadians have never even heard of him or his movies. Knowing and appreciating Arcand's work communicates comprehension of (at least one aspect of) high culture, which can help people acquire status and some power in influential circles, like those occupied by professors, film critics, and rich patrons of *avant-garde* art.

Movies, by contrast, are multi-million-dollar productions that usually fit within established genres and formats that are viewed by millions of people in megatheatres around the world. These movies epitomize pop culture: they are mass-produced with simple themes and well-known actors so as to attract as many viewers as possible. Blockbuster films are not meant to challenge or educate their audiences as much as entertain them. Although some of the directors of such films are well known—James Cameron and George Lucas for instance—they are the exception. More often, few people outside the movie industry even pay attention to who makes these movies.

So is there a difference between films and movies? Politically, yes. Whereas familiarity with Arcand's films might gain you some status and power because of his association with high culture, it is unlikely that such benefits will accrue from having seen all the movies in the *Twilight* series—because of their association with pop culture.

Note that the efficacy of any form of capital is dependent on the cultural or social context within which it is employed. Just as you would have a hard time persuading the cashier at the Gap to accept wampum (a form of economic capital that was valued in America some four hundred years ago) in payment for your new chinos, so too might your ability to swallow and then regurgitate goldfish bring you little favour among your grandmother's bridge club. But transport yourself back to colonial New England (where wampum was used as currency), or show up at a conference of circus performers or at a grade one class, and you might enjoy considerable status and power because of the material and cultural capital that you possess.

Sometimes Bourdieu's concepts of cultural and social capital are used synonymously, but they are different things. Simplifying somewhat, *cultural* capital is anything that reflects and facilitates cultural exchange between people; *social* capital is anything that eases or lubricates relationships between people or facilitates the creation of networks. Bourdieu (2001: 98) elaborated on this distinction further. Cultural capital, he said, could exist in three forms:

> in the *embodied* state, that is, in the form of long-lasting dispositions of the mind and body; in the *objectified* state, in the form of cultural goods (pictures, books, dictionaries, instruments, machines, etc.), which are the trace or realization of theories or critiques of these theories, problematics, etc.; and in the *institutionalized* state, a form of objectification which must be set apart because . . . in the case of educational qualifications, it confers entirely original properties on the cultural capital which it is presumed to guarantee.

Of these three forms, cultural capital in the 'objectified state' is perhaps the most intuitive. These are the things, symbols, or markers (for example, movies, clothes, or dialect) that people in different cultures choose to infuse with meaning and that bestow different statuses on people in different social contexts. But cultural capital also exists in the 'embodied state' because people learn cultural habits as children and carry them, in their minds and bodies, throughout their lives. These are habits that affect how they consume cultural and social products. People who did not have a TV when they were growing up and who only listened to classical music may be better able to decode elements of high culture as they move through life than their TV-watching peers but may fail to grasp or develop an interest in the pop-culture references of their co-workers. Each set of cultural knowledge, capital, can have implications for the status and power they enjoy in different situations and the value of other resources they can exchange for them. Of course, Bourdieu does not see these habits as fixed. Rather, he sees them as starting points that affect the trajectory of future cultural exchanges. Cultural capital also exists in the 'institutionalized state', that is, it is produced and reproduced through different social organizations. As an example, throughout his writings Bourdieu was particularly interested in the interrelation of the education system and cultural capital. He was concerned with how schools, their organization and operation, the curriculums they adopt and the behaviour they reward and punish, establish and perpetuate the value of some cultural knowledge and markers over others.

With respect to *social capital*, Bourdieu (2001: 102–3) wrote:

> Social capital is the aggregate of the actual or potential resources which are linked to possession of a durable network of more or less institutionalized relationships of mutual acquaintance and recognition—or in other words, to

membership in a group—which provides each of its members with the backing of the collectivity-owned capital, a 'credential' which entitles them to credit, in the various senses of the word.

To translate: who you know matters. Bourdieu said that social capital, resources that foster social relationships, is derived from your membership in groups. The number and nature of the groups you belong to affects the social capital you possess, and that in turn can affect the power you are able to exercise over your life and the lives of others. The soccer club or reading group you belong to or the university you attend can affect your life chances and opportunities. Soccer tournaments provide opportunities to meet people from different places who also love the game; reading clubs permit interaction with teachers and other professionals who have a common interest in books; and university affiliation is shared with people in many fields. These experiences can help forge connections between people and perhaps even encourage a sense of obligation and duty among them. Shared experiences can also cultivate feelings of loyalty and trust between like-minded individuals. Group members can then draw upon these connections, or exchange them, because they are political resources that can be used to forward their aims.

As we shall see, the concepts of cultural capital and social capital are useful for exploring how power is distributed among and exercised by individuals and groups. They are supple concepts that capture the flexibility that characterizes everyday manifestations of power. Unlike material resources, which you either have or you don't have, *everyone* has at their disposal at least *some* cultural and social resources which they can transform into power in one or another situation. In this sense, the concepts of cultural and social capital can help conceptualize power as less a **zero-sum game** and more as a situation in which power is distributed, held, and exercised more democratically. This has been especially helpful to political sociologists concerned with the emancipation of traditionally marginalized individuals and groups. These scholars look at how these groups can and should create and promote the cultural and social means to actively overcome, rather than passively accept, the continued subordination of their status.

Cultural and Social Capital in Action

The concepts of cultural and social capital provided a way for scholars to acknowledge and analyze power that did not derive from possession of material resources. The concepts also opened the way for researchers to explore how different forms of capital—economic, cultural, social—overlapped and influenced one another in different situations and conditions, or what Bourdieu called social **fields**. Bourdieu showed how seemingly unrelated preferences for different cultural products, foods, beverages, art, entertainment, and so forth, interrelated with economic and social interests. Bourdieu found that more specialized cultural and social markers tended to be related to higher status and wealth, and those which were less specialized were most often affiliated with the popular culture of the middle and lower classes. For instance, to most people, abstract art may not be appealing at first glance. To appreciate it one needs to have acquired at least some specialized knowledge about it, such as background information about its significance in relation to other works. Although this specialized knowledge is in some respects available to everyone, it tends to be monopolized by the wealthy. By contrast, the artwork on an album cover or movie poster does not need specialized knowledge to be appreciated—its appeal is usually self-evident. Because of this, everyone who consumes such art can enjoy it, but it is usually the less materially well-off who will embrace it.

Bourdieu observed that people who posses cultural and social capital wield much power. These forms of capital help to distinguish between those who 'know' things, and perhaps belong to the elite, and those who do not. They also distinguish between those who are posing or making false or unsubstantiated claims to those markers and those who embody them. The ability to distinguish in this way offers power that remains largely unseen yet structures many everyday interactions. This puts a slightly different spin on Sir Francis Bacon's (1597) claim that 'knowledge is power'!

If Bourdieu's work highlighted some of the ways that economic, cultural, and social capital were interrelated in the unfolding of power contests, feminist scholars have examined how they are tied, more specifically, to gender inequality. Although the Canadian federal government has enacted legislation to limit discrimination based on gender and sex and there is even an 'equality' clause (**s. 15**) in the Charter of Rights and Freedoms, these scholars say that women still face many obstacles in the informal cultural and social realms, obstacles that affect women's power on other fronts. Although federal and provincial legislation protects women's jobs if they need to take time for maternity leave, prohibits overt discrimination, and promotes equal pay for equal work, such laws cannot govern informal cultural and social interactions.

For example, a common practice in a number of Canadian workplaces is to hold an NHL hockey playoff pool. These are often seen as benign contests that promote workplace solidarity. Usually people select different players from teams that have entered the playoff competition and track their performance over the duration of the tournament until the last game is played and the Stanley Cup is awarded to the winning team. Although this practice does not preclude participation of any specific person within a workplace, it does generate boundaries of inclusion and exclusion that are based on knowledge of the sport—that is, cultural capital. It holds more salience for people who have played competitive hockey, even if they have not followed the NHL season or specific teams and players. This is because, as Bourdieu would note, they have an *embodied* knowledge of the game. Because of this, they might understand it despite not having played it for a number of years. In contrast, those who follow the game but have never played it may be up-to-date with current game statistics but may not appreciate more subtle norms that are part of the game, for instance, the ethos around fighting, norms of not bodychecking goalies when they leave their nets, or traditions like throwing an octopus on the ice at Detroit Red Wings playoff games. In fact, some like Gerry Veenstra (2007) have shown that knowledge of sports culture intersects inherently with gender and class.

Given the lack of women's, girls', and mixed-sex hockey leagues, women often do not embody such cultural capital. They are not as likely as boys and men to gain it at an early age nor to employ it throughout their lives. The same might even be said of the demographics of watching the game on television or attending them live in arenas. Both practices are largely dominated by boys and men, although we acknowledge that at least in amateur leagues this is slowly beginning to change (Theberge 2000; 2008: 122). But why does it matter who gets to play? Well, because playing creates cultural capital that often eases conversations in a workplace and that generates the pretext for informal social events, or the general work culture of the office (Oakly 2000: 329). In fact, cultural capital can even affect participation in the hockey pool itself—not to mention being successful in the pool. It is one thing for women to work alongside and with male colleagues but it is quite another to share similar points of cultural reference. The inability to do so can often lead to awkwardness or even alienation.

Let's consider another example. Perhaps the senior members of a firm have a tradition of going to 'happy hour' or '**cinq à sept**' drinks at a pub after a stressful day in the office. They may even invite the rest of the office to come and hang out. However, as noted in Chapter 2, the North American division of labour is gendered in that women often bear the brunt of child care and domestic labour. A young female colleague who is also a mother may not be able to participate in such an event because she has to pick up her child from daycare after work. Even if she did make arrangements with her partner to go to the pub, how might this affect relationships in her domestic life? And what about other colleagues who might feel excluded from such events if they do not drink alcohol or are uncomfortable in pubs?

Your first reaction might be: 'if they can't or don't want to go, what difference does it make?' But such informal events often generate both cultural and social capital for their participants, including the acquisition of undocumented historical knowledge of the firm, inside information on office politics and the alliances and disagreements that exist among colleagues, or even information on opportunities that might emerge in the company down the road. If a young worker does not participate in the after-hours informal interactions of an office, she may quickly find herself left out of the loop in workplace interactions and decisions, and that may hurt her chances of promotion to more senior positions and opportunities to advance her career. At the same time, joining the 'happy hour club' might unbalance her family relations or even lead to her being labelled an 'irresponsible mother'—thus placing her in a **catch-22** situation. She's damned if she does and damned if she doesn't. Much of the work environment still reflects a historical male-dominated culture (see Myerson and Fletcher 2000).

Although the examples offered are fictional, they reflect the experiences of many workplaces. If you doubt that this is a common experience, we suggest looking at Statistics Canada data on occupations by sex in 2006 (see Table 3.1). When these data are examined, we see that despite increasing rates of formal education and training among women, and years of employment-equity policy, women still hold only slightly more than a quarter of senior-management positions and only a little over a third of management positions as a whole. Clearly women are still not entering these positions, and most still work in occupations that have been dominated by women. In fact, 'in 2006, 67% of all employed women were working in one of the teaching, nursing and related health occupations, clerical or other administrative positions or sales and service occupations. This compared with just 30% of employed men' (Almey 2007: 9). In Chapter 2, similar data provided support for a materialist interpretation of gender power imbalances. Yet, as Bourdieu might have observed, these can also intersect with non-material influences. As a result,

TABLE 3.1 Distribution of Employment, by Occupation and Sex, 2006

	Women	Men	Women as % of Total Employed in Occupation
Managerial (Total)	7.1	11.0	36.3
Senior management	0.3	0.8	26.3
Other management	6.7	10.2	36.9
Professional (Total)	32.5	22.9	55.9
Business and finance	3.3	2.8	51.6
Natural sciences, engineering, mathematics	3.2	10.1	22.0
Social sciences, religion	6.7	2.4	71.3
Teaching	5.6	2.8	63.9
Doctors, dentists, other health	1.4	1.0	55.3
Nursing, therapy, other health-related	8.9	1.1	87.4
Artistic, literary, recreational	3.4	2.6	54.1
Clerical and administrative	24.1	7.1	75.0
Sales and service	28.6	19.3	56.8
Primary	1.5	5.3	20.5
Trades, transport, and construction	2.1	26.3	6.5
Processing, manufacturing, and utilities	4.1	8.1	31.1
Total	100.0	100.0	47.1

Source: Adapted from Statistics Canada, Labour Force Survey: www.statcan.gc.ca/pub/89f0133x/2006000/t/4064660-eng.htm.

differential possession of and access to cultural and social capital partially account for women's disadvantaged position relative to men.

Social Capital and Social Networks

Another understanding of social capital focuses more explicitly on social networks. This approach is largely American and is the one that has been picked up by popular commentators and policy makers. One notable figure on this front is Mark Granovetter (1973), who recognized not only the importance of social capital in determining the life chances of different individuals and groups, but also how different types or configurations of relationships can affect people's opportunities. Granovetter was particularly interested in relationships among people and the networks they tap into, and he distinguished between **weak** and **strong social ties**. Perhaps counter-intuitively, he argued that there is more benefit in maintaining weak ties than strong ones. Weak ties are essentially loose network connections—numerous but shallow connections to other people and groups. These, he argues, should be prized over strong ties with a relatively small number of people. He illustrated how this works in the job market (in 1974) by showing that people who are able to extend their networks and tap into a wide range of social groups and situations are more successful in landing jobs than those who have a few very strong ties to other people. In other words, his work helps show that it is important not only to develop cultural and social capital but also to be nimble and flexible in using it. The ability to maintain relationships with a diverse range of people can yield benefits.

Later scholars, including James Coleman and Robert Putnam, built on Granovetter's observations. They linked network ties and the forms they take to the notion of social capital and the way in which that influences political participation. Putnam (2000) theorizes a connection between membership in voluntary organizations like social clubs and bowling leagues, enhanced social capital, and political participation. Informal associations, Putnam argues, build social capital by fostering social interaction that produces reciprocity and trust and confirms social norms. These are qualities, he says, that are essential in well-functioning communities and democracies. Putnam laments that the US has witnessed declining rates of participation in these associations. This he interprets as an indication of the decline of **civil society**. With fewer people participating in informal and voluntary associations, fewer people are acquiring and cultivating the social capital necessary to sustain an effective political community.

Like Granovetter, Putnam recognizes that different types of social relationships produce different sorts of social capital. **Bridging social capital**, much like Granovetter's weak ties, extends networks and links different people and groups to one another. **Bonding social capital**, like Granovetter's strong ties, is more insular and characteristic of more homogeneous groups. Putnam believes activities that generate bridging social capital should be encouraged, because it fosters the formation of broad and inclusive associations. Bonding social capital, in contrast, holds the risk of over insularization, which can foster societal fragmentation rather than unity, something that Putnam hopes the US can avoid. In his most recent work, for example, Putnam (2007) fears that the over-insularization that is associated with bonding social capital in ethnic communities will lead to such fragmentation and be detrimental to North American society.

Putnam's recent writings reflect the observations of some of his earlier critics, such as Berman (1997), who describe how **vertical ties**, which generate strong but exclusionary bonds, contribute to radicalization, violence, and **xenophobia**. They also echo concerns expressed by Raymond Breton (1964), who many years ago wrote about both the benefits and disadvantages of the **institutional completeness** of ethnic minority communities in Canada. But not all scholars see bonding social capital as fostering division and animosity between dominant and minority groups. A number of political sociologists and some policy makers have cited an opposite trend and have looked to social capital as a tool with which immigrant and ethnic-minority communities can overcome inequalities (see Portes 1998; Aizlewood and Pendakur 2005; Couton and Gaudet 2008; Breton 2003; James 2003).

That scholars are divided on this issue is perhaps not surprising, because there is much disagreement over the definition of social capital, its influences, and its effects on societies. In part this is because the concept of social capital has fallen victim to its success. It has appealed to a wide range of social scientists and policy makers because it has pseudo-economic connotations (see Fine 2001) and at the same time can be applied to a wide range of phenomena, including education, voluntary associations, and informal networks. Few, sadly, have used the concept in the way Bourdieu originally articulated it. Fewer still have elaborated upon the notion of cultural capital or fields more generally. Some critics of the concept, such as Bezanson (2006), caution that current formulations of the concept ignore gender differences by focusing on the public realm while ignoring the private sphere and ignoring the fact that the language is overly determined by an economic imperative. A crucial puzzle for researchers that examine these issues is whether social capital produces other forms of capital, or whether it is a product of those other forms. An excellent review of these debates can be found in a book on the topic edited by Bob Edward, Michael Foley, and Mario Diani (1998).

Generally the concepts of cultural and social capital have allowed political sociologists to broaden the notion of power to allow consideration of non-material resources. The concepts have also allowed them to refine their focus to investigate more closely how power can operate and have repercussions for individuals and groups in different places and circumstances. But there are still questions around people's use of cultural and social markets in their pursuit of power that we have not yet answered. For example, how do individuals and groups come to lay claim to a cultural or social marker? And how do certain things, symbols, signs, and other phenomena come to be infused with cultural and social significance in the first place? We also need to discuss how some people and groups can influence and even change the status assigned to markers and challenge existing status hierarchies through collective action. It is to these questions that we now turn.

Presentation of Self

A lot of work around how cultural and social resources are transformed into power focuses on the description of large-scale and abstract cultural and social networks. But having knowledge of and evoking these networks is just one form of power; the ability and right to *lay claim* to them is yet another. Who gets to legitimately exploit different cultural and social markers in their interest, and who does not, is an important element of how power is negotiated. A key contributor to this discussion was Erving Goffman (1959). Much like Bourdieu, he recognized that the meanings and value of cultural and social markers are relational. They are by-products of a given social situation, the networks of people who produce them, and the people who interpret them. He compared the processes involved in different social interactions to dramatic performances, which he called **dramaturgy**. In any social interaction, Goffman said, people assume different **roles**, the demands of which compel them to behave in certain, almost scripted, ways. Take for instance the female flight attendants described by Arlie Hochschild ([1983] 2003). In one instance, Hochschild describes the flight attendant behaving as a caring and friendly service provider; yet, at the same time she may be an exhausted worker suffering from jet lag, hiding the fact from the passengers she is serving but showing it to the other flight attendants when out of sight from customers. Goffman would say that the flight attendant was **performing** different roles in each of these instances. The same can be said of other social roles, like doctors who are impersonal when they talk about illness, street people who are diffident when asking for change, or teenagers who who act irresponsibly at the mall. None of these are wholly accurate depictions of any single person. Rather, they are **stereotypical** interpretations of roles that people use to navigate and understand different social situations.

As with any role performance, Goffman recognized that there needs to be a stage: the social situation. And as in any stage production, there exists a **front** and **back** stage. In the front stage the actor is playing a role in the way he wishes his audience to see it or according to the expectations of the role. Interestingly North American slang often talks about people 'fronting', or acting out a role, which is very much in line with Goffman's use of the term. The back stage, in contrast, is the social space where people let down their guard.

The ability to convince an audience of a presentation of self in a given role in the front stage is what yields power and allows individuals to draw on different forms of cultural and social capital. However, there are instances where such performances are not accepted, or when the role is breached and the audience reacts harshly against those trying to lay claim to it. If we return to the example of a flight attendant, if he is courteous and brings you your gin and tonic without incident, all is well. He is playing the role of 'flight attendant' convincingly, and so he can legitimately lay claim to the cultural and social capital that flow from that performance. If, however, he is rude to you, he has breached the role of flight attendant and so surrenders his capacity to employ or enjoy the capital endemic to that role. Something similar happens when a doctor makes light of a chronic illness or when the street person is aggressive rather than obsequious, or when a teenager turns out to be an expert authority on astrophysics. In all these instances, the actor's performance either breaches their expected role or is deemed illegitimate. This can lead audiences to become disgruntled and perhaps even to retaliate. As Goffman so eloquently noted about **con men**, 'Perhaps the real crime of the confidence man is not that he takes money from his victims but that he robs us all of the belief that middle-class manners and appearance can be sustained only by middle-class people' (1959: 29). Thus, the ability to lay claim to cultural and social markers is very much an act of power in everyday life.

How the Cultural and Social Become 'Capital'

Although Goffman offered insight on how social interactions are shaped, he did not concentrate much on how cultural and social symbols come to be imbued with meaning in the first place. To do that, other writers, such as Stuart Hall, have turned to **semiotics** and structural linguistics as tools for understanding how elements of the cultural, social, political, and economic world are transformed into symbolic or discursive form when they are transmitted. He called this process **encoding** meaning. Hall was a member of the Centre for Contemporary Cultural Studies at the University of Birmingham, which was an influential hub for such analyses. Like many of its founding figures, he was interested in the authenticity of popular culture. But unlike many who looked down on pop culture in comparison to high culture, Hall was interested in understanding its value. In doing so, he theorized, not only how meanings are encoded into cultural and social markers, but also how they are interpreted, read, and decoded.

Hall uses the metaphor of language as a tool for understanding how meanings are produced, shared, and transmitted from one person or group to another. If you think about it, people are able to communicate, not only because they know the same words, but because they share an understanding of the *meanings* assigned to the words. If we use a word like 'apple', it will likely evoke a shared meaning between us, of fruit and maybe a brand of computers. The same can occur if we draw upon cultural and social markers and the performative roles affiliated with them. If we describe a person as 'rich' or 'North American' or any other marker of her or his cultural and social status, this too evokes some shared understandings. Hall argues that people and groups who generate or produce these shared meanings *encode* markers. He also says that people who interpret them or read them most often allow the meaning to stand. When meanings are not read, interpreted, or decoded the same way by everyone, it can lead to negotiation and even dispute.

For communication, and for that matter social interaction, to take place there must be some degree of shared meaning; however, it does not have to be exact. If we return back to the example of 'apple', it can mean a red fruit, or a green fruit or even a pink one, or it can mean something completely different, like a computer or smartphone. In fact, distortions or misunderstandings can themselves dictate a communicative exchange. One person will draw upon an encoded symbol, and another person, or many others, will try to interpret it. **Decoding** it also involves trying to understand other meanings that are indirectly associated with that symbol. Hall observes that in the process of this exchange, there are differences between *denotation* (the literal and intended meaning) and *connotation* (the changeable and associative meaning). He illustrated this with reference to Roland Barthes's (1977) example of a sweater. In its literal sense a sweater is just a garment worn for warmth. But in its connotative sense it can also mean the coming of winter, or a cold day. For Barthes, that is an illustration of the difference between the symbolic and semantic code of the sweater.

If we consider the diversity of human experiences and societies, it is clear that much misinterpretation is possible. Hall offers some categorical tools to help explain how communicative and social meanings are negotiated. He identified dominant (or preferred), negotiated, and oppositional meanings and readings. He argues that **dominant**, hegemonic, or **preferred meanings** are embedded in most symbols. These are the common, taken-for-granted meanings that make sense to most people. Hall stresses that these are 'dominant' rather than set or determined meanings because asymmetry exists within communicative structures and thus meanings and their readings can always be changed. In this sense, dominant meanings and preferred readings are those that are institutionally structured, as well as politically and ideologically ordered (Hall 2006: 169). They are in essence the common stereotypes or expectations of a given society.

As a result, when people read from the dominant position, they interpret texts or social situations in the preferred manner, the one with the expectations and legitimacy of the dominant society. For instance, as you were growing up you may have watched the children's television show *Sesame Street*. In that show Ernie and Bert are popular characters that live together. They are both male, and they often remark that they are 'best buddies'. If you take that dominant encoding at face value, it means that they are good friends and roommates. Yet Hall argues that there are two other positions from which meaning can be decoded, or read. One of these is from a **negotiated reading**. This occurs when audiences mix adaptive and oppositional elements into their reading, while at the same time acknowledging the legitimacy of the dominant definition (Hall 2006: 172). In this situation some elements of opposition against the preferred or hegemonic understanding emerge, but they are selective. They occur at different points, without fully questioning the integrity of the dominant meaning. Thus, there is some miscommunication, some argument or contestation of the dominant meaning but one that is reconciled into the dominant system. Returning to the example of Ernie and Bert, in different early episodes the two of them could be seen taking a bath together and sleeping in the same bed. This led some people to question whether they were in fact more than just best friends. An **oppositional reading** goes a step further in disputing the dominant meanings and evoking readings that are decoded in a way contrary to that of the literal and connotative meanings of the dominant encoders. That is, people in this position completely understand the dominant reading and preferred meaning but decide to recode it into a completely alternative framework of reference (Hall 2006: 172–3). Thus, Ernie and Bert not only sleep in the same bed and take baths together, but they also wear clothes that have multi-coloured, rainbow-like stripes, which are a symbol of LGBT pride, so they may in fact be a gay couple. This is an interpretation that led to much controversy and even some lobbying against the show and, ultimately, declarations from the show's producers that Bert and Ernie are not gay (Gikow 2009: 34).

Similar oppositional readings can been found in other popular culture icons too. As a result, unlike earlier political sociologists who treat cultural and social capital as outside the direct control of individuals and bound within structures controlled by the elite, Hall is optimistic about the power individuals have in contesting dominant meanings. He in fact argues, 'One of the most significant political moments . . . is the point when events which are normally signified and decoded in a negotiated way begin to be given an oppositional reading. Here the "politics of signification"—the struggle in discourse—is joined' (Hall 1980: 127). Hall believes that challengers to existing power arrangements can gain influence from decoding dominant meanings in alternative, counter-cultural ways (see Box 3.5).

Many people do not consciously recognize the power that comes with being able to encode and decode different cultural and social markers or interpret the social interactions and situations in which they can be drawn

Box 3.5 ⁕ Culture Jamming, Textual Poaching, and Empowering Language

Culture is always contested. People constantly challenge it through strategies such as *culture jamming*, *textual poaching*, and *empowering language*. In case you haven't heard of these, let us expand a bit.

Culture jamming involves playing with existing dominant media and cultural symbols to impart subversive or alternate meanings to them. It is a tactic that is often used against consumer culture by critics and activists. One of the best-known culture jammers is Adbusters, a group that produces alternative advertising, a magazine, and a website devoted to drawing attention to the moral dubiousness of consumerism. Their ads have jammed some of the biggest companies — Nike ('Don't Do It'), Wal-Mart (its smiley-face logo wearing a frown) — countering consumerism and promoting social justice.

Textual poaching is very much what it sounds like. It happens when fans of a movie, television show, or other cultural product begin to write their own texts in ways that the original authors would never have imagined or intended. Some of the oldest and most visible examples of textual poaching have been created around the *Star Trek* series, where fans have written about love affairs between different characters, including Kirk and Spock (Jenkins 1988). Other examples are love stories involving Gabriel and Xena from *Xena Warrior Princess* (Helford 2000) and re-writes of scenes from *Buffy the Vampire Slayer*. Textual poaching is a means for fans of a show to wrestle the direction of the show from the hands of more formulaic industry writers and take some control of its production and culture.

Empowering language happens when people in a group take control of a word used to label that group in a negative way and instead use the word to evoke positive meanings. The word 'queer' for example was once used pejoratively to demark difference and stigmatize gay and lesbian people. Over time, however, the word was embraced by LGBT communities as a means of *disempowering* the negative elements of the term and taking control of the labelling of their communities. Robidoux (2006) has found the same process happening in some Canadian Aboriginal communities around the 'Indian' images and symbols long used as mascots for North American sports teams, often in a cartoon-like or derogatory way. Rather than passively accepting such deprecating practices, these communities have adopted the logos and promote them as a means of self-referencing. Even as we are writing this book, there are women worldwide participating in 'slut walks', embracing the label and dressing the part, to seize control of the term rather than permit its continued use by police and justice officials as justification for rape (*Huffington Post* 2011).

All these groups seek to undermine the deleterious effects of the disparaging symbols or terms on group members by recasting them as empowering rather than offensive or abusive. As all these strategies and examples demonstrate, readings, texts, and meanings can all be contested in the negotiation of culture and power.

upon. Most of the time, this happens more or less unconsciously, without anyone telling us what and when to do and say things. As Michel Foucault (1991) put it, people largely regulate themselves in social interactions. Much in the same way that Bourdieu said that people embody cultural and social capital from an early age, Foucault theorized that people absorb and internalize the dominant views and symbols of their culture and are governed by them to the point that these ways of seeing and interpreting the world become the foremost **schemata**, or frameworks, of their consciousness. Foucault coined the term **governmentality** to signal the self-governing of one's own imagination. There are all sorts of ways and places where we govern ourselves. Have you ever tried to barter with the counter clerk at a fast-food restaurant? Why not? There is no explicit law that forbids bartering and prices are not governed by laws. No, economic interactions are actually dictated by social negotiation, in the same sense that Hall and Goffman illustrate with cultural and social exchanges.

Collective Identity and Challenges to Power

In the mid-1970s a number of scholars, in reaction to changing economic, cultural, and social practices, primarily in the post-industrial societies of the global North, began observing that many people were no longer mobilizing around material interests. Rather, identity and its recognition seemed to be emerging as the most important elements in the contesting of dominant power. They offered as evidence the cultural and social mobilization associated with the **New Left** of the 1960s, such as the second wave of the women's movement, or LGBT activism, or lifestyle movements like environmentalism or the **back-to-the-land** movement. The people in these movements were not interested in overthrowing the existing power structure—which was in stark contrast to the class-based mobilizations of the old left. In many cases, the goals of these movements involved recognition of identity, culture, social legitimacy, even mobilization 'for itself' rather than more tangible change as measured through transformation of the dominant institutions. Instead, the emphasis was on the creation of new cultural and social imaginations.

The earliest political sociologists to tackle these **new social movements** (NSMs) did not see how traditional Marxist social science could be of any help to them, given what they believed was its overly deterministic and structural focus. They also thought that the assumptions of resource mobilization accounts were too rationalized and bureaucratized to be of assistance. Instead, some saw the new forms of mobilization as manifestations of a burgeoning post-Industrial Revolution, which others such as Ronald Inglehart (1990) termed a **culture shift**. These scholars said the new movements were an outgrowth of the post-war baby-boom generation forming a large and unprecedented new middle class and fighting for the advancement of non-traditional goals. Later researchers carried on with the theme of 'newness' in these movements, theorizing that they were associated with the historical peculiarities of late modernity (see Touraine 2003, Habermas 1989, or Giddens 1991), the rise of the information or discursive age (see Melucci 1996a, 1996b, 1989), and the rise of networked society (see Castells 2004). These writers commonly cited increased communications among people across regions and countries, as well as travel and even new technology, as facilitating the rise of these movements.

Not all scholars agreed with these interpretations, however. A number were quite critical of the assumed newness of NSMs. In fact, Craig Calhoun (1993) went so far as to question whether these new social movements were indeed novel at all, citing the proliferation of cultural, lifestyle, and identity claims pursued by earlier movements throughout history. Such criticisms diminished much of the early enthusiasm of NSM scholars, prompting some of them, like Alberto Melucci, to switch focus and identify contemporary movements in terms of the more generic notion of collective identity. Melucci defined **collective identity** as 'the process of "constructing" an action system. Collective identity is an interactive and shared definition produced by a number of individuals (or groups at a more complex level) concerning the orientations of their action and the field of opportunities and constraints in which such action is to take place' (Melucci 1996a: 70). It is clear from this definition that, like earlier Western European thinkers, Melucci was focusing on how people constructed belonging or solidarity. Thus, he understood that processes of collective identity involved cognitive definitions, active relationships, and emotional investment by individuals and groups.

Since Melucci, others have elaborated on the concept of collective identity. Of those that do, few see it as trumping previous material and resource-based explanations and instead see it as complementing material perspectives to offer a fuller understanding of mobilization (Tilly 2008). In an excellent summary of this literature, Francesca Polletta and James Jasper argue that collective identity is 'an individual's cognitive, moral, and emotional connection with a broader community, category, practice or institution. It is a perception of a shared status or relation, which may be imagined rather than experienced directly, and it is distinct from personal identities' (2001: 285). As a result, although many people may self-govern their actions, shared imaginaries and the fight to have them recognized can contest the governmentality of dominant power holders. Many political sociologists who examine processes of collective identity focus on individual and everyday interactions to understand 'why' people mobilize. Polletta and Jasper (2001) elaborate upon this and argue that scholars who have turned to collective identity approaches tend to engage four broad types of questions: (1) Why do collective actors act when they do? (2) What are the motivations for action? (3) What strategies and choices are made? And (4) What are the cultural effects of social movements?

With respect to the first question, recall that in Chapter 2 resource mobilization theory (RMT) explained mobilization by identifying the material resources necessary for mobilizing. However, those approaches fail to account for why people mobilize around a given movement's issue and why they feel the need to act on some issues but not others. Just having the material and organizational resources to engage in collective action may be necessary for contentious action, but they are not sufficient to explain why people challenge dominant power holders. Moreover, the idea that people only mobilize because they are aggrieved or to maximize their material benefit loses sight of the complex motivations that drive human action. In many instances people also act on the basis of whether they receive *recognition* of their status or position.

Take Quebec nationalism, for instance. Have the more recent waves of mobilization witnessed in this movement been driven by Quebecers' desire to gain control of the state? Apparently not, because the province's leaders have long had control over taxation, education, language, and other formal institutions. What Quebecers did not have until recently, however, is recognition of their difference. In fact, as Charles Taylor (1992) notes, such recognition by dominant power holders is an essential element to maintaining multicultural societies. We will pick up on the more specific case of Quebec in the next section and then again in Chapter 4. But for now note that the desire for recognition of one's identity can help account for the timing and cohesion of a social movement.

Recognition of a collective identity can also address Polletta and Jasper's second question pertaining to the *motivations* behind collective action. It makes sense that people would join and be active in a social movement because they feel a sense of solidarity with or membership in an aggrieved group. People may mobilize on the basis of their network or emotional ties to others, drawing upon trust and obligation, perhaps social capital. However, as Polletta and Jasper rightly note, the assumption that this is an automatic or natural occurrence is perhaps a little naïve. As Goffman showed us, identity or solidarity is a process that must be continually performed, managed, and maintained. Otherwise, like other things, it will become extinct. Thus, what this approach recognizes is that identity can provide an additional explanation for why people act contentiously.

Collective identity, cultural capital, and sense of belonging also influence the kinds of choices people make when engaging in collective action. These concepts can help us to engage Polletta and Jasper's third question pertaining to the *strategies* that social movement actors employ. Accounting for culture and identity adds additional criteria by which people make tactical decisions about the types of actions they engage in. For example, people who identify as rebels might be more likely than others to participate in violent or radical actions. Conversely people who identify as pacifists may participate only in actions that are non-violent. Collective identity and the culture that comes with it can thus frame the boundaries of the types of things people are willing or unwilling to do (Polletta and Jasper 2001: 195).

Finally, the desire on the part of movement members to acquire recognition of their collective identity speaks to Polletta and Jasper's last question regarding the *cultural effects of social movement*s. Identities are situational (Polletta and Jasper 2001: 294). Just as Goffman and Bourdieu showed us, identities manifest themselves in the social interactions between those who are exerting a given identity and those with the power and legitimacy to recognize it. It is an aim and activity that is expressive, and such expression can often be the ultimate goal of a movement. Because of this, the various movements based on collective identities often pursue very different, sometimes contradictory, outcomes. Whereas materially oriented movements sought to maximize their control over physical and financial resources, movements dedicated to collective identity recognition may be driven by people's desire just to *be*.

For instance, most LGBT activists do not mobilize in order to destroy the heterosexist capitalist state but rather to get the state and others to recognize LGBT people as legitimate members of the community with the right to participate fully in these communities. Thus, a **gay pride** parade is more than just a colourful and exuberant (and often racy) event. It is a political act, an example of a collective action held to encourage recognition of the existence and legitimacy of people with diverse lifestyles. Thus, the creation, maintenance, framing, and exhibition of identity can be goals in and of themselves. The ability to gain economic prominence or influence or to change the state or policy thus becomes a less direct goal and, in some senses, is less important than achieving recognition. Thus, members' personal desire to be acknowledged by the community as legitimate is expressed in a political act designed to change existing culture.

Post-colonialism and Nationalism

Although collective identity approaches build upon many insights pertaining to cultural and social power, they tend to focus on individual status, prestige, and recognition, and small-scale mobilization and action within a given state. Identity, however, also exerts an influence in different and larger forms. Many political sociologists have seen the rise of broad-based identity movements based on historical communities or nations through the rise of **post-colonialism** in the post–Second World War era and **nationalism**, which are perhaps two of the most prominent trends that reflect these attempts to gain recognition of identity.

As you may be aware, colonialism and **imperialism** were major forms of international relations and of the expansion of European states until the twentieth century. Both are practices in which powerful states exert control over less powerful ones and that often involve the annexation of land, resources, and peoples. The history of colonialism is also associated with asserting and prizing the culture of the dominant power holders over the masses that have been colonized. This happened in Canada with the English colonization of North America in the seventeenth and eighteenth centuries, processes that established the dominance of English culture and traditions over territories formerly controlled by the French, Acadians, and Aboriginal peoples. As a result, the French language and culture—which are at least as old in Canada as their English equivalents—were marginalized relative to the English language and culture, which were practised by the most powerful in the country (Warren 2009). In its most extreme forms, Anglo colonialism in Canada fostered discriminatory policies like the **Indian Acts**, which as Ramos (2007) notes, led to the legal definition of 'Indian', the displacement of Indians to reserves (Miller 1989), their disenfranchisement (Canada 1996: Sec. 9.9.12), their forced placement in residential schools (Haig-Brown 1988), the banning of Aboriginal cultural practices (Canada 1996: Sec. 9.9.5), their transfer from state to state without consultation (Grand Council of the Crees 1998), and discrimination against Aboriginals in employment and daily life (Fleras and Elliot 2003: 175; Langford and Ponting 1992; Ponting 2000).

The armed forces of former colonial powers became weaker after the First World War and especially after the Second World War, and the **United Nations** adopted the Universal Declaration of Human Rights in 1948. This signalled the beginning of the era of post-colonialism. It was an era in which colonized peoples around the world began to take action against the states that had once dominated them.

Political sociologists have accounted for this mobilization in a number of ways. Some such as Susan Olzak (1983), looking at the Quebec case, argued that it was a result of **ethnic competition**. She observed that as the Catholic Church came to play a smaller and smaller role in provincial and institutional affairs, and as Quebec experienced the **Quiet Revolution**, the province witnessed unprecedented educational attainment, a growth in middle-class wealth, and urbanization among its colonized francophone majority. Nagel and Olzak (1982) posited that these cultural factors, in addition to control over material and organizational resources, contributed to the mobilization of French-speakers in Quebec. Rima Wilkes (2004) examined whether the ethnic competition model can be extended to Aboriginal populations in Canada. Others, such as Michael Hechter (2000) and John Meyer et al. (1997) argued that such mobilization was a by-product of nations' seeking to become states. In modern international relations, states are typically the only entity recognized as legitimate holders of ethnic and national power. These scholars argue that groups whose members identify with a particular culture or ethnicity and desire more power over their own destinies are in a sense compelled to mobilize for recognition of their own state to acquire that power.

Yet other political sociologists, many of whom were colonized people themselves, located the impetus for post-colonial mobilization in the social and psychological consequences of colonization. One of the most prominent of these thinkers was Frantz Fanon. He was a Martiniquean-born French citizen, who was trained as a psychiatrist and worked in colonized Algeria, where he wrote many of his key works. Fanon was influenced by other French Caribbean and African writers like Aimé Césaire and Léopold Sédar Senghor. As a Black citizen of France, he experienced and eloquently documented the double standards of French society. He found that rather than a society based on liberté, égalité, fraternité, slogans of the French Revolution, it was a society that was hierarchically ordered by class, ethnicity, language and race. Like Bourdieu, who also spent time in Algeria, Fanon recognized that the most important cultural and social markers were largely monopolized by dominant power holders, in this case, the almost exclusively White aristocratic elite. He found that in order to succeed in France, one had to endure a devaluing of one's own cultural and social identities, and embrace those of the dominant colonizers. This led him to use the phrase 'black skins, white masks', which is also the title of one his most famous books (1967), to describe the psychological turmoil suffered by racialized people in France as they came to terms with the feelings of dependence and inadequacy promoted by the dominant colonial culture. For this reason, in his writing, Fanon advocated raising people's self-awareness and consciousness of the values of colonized identities. He believed that the first step to their emancipation and recognition by dominant power holders was for people to recognize their own identities.

Similar observations were made by scholars looking at other colonial relationships, such as Edward Said in his book **Orientalism** (1978). Like Fanon, Said's work noted how Western European colonizers and their scholars and artists often described the colonized as 'inferior, irrational, deprived, and childlike' (Sardar and Van Loon 1999: 107). His attention was focused on the Middle East, Asia, and the Muslim world; hence his choice of terminology. Said observed that culture, literature, and art about these parts of the world reflected ideas of the Orient that were shaped by the imbalance of power between dominant colonizers and the colonized. Rather than portraying Middle Eastern and 'Oriental' peoples as complex, with rich histories that rivalled those of the colonizers, they were instead often portrayed as subservient, backwards, and exotic, descriptions that had detrimental effects upon those who were portrayed in such ways. Thus, Fanon and Said show us that repression of identity and culture can have damaging influences on entire nations of people.

Within Canada similar observations can be seen in the discourse of the Quebec nationalist movement in the 1960s and 1970s. The movement, like so many identity-based movements, was committed to raising the consciousness of Quebecers to gain a pride in their culture and traditions and to re-establish their self-worth, through actions like the romanticization of **joual**. That was the dialect of French spoken by working-class Quebecers, and it was deliberately spoken and celebrated by Quebec nationalists in preference to more standard international French or English, which at that time was the dominant language of business in Quebec. And there is little question that Pierre Vallières (1967), a leader of the Front de libération du Québec (FLQ), was trying to shock Anglo culture into recognizing the colonized status of the Québécois when he called his book about the Québécois *Nègres blancs d'Amérique* (or *White Niggers of America*). Similar mobilization of consciousness and identity appear in the writings of prominent Canadian Aboriginal activists of the same period, such as Howard Adams (1995). The importance of exerting and preserving identity can also be seen in the recent writings of Taiaiake Alfred (2005) on **Wasase**, which advocates for Aboriginal mobilization around Indigenous culture, traditions, and identities instead of ones that play into the established colonial order of the Canadian state.

Although mobilization can occur around claims for recognition of postcolonial identities, it can also occur around assertions of nationhood and nation building. Benedict Anderson (1991) argued that culture, language, and media play important roles in the generation of national identities and nationalism. Unlike ethnic identities, which can exist among people living in different states spread out across the world, or racial identities that are ascribed, national identities have associated with them an enduring history, a defined territory or 'homeland', and shared culture, language and social relations. Unlike earlier scholars of nationalism, such as Ernest Renan ([1882] 1990), who argued that nations are built on a 'collective loss of memory' (in that nationalists can 'forget' their 'real' history to promote the national myth), Anderson argues that nations are built through a shared **imagining of communities**. That is, most nations are the product of generating shared cultural and social capital, through which people begin to identify with one another. Others, such as Brubaker, Loveman, and Stamatov (2004) extend this idea to consider also how mental schemata, by shaping how people see the world and relate to one another, contribute to nationalist identities and, ultimately, movements.

Ernest Gellner (1983) and many other political sociologists looking at nationalism, however, would contend that identity is only one among many elements that constitute nationalism and national mobilization. As we will see in the following chapter, the state and its institutions are important sites of power. Gellner and other state-centred theorists of nationalism (see Hall 1998, 1993; Mann 1986, 1993; Dunleavy and O'Leary 1987) argue that education systems and other state-run institutions play important roles in legitimizing identities, cultures, and social practices and in turn are necessary for creating nations.

Summary

Clearly, we have come a long way from Weber's observation that power derives from sources other than just material resources and that social markers can confer power independently of people's possession of material assets. Political sociologists have taken up Weber's original formulation and elaborated on how different cultural and social phenomena become infused with meaning, and then act as markers of status that bestow power on different individuals and groups in the process of social interaction. Gramsci, Horkheimer and Adorno, and Herman and Chomsky all recognized the importance of controlling cultural production and in turn the valuing of different forms of knowledge that can be used to pacify opposition or mobilize contention. Others have showed us that culture and social ties can be exchanged and transformed in the negotiation of power. Bourdieu showed us that cultural and social markers contribute to a person's status and power. Putnam extended these insights by looking at how social ties contribute to healthy democracies and communities. Yet others have highlighted the importance of social and cultural practices in the negotiation of power, both at the micro- or individual and small-group levels, and at macro- or national and even global levels. Erving Goffman did this by using the analogy of drama, and Stuart Hall looked to semiotics to understand why different cultural and social markers gain value. Together these scholars have drawn attention to the often 'hidden' meanings that shape social interactions and in a way, have democratized power holding by acknowledging that everyone, as possessors of at least *some* forms of cultural and social capital, are capable of exercising power *sometimes*, depending on the circumstances.

Questions for Critical Thought

1. What forms of cultural and social capital do you possess?

2. Why is it difficult for young women to advance their careers in male-centred workplaces?

3, What underlying processes shape social and cultural resources negotiated in your everyday life?

Suggestions for Further Reading

Brissett, Dennis, and Charles Edgley (eds). 2006. *Life as Theater: A Dramaturgical Sourcebook*. New Brunswick, NJ: Transaction. This book introduces concepts and works related to Goffman's symbolic interaction and later approaches to dramaturgy.

Gagnon, Alain. 2004. *Québec: State and Society.* Toronto: Broadview Press. A one-stop reference to familiarize yourself with issues and scholarship related to Quebec and its broader historical and contemporary relationship with the rest of Canada.

Hier, Sean P., and B. Singh Bolaria (eds). 2006. *Identity and Belonging: Rethinking Race and Ethnicity in Canadian Society.* Toronto: Canadian Scholars' Press. A collection of research that deals with identity, nationalism, and the politics of recognition. It includes a number of significant Canadian writers.

Polletta, Francesca, and James Jasper. 2001. 'Collective identity and social movements'. *Annual Review of Sociology* 27: 283–305. A summary article that covers some of the key concepts related to NSM and collective-identity approaches to mobilization.

Websites

Canadian Association of Cultural Studies
www.culturalstudies.ca/english/eng_about.htm

Egale Canada
www.egale.ca

Historica (on Nationalism and Separation in Canada)
www.histori.ca/peace/page.do?pageID=242

International Network for Social Network Analysis
www.insna.org

4 Institutions

Learning Objectives

⊛ To understand what social institutions are and how they affect power relations
⊛ To recognize the important role that the state plays in power contests
⊛ To learn about 'new institutionalism' and related fields in political sociological research and review some of the works of key scholars in this field, including Theda Skocpol and Michael Mann
⊛ To see how paying attention to institutions can shed light on genocide, nationalism, and participation in voluntary associations
⊛ To learn how institutions can affect challenges to power by providing both barriers to and the means for mobilization

Introduction

In the previous chapter, we introduced you to political sociologists who explore how cultural and social markers become means by which people and groups exercise and challenge existing power arrangements. Their work has helped reveal many of the 'hidden' or previously unacknowledged ways that people exercise power over others every day. It has also broadened our understanding of collective action, as including the pursuit of ends that don't seem to be directly related to material power.

But these perspectives are not without their critics. Although most political sociologists now recognize that it is important to consider how cultural and social processes shape power relations, some say that if such factors are given too much prominence they can misrepresent the capacity of different people and groups to wield power and effect change. Some of these critics say that studies which privilege cultural and social factors in their analyses of power are overly **reductionist**. That is, they incorrectly reduce power relations to inequalities in people's access to and ability to control things like ideas (cultural capital), and social networks (social capital). These scholars sometimes extend this criticism to materialist perspectives too. This is because such approaches say that the material resources that people and groups possess are the primary means by which they employ and resist power.

But what else can social actors use as a means of acquiring power besides the material, cultural, and social capital that they possess? They can use **institutions**. Overly materialist and cultural and social accounts of power under-specify how institutions can affect power negotiations. It's not that these perspectives ignore institutions. Recall that Marxists and materialists maintain that institutions like the state, religion, media, and the education system operate in the interests of the materially well off. Feminist scholars and scholars of race and ethnicity add that institutions also function to sustain the power of culturally and socially advantaged groups, like men or non-racialized people, over women and the racialized. But both traditions treat institutions basically as reflections of the power inequities generated between individuals and groups. They do not delve as deeply as these critics say they should into how institutions themselves can serve as means of exercising and contesting power.

In this chapter we provide an overview of the institutionalist perspective in political sociology. We begin with a discussion of what an institution is in political sociological terms, with a focus on the state as the most important institution affecting power relationships in contemporary societies. We then move on to show how the main ways that political sociologists understand institutions that influence power contests have their origins in Weber's insights into the structure and characteristics of *bureaucracy*. As you will see, these insights are evident in the scholarship of the 'new institutionalists', such as Theda Skocpol and Michael Mann, and in the related fields in political sociology that we review, including organizational analyses and studies of nationalism. That violence often erupts in power contests fostered by or launched against the state means that its analysis by political sociologists has been unavoidable. We note some of the key observations that scholars have made about the use of violence in power struggles, with an emphasis on the important, sometimes surprising offerings that institutionalists have made to the dialogue. The chapter then turns to a discussion of how institutions affect challenges to power. Here we engage Weber's notion of 'party power' more explicitly and explore how the power of a collective can be enhanced or hindered by institutions, especially those that constitute the state. This is illustrated by means of Jane Jenson's work on 'citizenship regimes' and an appraisal of how the *political opportunities/political process* school in social movement studies understands institutions as acting both as barriers to and means for mobilization efforts.

Institutions

How do institutions affect power relations independently of the money and cultural and social assets that people and groups command? They do so by setting the bounds of social interactions, the 'rules' and guidelines that govern the manner in which social relations unfold, and by delimiting the choices of action available to people at any given time and place. In this way, institutions do not determine the outcomes of power negotiations, but they shape them to a much greater degree than a purely materialist or cultural or social approach may allow.

Let's think about this for a moment. We know that the materially advantaged wield a lot of power in contemporary societies. But can they really do anything they want, any time? Well no, they can't. In Canada, they can't go around driving on the left side of the road, or killing people; they can't legally pay their employees below the minimum wage, or simply install the Prime Minister of their choice. The same can be said of those who hold high status because of the cultural or social resources they possess. Leaders of religious organizations, such as the Pope, for instance, or modern-day monarchs like Queen Elizabeth, must still observe the laws of their societies, regardless of how much social honour is granted them by their followers. They cannot order their flock to stop paying taxes or rally those loyal to them to overthrow the sitting government, without consequences. Similarly, celebrities who enjoy a high level of cultural prestige and can exert their will more often and easily than the non-famous, might still be obliged to take part in the annual family Christmas sing-along if their mothers and fathers expect them to. In other words, just because a person is rich, well networked, or popular, there are norms, rules, and social practices that even she is compelled to follow. Those rules will invariably shape how power negotiations unfold and the outcomes that come about. Now, the materially, culturally, or socially advantaged may be able to circumvent institutions or change them more easily than the less advantaged. But they still need to take into account the 'way things are done', the regular and predictable patterns by which a society is ordered, when they exercise their powers. Put another way, individual advantage does not give a person licence to ignore the institutions ordering a society.

When sociologists talk about institutions, they often refer to formal organizations like the state, a workplace, or a university. But they also mean things that you might not automatically think of as institutions, like the economy, family, religion, or the education system. These are phenomena that may not always be characterized by an identifiable administration or bureaucracy, but they nevertheless *order* people's behaviour in enduring and relatively predictable ways. Much of the time, this happens not because people are forced to do so, but instead because they are following the social practices or norms making up and maintaining institutions. When norms and social practices have 'calcified' to the extent that they create a predictable pattern or map of the behaviour that people will usually follow, they compose an institution.

The degree of calcification can vary. Institutions can be informal, fairly loose arrangements that people stick to by choice or habit. Friday game-and-pizza night would be an example of an informal institution among the members of a family; the Thursday pub crawl might be an institution among university students. These are institutions that the people maintaining them can change or choose to participate in quite easily. Institutions can also be formal, stricter arrangements that configure people's behaviour more rigidly. Examples of formal institutions are the organizational hierarchy at a workplace or the manner in which education is delivered to children though a series of age-restricted classes taught and assessed by teachers and administrators in well-defined ways. Such institutions are more difficult to avoid or change because they tend to have been around, and affecting people's behaviours, for a long time. Sometimes it gets to the point that the people participating in them view them as given or 'natural', or cannot imagine—indeed may not have even thought of—other ways of going about the same thing. Nevertheless, even the most durable social institutions have their origins in the regularized, patterned, behaviour of groups of people. They are perpetuated by people who abide by and take account of these practices in their daily lives, over and over and over again, sometimes to the point where the practices become habitual, second nature, or more or less unquestioned.

Sociologists of all stripes study institutions, but political sociologists study them because they shape the negotiation of power. Because institutions order and assign roles to people, they can have a major impact on the capacity of a person or group to exert their will in power contests. In the case of formal organizations this is pretty obvious. If you are in one of the entry-level positions in your workplace administration, as mail clerk for example, you will for various reasons have less power in that organization than the people who occupy higher positions, like the executive director. But this is also true of less formally defined institutions, like the family. Parents are expected to make decisions about how family members will interact; children are supposed to follow their instructions. In both examples, the institution configures the roles occupied by the people that constitute and sustain them as well as the responsibilities, expectations, prestige, and hence, power, associated with those roles. They do not always determine exactly how social interactions will unfold. Children exercise power in the family all the time, as when crying babies compel their CEO fathers to come and care for them in the middle of the night. Even in workplaces where employees' powers are very strictly defined, a mail clerk can legitimately hold up an executive meeting when the union he belongs to permits him to take a mid-morning break. But by serving as the rulebook that guides the social interactions that encompass them, institutions will direct how power is exercised and negotiated most of the time in fairly predictable ways.

A defining feature of an institution is its durability, but it would be wrong to assume that institutions do not change. Institutions, even those that seem the most natural or longest-lived, change all the time. Recall from Chapter 2 that Marx, like other social thinkers of his time, pondered how and why the institutions that configured work in the past were transformed with the coming of the Industrial Revolution. Before industrialization, most people worked on subsistence farms in rural areas, where the division and scheduling of their labour was determined, in the main, by the demands of family and nature. This changed with industrialization, when workplaces moved to factories in urban areas and labour became increasingly gendered (in that men came to dominate work in the public sphere, women in the private sphere)and more highly structured with respect to when and how work was done. Although we take the separation of home and work for granted today, and although we accept as commonsensical the different norms and social practices we abide by in each place, the institutions that governed people's working lives were once very different. Families too have changed. The nuclear family—man, woman, and two or three biological children living in the same household— may seem the natural way that families should be organized, but they are rather recent phenomena in the West. In traditional societies, couples typically had more children, and an extended family may have been included in the household, even with some servants or farmhands thrown in. Today in most developed or industrialized societies, smaller families are the norm, and forms of family that are different from the nuclear structure have emerged, such as lone-parent families or same-sex partnerships, and partnerships with or without children. These changes are still occurring, as seen in Figure 4.1. Since 1981, the number of married couples with children has decreased while common-law relationships with children have increased and lone-parent families with children are more common.

That today's workplace and family look very different than they did two centuries ago, or even thirty years ago, shows that social institutions, as stable and enduring as they may seem, are not timeless and are subject to change. It follows then, that the power relationships that characterize institutions must change too. The power relationship that existed between the dominant

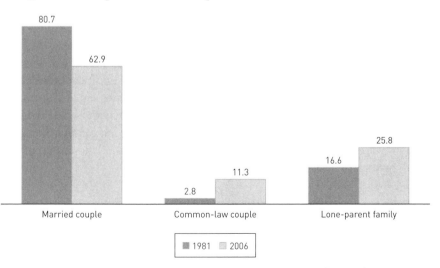

FIGURE 4.1 Families with children, by family structure, 1981 and 2006 (per cent)
Source: Statistics Canada. 2006 Census. (Cat. No. 97-554-XCB2006007). Ottawa, 2007.

landlord and his subordinate peasantry was different than that which exists today between boss and employee. Although peasants were undeniably less powerful than the nobles on whose land they toiled, the noble nevertheless had some personal responsibility to protect them from harm and ensure their well-being. Moreover, the peasants were more or less self-sufficient since they were permitted to keep some of the agricultural product they produced to survive. Today, workers seldom have any alternative means of surviving, outside the wages they receive, to purchase the things they need in order to live, and bosses, although they must abide by labour laws, are not in any way personally responsible for them. Thus the nature of the power relationship between superior and subordinate has changed. And although children are still subordinate to their parents, families, especially middle-class families, are much more democratic than in the past. That is, children can exert much more power and influence in the family today than they did even a generation or two ago. For example, 'pester power', the ability of children to nag their parents into buying things that they wouldn't otherwise buy, has grown significantly over the years as family structure and roles have changed, parenting styles have become more 'child-centred', and the focus of marketers on children has intensified (Media Awareness Network 2011).

So institutions change, as do the relative powers of the people who constitute and sustain them. But how do they change? What causes them to change? And come to think of it, where do institutions come from in the first place? We know that the modern economy, schools, governments, legal systems, and other institutions did not materialize fully formed when humans appeared on earth, so who made them, and why? These are big questions, but political sociologists who focus on how institutions affect the negotiation of power take them on. They do this by **deconstructing** institutions, and they try to make sense of where they came from, how they work, and in whose interest they operate. They also explore how institutions change, what social forces and factors combine to help alter existing institutions, and how individuals and groups promote the creation of new institutions or the modification or abolition of old ones. Political sociologists do all this to assess how institutions contain power negotiations and direct them and to see how those negotiations will unfold. Institutions, these scholars show, shape the nature and outcomes of power contests between social actors, independently of the material, cultural, or social resources those actors command.

The State

Although political sociologists examine all sorts of institutions, the one that they are especially interested in and that almost always figures in their analyses in some way is the **state**, or what people usually call 'the government'. This is because political sociologists study power, and the state is, arguably, the most powerful institution found in contemporary societies. You probably don't go around thinking about this all the time, but the state is the only institution whose leaders and personnel have the legal right to tax you, to assault you through its police and military, to permit or force you to commit murder if they conscript you into the armed forces and send you to war, to legally detain you in prison, and in some places even to kill you by means of capital punishment. It is also the only institution that can set policies and laws governing your behaviour, restrict the ways you conduct business and even your personal and love relationships, authorize your credentials and license your activities, and so on. Of course, we permit states to do these things because they are supposed to provide us with needed services like schools, roads, and health care, ensure a safe and orderly society, and protect our national interests. But given the strength and breadth of authority the state is sanctioned to exercise, there is no denying the power that the people who control state institutions have. This is why the right to manage and influence a state is relentlessly fought over by the leaders and members of various political parties and groups wanting to promote their own ends. It is also why political sociologists keep at least one eye firmly focused on state activities.

The primacy of the state in institutional perspectives on power also permits us to examine another process that people and groups employ to exercise and challenge power that we have not yet touched upon. That is, *violence*, or actions that result in people getting injured or killed. We include it here because any political sociologist who wants to understand the use and abuse of violence in negotiations of power will invariably engage state institutions in some way. This is because these days violence is not available to very many social actors as a legitimate means of shaping power contests. In the majority of countries in the world, state leaders are the only people who have the legal right to use violence, through state-sponsored police forces, the military and court systems, to maintain social control and defend the interests of their nation. And even they need to provide proper justification to their citizens and sometimes to the international community for ordering or allowing police or military aggression at home or elsewhere. If they don't, they face the possibility of citizen unrest, sanctions from the international community, and even a decline of state power.

Violence in this sense is quite strictly, albeit imperfectly, regulated in contemporary societies and so any time it is used as a means of influencing power negotiations, it has to be examined in light of the state institutions that have either enabled or inhibited its employment. This is true whether the violence is undertaken by the state in its normal capacity as the monopolizer of physical force; by state leaders who employ violence unlawfully in power contests with other groups or state interests; or by non-state actors who use violence as a means of challenging existing power arrangements or even the state itself (see Box 4.1).

BOX 4.1 ❋ THE G20 PROTESTS AND THE CANADIAN STATE

Max Weber said the power of the state ultimately flowed from its monopoly on the legitimate use of violence. But here in Canada we often forget that when we elect state officials to office, we are granting them, by virtue of their control of the state, the power to use police and military forces as they see fit. Even against us.

Each year, leaders of the Group of 8 and Group of 20 countries get together to discuss and debate issues of common concern. In June 2010, it was Canada's turn to host the meetings, so the leaders of these most powerful states descended on Huntsville (for the G8) and Toronto (for the G20) in Ontario to engage in several days of talks. And as has become common, the meetings were accompanied by large protests by people opposed to the economic, social, environmental, and military decisions that these leaders have made over recent years.

The meetings and protests unfolded largely as expected, but the response of the Canadian state through its security and police forces did not. Throughout the weekend of the G20, heavily armed and suited officers retained by the various levels of governments to provide for summit security engaged in aggressive actions against Toronto protesters that shocked many Canadians watching the events unfold. These included the repeated and violent dispersal of protesters, even from areas designated as 'protest areas', mass detentions, and arrests of demonstrators. In all, over 1,000 people were arrested, the largest mass arrest in Canadian history during peacetime, the vast majority of whom later had their charges dismissed (Canadian Civil Liberties Association 2011).

To some Canadians, the protesters only got what was coming to them for creating a disturbance. To others, the scene reminded them of how fragile our 'right' to freedom of expression and assembly actually is. Concerns only intensified when it was discovered that these actions had been approved by state officials. At the request of the police, the provincial government, quietly and without debate in the legislature, passed a regulation before the summit that gave the police the power to search, detain, and arrest anyone inside the fence that encircled the summit site. The police then announced, incorrectly, that anyone within five metres of the fence could be arrested.

In a report released some months after the meetings, Ontario's Ombudsman, André Marin, said it was 'opportunistic and inappropriate' for politicians to enact what amounted to a 'war measure' allowing 'extravagant police authority' without publicizing its passage. 'By changing the legal landscape without warning,' Marin wrote, '[the regulation] operated as a trap for those who relied on their ordinary legal rights.' More than this, he said, the misapprehension by police officials and officers of the regulation's reach meant that '[t]hroughout the weekend . . . police

Box 4.1 ⁕ CONTINUED

exercised their powers under the Act well beyond the limits of the security perimeter, even after the misinterpretation had been corrected' (Ontario 2010).

At least five separate reviews into the events around the summit have been held, together with legal challenges by a number of the protesters who were arrested or injured by the police. And for now, the politicians involved are satisfied with the process. David Miller, who was mayor of Toronto at the time, has remained steadfast in his support of the Toronto police, and Ontario Premier Dalton McGuinty recently rejected a call from the Canadian Civil Liberties Association for a public inquiry into police actions. McGuinty admits, however, that there were 'some shortcomings' arising from his government's decision to pass the secret security law (Jenkins 2011).

Let's now take a look at the work of some political sociologists who explore how institutions, especially state institutions, influence power contests. As in the previous chapters, we will begin with Max Weber. You already know that Weber was critical of materialism for claiming that power inequalities stemmed ultimately from material inequalities. You also know that he acknowledged people's use of cultural and social markers in their pursuit of status power. But he also recognized the power residing in institutional arrangements. Weber elaborated on two elements of institutions—their **inertia** and their *role as containers or the framework of social action*—that are reflected in present-day political sociological studies around institutions. The first is evident in his writings on bureaucracy; the second, in his articulation of party power.

Bureaucracy and Institutional Inertia

Weber travelled to the US in 1904 and was impressed by the way American businesses were organized. **Bureaucracy** was fast becoming the primary way to order businesses in Europe, but it was in the US, Weber thought, that this modern organizational form approached its ideal. These days, the word bureaucracy has become almost synonymous with inefficiency, rigidity, and obstruction. Bureaucracies produce all the 'red tape' around people's activities, the paperwork, the lineups, the endless rigmarole that seems to accompany anything to do with governments and large corporations and organizations. But in Weber's day, bureaucracy was still quite a novel development, especially to a European coming from an area of the world that had only relatively recently emerged from a system organized around hereditary rights, and there were many things about it that Weber liked. There were also, however, many things that Weber disliked about it, features that he predicted would result in negative outcomes.

Weber recognized bureaucracies as unique to the modern period and wanted to understand them better. To do this, he came up with the **ideal-type** bureaucracy. The ideal type was a methodological tool that he conceived of and used to assess a variety of social phenomena. As its name suggests, it was, basically, a model of the phenomenon as it would exist in its ideal or perfect form that could be used as a tool for comparison among cases. In the case of the ideal-type bureaucracy, it was a representation of what a bureaucracy is and how it operates when it is working the way it is supposed to.

It feels strange to read Weber's (1946: 196–244) discussion of the ideal bureaucracy these days because what he says seems obvious: a bureaucracy in its ideal form is *hierarchically ordered*; that is, power is concentrated at the top of the organization and flows down; it consists of various *offices* or jobs that are occupied by different *officials*, or people who have obtained their position because of the *skills* and *experience* they possess; each of these positions has associated with it a *job description* detailing the officer's powers and responsibilities, as well as information, data, and documents—what Weber called the *files*—that exist independently of the person occupying the position and remain attached to the organization even when the person currently occupying that job leaves. Officials of the organization do their jobs according to their job descriptions, unaffected by emotion or personal ideals, they enjoy some *status* from their position, and they receive a *salary* (as opposed to an hourly wage). And there is an **esprit de corps**, a spirit of camaraderie, that is evident in the ideal-type bureaucracy that springs from officials working together with others toward a common goal and from the knowledge that, with time and experience, their hard work and loyalty to the organization will allow them to move up the hierarchy to more powerful and better-paying positions.

Weber liked the impersonal nature of the modern bureaucracy. Older forms of organization that had distributed power on the basis of chance (by heredity, for example) or superstition (by 'divine right' for instance) were more prone to inefficiencies and inequalities because of the favouritism and corruption they permitted and fostered. That said, Weber recognized that the dispassion that characterized the modern bureaucratic organization also had a dehumanizing effect on the people who came into contact with it and who occupied its positions. By regulating more strictly the ways in which people were appointed to its ranks and how business was done, it limited the range of actions, choices, and sentiments that could be taken and expressed in regard to the organization's activities.

For Weber, then, the modern bureaucracy was a double-edged sword, both good and bad, and its contradictory nature was nowhere more evident than in the modern state. Though modern state leaders no longer enjoyed unlimited powers since their authority had not been granted by God, they did not inspire the personal loyalty and devotion that many past leaders had evoked. While things like tax collecting, law making, and waging war were monitored more strictly and undertaken more justly by the modern state, the execution of these tasks happened in a more dispassionate manner, through means spelled out by formal legislative and constitutional principles. And while the jobs of modern state officials, politicians, and civil servants were more defined and predictable than those of their pre-modern counterparts, they were also more delimited since they were bound by the rules dictated in their job descriptions.

The last was of special concern to Weber because he foresaw the work conditions of bureaucrats becoming even more regimented over time. The rules that structure a bureaucracy may make it a very efficient way of achieving goals, thought Weber, but those same rules can make it a very restrictive place composed of boring jobs that demand that officials engage in tedious, repetitive tasks. This has implications not only for the workers, who are compelled to labour in positions in which they amount to little more than robots, and for the people who interact with bureaucracies, who are reduced to numbers in the name of fairness and predictability, but also for future societies, the ordering of which becomes increasingly difficult to change once it is established. This is because bureaucracy, by its very impersonal and mechanical nature, discourages creative, 'out-of-the-box' thinking. It, along with other modern 'rational' phenomena, combine to produce an **iron cage** as Weber called it, or 'steel-hard casing' (2002: 123) of thought and action. Bureaucracy limits the possible means by which activities are undertaken and fosters a rigid mindset among staff and those with whom it comes into contact. As a result, it holds people captive, undermining their attempts to alter, or even think about alternatives to, the way things are done. It can also, paradoxically, lead to practices that are quite inefficient and irrational, the very opposite of its intent. This can happen when adherence to rules and procedures becomes more important than achieving the ends the bureaucracy was set up to meet in the first place.

Weber's hopelessness about bureaucracy and its effects on humankind has been criticized by a number of scholars, including Trevor Noble (2000: 140–2), who says that Weber's pessimism was mistaken because it derived from his depiction of the *ideal* bureaucracy, and not *real* bureaucracy. At the same time, there is no question that jobs in bureaucratic organizations can be mindless, tedious, and taxing affairs and that people who occupy those jobs can become so wrapped up in the regulations guiding their tasks that they can become a misery to themselves and others. Many of us have been subject to the bureaucrat so wedded to the rules, either because of fear of reprisal or just plain habit, that they have refused to bend, even just a little, to accommodate us. In fact, some scholars, such as Robert K. Merton (1949), have noted that this is one way of exercising power for those who are mere cogs in a machine (Bruce

Box 4.2 ⁂ Bureaucrats and Bureaucracy

In the television series *Futurama*, Hermes Conrad is an accountant and 'certified 37th class bureaucrat' who works for the Planet Express delivery company. According to *The Infosphere* (2011) Hermes was a born bureaucrat, 'crying when his alphabet blocks [were] knocked out of order as a four-year-old, and making friends and family file long applications to get into his tenth birthday party'. In the show, he spends his time filling out forms in triplicate, stamping requisitions, informing next of kin, and all the other repetitive tasks that we typically associate with bureaucracy. Far from unhappy in his job, Hermes relishes his work, concerned only with not making a mistake that might demote him back to a lower grade. Aside from his rigid adherence to bureaucratic rules, Hermes hardly resembles the alienated official that Weber predicted would populate modern bureaucracies. Which one best captures the real bureaucratic experience?

If we look to government workers in Canada, it appears Weber wins. A 2010 study of Canadian public-service workers declared that depression among the country's nurses, teachers, police officers, and bureaucrats had reached epidemic levels. Stress, burnout, and other forms of mental distress among employees of the federal government represents Canada's 'biggest public health crisis,' reports Bill Wilkerson, founder of Global Business and Economic Roundtable on Addiction and Mental Health. These disabilities are fostered by 'an inertia and paralysis [that] have gripped the public service.... Such an environment takes its toll on people, many whom leave work every day frustrated and feeling they have accomplished nothing' (May 2010). The sterility of the workplace and the employees' powerlessness that Wilkerson says faces public service workers sound a lot like what Weber's bureaucrats were experiencing over a century ago: 'The individual bureaucrat cannot squirm out of the apparatus in which he is harnessed.... In the great majority of cases, he is only a single cog in an ever-moving mechanism which prescribes to him an essentially fixed route of march. The official is entrusted with specialized tasks and normally the mechanism cannot be put into motion or arrested by him, but only from the very top' (Weber 1946: 228).

In the *Bureaucrat Song*, Hermes sings of office work, 'When push comes to shove, you gotta do what you love....' Maybe that's how bureaucrats will feel in the thirty-first century. But we're clearly not there yet.

2000: 74; Harary 1966). People often follow the rituals of an institution zealously even if they do not believe in them, just because they can!

Weber's ideas about bureaucracy can help us to grasp some of the key features of institutions on which political sociologists focus. The *durability* of the bureaucracy, as well as its tendency to *limit the range of actions* available to individuals who maintain its existence, are traits most evident in the research of scholars interested in how institutions affect the exercise and negotiation of power. Scholars sympathetic to 'new institutionalist' or '**state-centred**' perspectives wish to expose and address the reality that institutions affiliated with the state tend to be slow to change and so shape social and political outcomes in sometimes unexpected ways. Some even argue that the state, because of its stable and predictable organizational structure, is itself an autonomous **agent**. This is because its institutions can compel the people staffing them to act in ways and take decisions they wouldn't otherwise. That is, if they were not bound by the procedures and conventions that characterize them.Others who may not identify themselves as institutionalists have elaborated on the crucial role that state institutions play in the rise of phenomena such as nationalism and state-sponsored and anti-state violence and even on the way non-state organizations are structured.

The New Institutionalism

You might think it's funny to call a perspective that arose in the late 1970s and the 1980s 'new'. But the new in 'new institutionalism' refers not to its recentness as much as to its contrast with the 'old' institutionalism. Whereas the old institutionalists in sociology were primarily concerned with describing and charting the legal and administrative mechanisms of the state, the **new institutionalists** are interested in exposing the ways that state institutions, the formal and informal patterns of interaction that constitute state activities, shape the ways that power is exercised, challenged, and negotiated.

The main message in the new institutionalist literature is: institutions matter; they are not just simple reflections of the preferences of the people who are in them or tools of this or that powerful group in a society. Rather, because institutions determine how power is negotiated, the groups that can legitimately take part, the rules they must abide by or take into account, even the kinds of issues and approaches that these groups are authorized to take up, they will have an effect on how those negotiations unfold. They have this effect, say the new institutionalists, because institutions encourage **path dependency**. In other words, once established, institutions tend to encourage social relations to proceed in certain ways that promote consistency at the expense of other relations and actions that deviate from them. With regard to the state specifically, it is the idea that, once state officials decide to do something in a particular way and set up the administration to support that decision, state action will usually continue to abide by those arrangements and continue down that 'path' of action without any huge or sudden changes. There are occasions, certainly, when institutions will be confronted with forces or pressures that will result in their significant modification. At these **critical junctures**, decisions made by institutional leaders will establish new patterns of interaction, new 'rules of the game', that themselves will eventually exhibit path dependence. They will also, however, close off whatever alternatives may have been available at that decisive time. Thus, institutionalists take very seriously the inertia that Weber identified in formal organizations or the modern bureaucracy. Simply put, institutions are slow to change, and because of that, they will exert an influence on power negotiations independently of the relative powers of the individuals and groups involved in the contest. Institutionalists also recognize the tendency for institutions to limit the number and nature of actions that the individuals who constitute and maintain the institution have available at any given time (see Brinton and Nee 1998; Clemens and Cook 1999; Peters 1999; and Steinmo, Thelen, and Longstreth 1992).

One of the best known institutionalists in sociology is Theda Skocpol. In 1979, she published a comparative-historical analysis of the revolutions in France, Russia, and China. The subject may sound obscure to you, but the book had a huge impact on the discipline. Skocpol was responding to the traditional Marx-inspired understanding of revolutions as class-based conflicts fostered by changes in the nature and ownership of the means of production. Such 'class-struggle reductionist' (1979: 28) accounts, she said, may provide us with a general framework that calls our attention to the condition of class relations leading up to revolutions. But how do we explain differences in the timing and unfolding of revolutions in different places? This, said Skocpol, required a closer reading of specific events, with special attention to how the state institutions that configured each situation contributed to each outcome. Her careful historical analysis revealed that, in each case, state powers were weakened by the inability of existing state institutions to meet or resolve crises arising in the international realm, especially wars or economic troubles. In other words, the way things were done in these states, such as the way they were administered, the manner in which interactions between individuals and groups in and outside the state were managed, and the procedures that characterized state business, could not withstand the pressures of warfare or disruptions to the economy. Which class or classes ended up exploiting this situation and fostering revolution depended on the distribution of power among them. The different outcomes of revolution in each case were affected by the legacies of state institutions prevailing before the conflict, the power arrangements they had fostered among classes, and the international relations they had configured. Thus, Skocpol argued, state institutions in France, Russia, and China had not only helped generate external and internal conditions that enhanced the potential for revolution but had also helped shape the nature of the new regimes after the revolutions.

Skocpol's study was a watershed in institutionalist and state-centred research because it 'brought the state back in' to political analyses. It is a phrase that echoes the title of a book edited by Skocpol and colleagues (Evans, Rueschemeyer, and Skocpol 1985). Before their work structure had been marginalized in favour of reductionist materialist or voluntarist perspectives on the state like **pluralism**. Pluralism understands the state and its operations as the manifestation of the will of groups in civil society freely and 'voluntarily' competing to affect government policy. The pluralist state acts a sort of referee, a neutral mediator in the conflicts between interest groups, which ensures that the competition is fought fairly and then acts in accordance with the wishes of the winner(s). Skocpol's (1979) work was an important challenge to these views. It showed that the state is not just a tool in the class struggle or an arena for contests between interest groups, but that it can influence the progress and outcomes of these conflicts in significant ways depending on the institutional arrangements that characterize the state.

If Skocpol's study is a good example of how the inertia and path dependency of state institutions shape power contests, other scholars in this tradition reveal how they can also place limits on the range of actions available to social actors in power contests. State institutions do not determine the actions of people in some direct or causal way. Rather, people exercise choice within the constraints imposed by the formal and informal rules that govern state-related business (Ingram and Clay 2000). Charles Tilly (1995), for example, showed how the array, or **repertoire**, of protest tactics used in popular protests in Britain changed over time with, among other things, changes in the nature of British state power. As British governance became more democratic and the state's institutions developed to include more and more people, the techniques of protest available to people challenging state power were transformed. It changed from a repertoire that in the 1760s included few if any 'mass' interventions, to one that by the 1840s comprised a set of tactics familiar to most of us: mass marches, petitions, and public meetings. The idea here is that state institutions at both times did not determine how people engaged in popular protest, but set bounds on the choices of protest tactics available for them to take up.

In addition to Skocpol and Tilly, there are many other political sociologists who privilege institutions, especially state institutions, in their analyses of power. Michael Mann (1984) identifies the mechanisms that lend people who control the state an independent basis for the exercise of power. The ability of state leaders to exercise sovereign and final power over a given territory he terms *despotic power*, which is the authority that leaders enjoy simply by occupying the top state position. *Infrastructural power* derives from state leaders' control over the massive state bureaucracy that penetrates society and allows leaders to actually implement the directives they pass and ensure everyone abides by them. The former is not much use without the latter, says Mann, comparing such a scenario with the Red Queen in *Alice in Wonderland* yelling, 'Off with her head!' but getting little response from people out of earshot. His point is that state institutions serve as means of exercising power that are separate and autonomous from other kinds of power, such as material or cultural and ideological power. (For an application of Mann's typology see Stanbridge 1997.)

Although Mann's distinction between the despotic and infrastructural powers of the state has been taken up widely in the field, he is perhaps best known for his work *The Sources of Social Power* (Mann 1986, 1993), in which he traces no less than the development of power in human societies. In the first two volumes he identifies and tracks the progress of what he says constitute the four primary bases of power in human societies, namely, control over ideological, economic, military, and political resources. Although groups that controlled ideological resources, especially religion, may have dominated in past (pre-1760) societies, Mann shows that it is command of military, economic, and, most significantly political resources that defines the nature of power in the modern era. Most important here was the rise in the West of modern states, whose territorial boundaries and sovereign power were forged through centuries of warfare, and their centralized administrations (and eventually, bureaucracies), which were formed to extract money from the citizenry and manage new capitalist economies to help fund those same wars. Mann shows that the modern Western state is at once the product of power and the primary producer of power in the contemporary period. Its authority is not separate from the rest of a society; rather it is at once reliant on and constitutes the primary power arrangements in a society in important ways.

So for Mann, the modern state is an institution that, through its officials, helps to sustain the distribution of power among significant groups, for instance classes, in contemporary societies. Yet, at the same time it is dependent on those groups for the money and legitimacy it needs to exercise its own power. This does not mean that every state is structured in the same way or that state officials everywhere will respond in an identical manner to power struggles in their constituencies. Indeed, the power struggles themselves, the groups involved, and the issues that matter to them are, like the institutions of each state, shaped by the unique history of each place. Mann's analysis, however, maintains that state institutions are involved regardless, even in cases whose origins are not normally taken to be state-related.

New institutionalists such as Skocpol and Mann are committed to exploding the '**black box**' of the state to reveal how the formal and informal patterns of interaction that characterize state business shape power contests, which in turn modify those same institutions. Other political sociologists, who may or may not embrace the institutionalist label explicitly, are similarly interested in how the inertia, path dependence, and other traits displayed by state institutions affect the negotiation of power. In Canadian sociology, these include Samuel Clark (1995) who takes up the study of how status power accrued to Western European aristocrats in the early modern period (see Box 4.3). He shows how the development of centralized state institutions in the British Isles, France, and other countries in between 1500 and 1800 caused aristocratic

Box 4.3 ❋ CANADIAN SOCIOLOGISTS AND INSTITUTIONS

Canadian political sociologists who adopt an institutional approach to their sub-ject often take Canadian power contests that are typically understood as stemming from class or cultural antagonisms and recast them from an institutional perspec-tive. Take Quebec nationalism, for example. In *Nationalism and Social Policy*, Daniel Béland and André Lecours (2008) make the argument that, while cultural factors have obviously played an important role in the emergence of Quebec nationalism, it has been strengthened by the way the Canadian state is organized and the judicious use of state policy by nationalist leaders. The Canadian federal system grants certain powers to the provinces, thereby providing an institutional context that permits Quebec nationalism to exist alongside a pan-Canadian nation-al sentiment. Such a context also permits nationalist politicians to promote poli-cies that they regard as consistent with Québécois culture and identity. Since the 1990s, say Béland and Lecours, it has been progressive social policies that have fit the bill. Now, institutionalized programs like the province's publicly funded child care and its universal drug plan are embraced by many Quebec nationalists as rep-resentative of the unique values and priorities and hence, distinctiveness, of the Quebec nation as compared to the wider Canadian nation.

But institutions can produce unintended consequences. In the 2011 federal election, Jack Layton, the late leader of the New Democratic Party, experienced a surge of popularity in Quebec. For the first time in decades, many Quebecers—including ardent nationalists—considered changing their vote from the nationalist Bloc Québécois to the NDP. Why? According to two *Globe and Mail* journalists, 'Mr Layton's . . . commitments on health, education, seniors, and the environment are a natural fit in the left-leaning province' (McKenna and Marotte 2011). Despite a warning from Pauline Marois, leader of the nationalist Parti Québécois, that the NDP was a 'federalist, centralizing party from Toronto', some voters said they had become weary of the Bloc's overtly nationalist agenda and found the NDP's social policy focus appealing. Whether the NDP has managed to channel the social con-science of the Quebec nation away from the Quebec nationalist parties that have cultivated it remains to be seen. But it indicates the strength that institutionalized policies can have on the beliefs and identities of those at whom they were origin-ally targeted.

status to evolve in different ways in each place. Karen Stanbridge (2003a) challenges some traditional interpretations of the increasingly tolerant policies enacted toward Catholics by the British state over the eighteenth century. She argues that these policies were not the outcome of the growing tolerance of state officials, but of the gradual institutionalization of more liberal treatment of Catholics after the generous policies implemented in Quebec (1774) and Ireland (1778) proved successful (see also Stanbridge 2003b). Daniel Béland (2005, 2006, with Lecours 2008) explores how political 'institutional legacies' in the US, Canada, Belgium, and other countries have shaped a range of social phenomena in these places, including nationalism, fiscal policy, health and pension programs, and welfare regimes. Jeffrey Cormier (2004), shows how lobbying by academic associations led to changes in federal laws on the hiring of new academics in an attempt to 'Canadianize' universities. This lobbying led to significant changes in employment legislation and practices that established patterns in hiring that are still felt today. And Dominique Clément (2008) offers an overview of how federal policy and funding interacted with and influenced the rise of what he calls Canada's 'rights revolution', or the rise of civil-liberty and human-rights organizations during the course of the twentieth century. Clearly, the state as an institution has much influence over the form of civic engagement and the repertoires of tactics taken up by different groups. It also contributes to the slowness of the pace of change that occurs in civil society and the homogenization of various forms of political engagement.

State Institutions and Nationalism

Some political sociologists interested in how institutions shape power contests are not as concerned as the new institutionalists about institutional inertia, but they still highlight the durability and organizing capacity of institutions as factors that can influence the negotiation of power in important ways. Take the study of nationalism for instance. Nationalism includes those feelings of belonging that people can experience as members of a distinct nation or ethnic group—for instance, Canadians, Newfoundlanders, Acadians, or Cree. We have already introduced you to some of the explanations for nationalism put forth by political sociologists in our discussions about Québécois and other nationalisms in Chapter 3. Whereas materialists locate the impetus for nationalisms in the unequal distribution of or access to material resources and others maintain that nationalism is a response to differences in the values people place on cultural or social markers, political sociologists interested in institutions investigate how institutions can fashion nationalisms. Certainly the most famous in this regard is Ernest Gellner.

Gellner ([1964] 1994, 1983) argued that nationalism was a strictly modern phenomenon, only as old as the modern state itself. As power was consolidated among the leaders of the modern states emerging in nineteenth-century Western Europe, the administration of their territories became increasingly centralized. Centralization of state power was accompanied by and facilitated industrialization, a system that, compared to past agrarian societies, was more technical, specialized, and subject to rapid change. Both of these processes, said Gellner, demanded greater cultural homogeneity in a population. A common culture, he observed, makes cross-cultural communication and social control easier. Shared skills and knowledge also ensure a store of interchangeable workers for the new economy. Nationalism was constructed as a means to achieve both common culture and shared skills, through state-run education systems to which populations were exposed, and through the creation and promotion of national-origin myths. Such myths, Gellner (1983: 55) colourfully noted, stem from 'shreds or patches' of history and memory that leaders choose. Even the emotions that people feel toward the nation and other nationals, Gellner said, are a function of the institutions that accompanied modernity. As people come to recognize that their self-interest and livelihoods are inextricably connected, their emotional attachment to the nation-state grows.

In locating the origins of modern nationalism in the institutions of the modern state, Gellner ran straight up against scholarly accounts (and popular ones) that nationalism derived from long-lived ethnic, tribal, or cultural groups. Many doubted that the passions and fervour that often characterized nationalist sentiment could be generated otherwise. But **modernist** accounts of nationalism and other institutional perspectives on nationalism have proliferated in political sociology in recent years. Benedict Anderson (1991), whom we have already seen in Chapter 3, acknowledges that cultural and social factors help to cultivate nationalist feeling. He also agrees with Gellner that nationalism is largely a modern phenomenon supported by the institutions of the modern state. Whereas Gellner privileged mass education in this regard, Anderson highlights the need for a common communications mechanism to help forge connections and familiarity among far-flung populations and create the sense of an **imagined community** that nationalism evokes. He says the spread of literacy and print technologies developing within and fostered by centralizing states encouraged people who inhabited these new political configurations to conceive of each other as alike and equal in time and space. Rogers Brubaker (1994, 1996), like Anderson, acknowledges that nationalism is realized through cultural and social processes. But he highlights the role of institutions in cultivating nationalism and national conflicts like those that arose in many countries after the Soviet Union collapsed in 1991. A common interpretation of these rivalries sees them as stemming from deep-seated ethnic animosities that were held in check only as long as populations were under communist rule (Brubaker 1998). But Brubaker argues that the Soviet state's practice of identifying and codifying different nationalities had the unintended consequence of cultivating feelings of nationhood and nationality among the various groups. Thus, administrative practices employed by the Soviet state, such as enumerating the members of different ethnicities in state censuses to facilitate its rule over those groups, created 'institutionalized definitions of nationhood' (Brubaker 1994: 47) among these different groups. To use some of the terminology introduced in the previous chapter, the recognition received by these groups from Soviet state institutions took on real significance and served as a basis for mobilization among their members. To offer one last illustration, John A. Hall, who has published extensively on and with many of the field's key scholars (see for example, Hall 1993, 1998, 2006, 2010; with Gellner and Jarvie 1992; with Schroeder 2006) has elaborated on the link between small states, their institutions, and the strength of their national identities. Hall builds on Gellner's argument that the industrializing societies of the nineteenth century fostered the emergence of nationalism as centralizing states homogenized the culture and training of their populations. He notes that small states often developed stronger national identities, as well as state institutions more capable of managing state-society and international relations, than larger states. The first, he says, is because smaller states tended to be more culturally homogeneous to begin with, forming a more ready and sound basis for a unifying nationalism. The strong nationalisms emerging alongside the new state institutions in these places, resulted in a more conciliatory 'social partnership' between the state and civil society, enhancing state-society relations.

In all of these examples we see how institutions shape large-scale political movements and organization. The procedural practices of institutions, such as those that surround the practice of democracy in a given state, the promotion of language and curriculum in state-sponsored schools, the use of media to create a common identity, and the size of institutions all influence how politics are practised, how people live their daily lives, and how power is contested.

Organizations and State Institutions

But if, as the preceding discussion shows, political sociologists explore how (state) institutions shape power contests more or less directly, they are also interested in plotting their indirect effects. Some scholars, for instance, examine the ways that state institutions come to influence power negotiations unfolding outside the 'container' of the state by helping to configure non-state organizations. In 1983, Paul DiMaggio and Walter Powell took up Weber's observations on the modern bureaucracy. While agreeing that bureaucracy had become all-pervasive, they found that it had spread, not because of capitalism's demand for efficiency, but rather because of wider processes that encourage *homogenization* of organizational forms. But why would organizations purposely structure themselves to resemble *other* organizations? Well, think about it. Say you and some friends wanted to start a group on campus for students who juggle. To acquire 'official' status so that you could secure a space on campus for your meetings, you would likely have to fill in some forms requiring you to list the president, vice-president, and treasurer of your group, and detail the powers and duties of each. Even though you and your friends had not thought about your positions in the group in this way, the requirements of the university demand that you impose a bureaucratic structure on your club in order to align it with the structure of other clubs and to facilitate the club's communications with the university. *Voilà!* Your organization has been bureaucratized, and by a process that has nothing to do with its intent! DiMaggio and Powell call this **institutional isomorphic change**, and it is especially prevalent among organizations that have to deal with the state. Which these days is most of them. Over time, as the state became more bureaucratized and its (infrastructural) power increased, it came to influence more and more non-state areas of societies, and that in turn encouraged non-state organizations to mimic the (bureaucratic) institutional structure of the state so they could communicate and interact with state officials more easily.

Given the state's key role in driving the isomorphism that occurs across modern organizations, you can see why political sociologists like Theda Skocpol might wish to explore this process further. And she has, in her study of **voluntary associations (VAs)** in the US (Skocpol 2004). Recall from the last chapter that Robert Putnam (2000) observed a decline in the membership in VAs over the years and concluded that this was detrimental to the civic health of the nation. Skocpol does not contradict Putnam's thesis so much as supplement it, showing that it is membership in specific types of VAs that has fallen off since the 1960s. In particular, 'broad-based, popularly rooted' VAs, like church groups, women's clubs, veterans' associations, fraternal organizations, and fellowship associations have suffered. Elite professional societies, in contrast, have actually seen increases in participation rates over the last decades as have national and international environmental and anti-poverty groups and pro-choice and family-values associations, for example.

Why is this so? Skocpol says that it's because the latter groups, with their professional staff and management and more formal bureaucracies, have developed organizational structures that are aligned more readily with the offices of the state. Such isomorphism has facilitated their communication with the state and their capacity to secure rewards like state recognition and funding. Their successes have meant that community organizers and activists are now less likely than in the past to create vast federations with local branches to recruit active citizen members in the name of their cause. Today, they work toward establishing a national office from which they manage national projects from the centre, a model more amenable to interaction with powerful and legitimating state officials. Active citizen participation in these top-down types of 'mailing-list organizations' is not really required; members only need to write a cheque or click a 'like' button to join and 'be active'. The results are much the same as those Putnam laid out: a decline in the number of people directly engaged in civic as well as political, pursuits. But Skocpol shows how shifts that look as if they stemmed from non-institutional sources—changes in the independent choices made by Americans to join or not to join voluntary associations—in fact have institutional origins.

The State and Violence

Another area of study that interests political sociologists concerned with the ways state institutions shape power contests is people's use of violence as a means of maintaining or challenging existing power arrangements. In trying to come up with a general definition of the state, the best Max Weber could do was to remind us that states claim 'the monopoly on the legitimate use of physical force within a given territory' (1946: 78). While the *ends* or aims of states have varied widely over time and place, Weber observed that the *means* by which state leaders exercise their power has remained consistent: they rule, in the final instance, through violence or the threat of violence. They are the only people in a given territory that are legally permitted to order or engage in violent acts against others. This has meant that, in the modern era, anyone else who engages in violent acts without the endorsement of state leaders does so *illegitimately* and often illegally. Groups that commit violence, be they nationalist groups who want to secede or separate from an existing state and establish 'their own' state, aggrieved minorities wishing to draw attention to the way they are neglected or abused by state powers, or social movements determined to communicate the gravity of the issues that concern them, are inherently anti-state because they challenge the state's monopoly on physical force. Therefore, they must be analyzed in relation to state institutions.

Certainly the most publicized form of anti-state violence these days is *terrorism*, that is, violent actions taken by individuals and groups in society to challenge the authority of state powers they perceive to be unrepresentative, unjust, or immoral. Terrorism is by no means a recent phenomenon. In Newfoundland and the UK, people still commemorate Guy Fawkes's unsuccessful attempt to blow up the British Parliament in 1605 by celebrating 'bonfire night' every year! The Irish Republican Army, Basque nationalists, the Tamil Tigers, and of course al-Qaeda—are all groups that have employed violence to try to win power contests with the states that hold legitimate sovereignty over them, with varying results.

What are the institutional conditions that compel people to use violence rather than other means to achieve their ends vis-à-vis the state? Mark Cooney (1997) has found that violence tends to happen more in places where state institutions are weak, but also in places where state institutions are oppressively strong. Note that in both circumstances, the violence may not only be committed by non-state groups but by the state itself. Armed **warlords**, for example, may engage in violence to take advantage of power vacuums created by weak or non-existent states. But so too may the leaders of such states inflict violence on their enemies or citizenry because of the absence of institutions preventing them from doing so. The 2008 Brookings Institution report on state weakness of 141 developing countries shows this to be all too true (see Table 4.1). The report showed that Somalia, Afghanistan, the Democratic

TABLE 4.1 Ten Weakest States in the Developing World

Rank	Country	Overall Score	Economic	Political	Security	Social Welfare	GNI Per Capita
1	Somalia	0.52	0.00	0.00	1.37	0.70	226
2	Afghanistan	1.65	4.51	2.08	0.00	0.00	271
3	Congo, Dem. Rep.	1.67	4.06	1.80	0.28	0.52	130
4	Iraq	3.11	2.87	1.67	1.63	6.27	1134
5	Burundi	3.21	5.01	3.46	2.95	1.43	100
6	Sudan	3.29	5.05	2.06	1.46	4.59	810
7	Central African Rep.	3.33	4.11	2.90	5.06	1.25	360
8	Zimbabwe	3.44	1.56	1.56	6.81	3.84	350
9	Liberia	3.64	3.39	3.91	6.01	1.25	140
10	Côte d'Ivoire	3.66	5.23	2.12	3.71	3.56	870

Source: Based on Brookings Institution Index of State Weakness in the Developing World (www.brookings.edu/reports/2008/02_weak_states_index.aspx).

Note: the 10 weakest states and their index basket scores are presented. A basket score of 0.00 represents the worst score of the 141 countries sampled, a score of 10.0 signifies the best.

Republic of Congo, Iraq, Burundi, Sudan, Central African Republic, Zimbabwe, Liberia, and Côte d'Ivoire are the ten weakest states in the world. Sadly, each is a country that is wracked with war, ethnic conflict, or state violence. Having a weak or absent state is obviously related to the degree of violence experienced by a region. But violence is also more likely to occur in places with overly domineering states. Here, rebels may take up arms to topple the authoritarian government. But state authorities may respond with violence because of the presence of repressive institutions that give them the capacity to do so. Hence, Cooney concludes that the relationship between violence and state institutions is not linear but U-shaped. States through their institutions must hold a monopoly on the legitimate use of violence to discourage state and anti-state violence, but not so strongly as to foster dissent or authoritarianism among a country's citizenry and state officials (See Figure 4.2.).

We are fortunate in Canada that current political circumstances are such that violence is seldom employed by groups in civil society or by our state leaders to enforce social order or maintain their authority. But it does happen here occasionally as noted in Box 4.1. Likewise, Prime Minister Pierre Trudeau instituted the *War Measures Act* in 1970, ordering the stationing of armed soldiers and military vehicles on the streets of Montreal. He was responding to requests by state officials in that city and in the province of Quebec to secure Montreal in the face of a perceived threat by members of the FLQ, but it had repercussions for the rights of people across the country (Clément 2008). The armed forces and the police have also been used when Aboriginals have taken up arms in defence of their land and treaty rights, as in the case of the seventy-eight-day Oka standoff in Quebec (Ramos and Wilkes 2010; Wilkes 2006), the Ipperwash crisis of 1995 in Ontario (Edwards 2001), and the Gustafsen Lake standoff of the same year in British Columbia

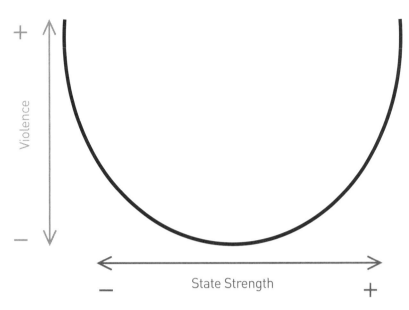

FIGURE 4.2 U-Shaped Distribution of Violence and State Strength

(Lambertus 2004). These events thankfully do not compare to the state violence that has been meted out by such past and present political leaders as Joseph Stalin, Augusto Pinochet, Moammar Gadhafi, and Kim Jong-il. Nevertheless, they are all examples of the use by state leaders of their positions as controllers of the state to threaten or inflict harm and even death on their citizens to gain advantage in power contests.

Notice that the capacity of state leaders to employ physical force against their citizens and 'enemies' derives not from the personal powers of state leaders. It does not flow from their personal material, cultural, or social advantage. Rather, the permission to use violence as a means of dominating power negotiations is, in a sense, granted to state leaders by the state institutions themselves. Indeed, it is the sovereignty of states and not the individuals who control them that is enshrined in historical precedent and international laws. These guarantee that institutions recognized by the international community as states will bestow on their leaders the ultimate power over the people and territories that fall within their jurisdiction. As long as state leaders do not abuse this privilege excessively—and unfortunately even when some do—the international community, as represented by the United Nations, will allow them more or less free rein to use the powers granted them by state institutions, including the right to employ violence against citizens in their attempts to maintain or re-establish their advantage in national power contests.

The power of state leaders vis-à-vis other groups in a society is clearly enhanced by their control of state institutions that authorize their use of physical force against their citizens through the police and military. But political sociologists have revealed other, less direct, ways that state institutions can shape how and when violence is used by state leaders as a means of dominating power contests. **Genocide** is the purposeful and systematic elimination, by murder or other means, of a group of people identified by another as being somehow distinct. The mass killing of Jews by the Nazis during the Second World War, the slaughter of Tutsis and their supporters by Hutus in 1994 in Rwanda, the massacre of Bosnian Muslims by Bosnian Serb forces in the former Yugoslavia in 1995, and the purposeful annihilation of indigenous nations during the founding of North American states are vivid examples of an all too common occurrence in modern times. Michael Mann (1999, 2004, 2005) challenges the typical popular explanation of genocide as a terrible manifestation of rabid 'tribal' racism. Instead, he points to **democracy**, and the state institutions that facilitate it, as catalysts for genocide. Mann says that democratic state institutions do not always foster peace by permitting everyone access to the state so they can resolve group conflicts in an orderly manner. Sometimes, these institutions can encourage whoever is in power to define 'we the people', that is, who is considered a legitimate citizen, in ethnic terms. As 'non-persons', then, members of the marginalized groups, the 'minorities,' become prone to persecution or, worse, repression or mass murder. Mann believes that this stems, not from the use of state institutions as a tool of oppressive leaders, but from the state institutions themselves. This is evident from his observation that '[t]he dominant Western system of liberal democracy has made sacred a majoritarian and territorial form of sovereignty. It has often added a high degree of state centralization. . . . These qualities have never been good at dealing with spatially concentrated minorities' (Mann 1999: 44). Genocide is more an administrative and institutional problem than an outcome of racist zealotry, says Mann. We need to recognize this and deal with its link to the Western state form or else 'be confronted again with mass murder' (Mann 1999: 45).

When and under what conditions state leaders and their opponents resort to violence as a means of maintaining or challenging power are matters that continue to be taken up by political sociologists in their efforts to reveal how power contests unfold. They also draw attention to the more general question of how institutions shape *challenges* to power and how the patterned interactions that constitute institutions like the state influence people and movements dedicated to *resisting* existing power arrangements. Let's look at how some political sociologists have responded to these questions.

Party Power and Institutions

We have already talked about how when most people think of 'politics' they usually think of formal politics. Formal politics encompass activities that are associated with what Weber called '**party' power** (Weber 1946: 194–5). It is a type of power that comes from the capacity of a group to pursue a goal in circumstances characterized by what Weber called an 'existing dominion', or some existing social order. Notice there are two components of party power: a goal-seeking group and an existing social order, or what we could call an institutional context.

The most obvious example of party power is that exercised by formal political parties. In Canada, political parties like the NDP and the Liberals are composed of people who spend their time working together to try to influence (and ultimately, take over) the Canadian state. At any given time, the state, its offices, and officials operate in accordance with laws and policies set by past administrations and court decisions and by means of a fairly stable organizational structure. Because of these enduring features of the state, there are certain rules and practices of engagement by which political parties have to abide to try to affect what the state does, or ideally, acquire control of the entire institution. The leader of a political party in Canada cannot just one day decide that his or her party should seize control of the state; she has to wait until the ruling Prime Minister or Governor General calls an election, then rally her supporters to lobby for our votes and hope that Canadians will elect more members of her party to the House of Commons than of other parties. There are even rules on how one registers as a candidate in an election. Until then, she and her fellow party members must introduce and promote policy ideas by appealing to the public through the media and other means, try to undermine their opponents through critique and rhetoric, lobby key politicians and civil servants to acquire support for their programs, and acquire positions on crucial committees and commissions, and so on. When a political party successfully influences or achieves control over the Canadian, provincial, or territorial state, that political party exercises party power.

Both components of Weber's conceptualization are evident in this example: the goal-seeking party (the NDP and Liberals) and the institutional context (the existing rules and organizational structure characterizing the Canadian state). Yet, you do not have to be a politician or belong to a political party to exercise party power. In fact, any time a group to which you belong influences the activities of an existing organization, you exercise party power. So if you and your friends go through the steps of lobbying your university's administration to stop using bottled water at university functions, you are building on party power. Similarly, if people in an urban neighbourhood come together to try to persuade their city officials to allow backyard chicken coops (see Box 4.4), or if a group of parents press the makers of a children's medicine to stop

Box 4.4 ⁕ Chickens and Party Power

Food has become a politically explosive issue in recent years. Although access to food has always been a part of the mandate of anti-poverty groups, human rights organizations, and so on, people are increasingly mobilizing around matters pertaining to food more directly. 'Foodies' affiliated with groups like the Slow Food and Locavore movements encourage individuals in privileged countries, who seldom think about the origins of the food they buy or the conditions under which it is produced, to become more conscious of the food they eat.

One such movement gaining widespread popularity in North America encourages people to raise chickens in urban areas. People in cities across the US and Canada who are interested in issues such as food sustainability and the health and animal-welfare concerns around factory farming have come together to lobby officials to change municipal regulations and permit urbanites to set up chicken coops for egg production in their back yards. These groups have met with varying success. In Vancouver, Victoria, Brampton, and Niagara Falls, for example, residents have managed to convince city officials that urban chickens are a good idea. Officials in Calgary, Windsor, Toronto, and Halifax, however, have so far not been moved to change city regulations.

Aside from providing the media with fodder for clever headlines ('Windsor cracks down on backyard chickens' or 'Plan to study backyard chickens scratched'), these movements and their progress offer an excellent study of the features and workings of party power. What becomes especially clear in the response of people and politicians opposed to urban chickens is the countering effect that the existing institutional context has on the ideals and goals of the pro-chicken groups. This of course takes the form of practical bounds on the ways changes can be sought: the public must be consulted, committees must be struck, feasibility studies must be undertaken, and the positions of city councillors must be expressed and considered democratically. But institutions can also place limitations on the ways that people even conceive of or think about the issue. State regulations long designating chickens as 'farm animals' and hence subject to different rules than animals administered by cities as 'pets' have no doubt contributed to the impression, for example, that chickens are smellier and pose a greater public health risk than dogs and cats. This is despite the fact that according to a website promoting urban chickens in Fredericton, five chickens produce less manure than one medium-sized dog and that manure, unlike the droppings of dogs and cats, can be easily converted to lawn and garden fertilizer (Fredericton City Chickens 2011). This may explain, in part, one Windsor city councillor's quip that debating urban chickens was 'clucking ridiculous' (CBC 2010b), but also, more broadly, why some groups have a more difficult time exercising party power than others.

Red Dye 40 in their formulas, they are all engaging in activities that seek to influence or alter the operations of an existing organization to bring about a desired end.

But don't forget, the other part of party power is the institutional context in which parties form and operate. This will configure the formation and progress of parties in a number of ways. Most directly, it will define the structures that parties generally work *for* or *against* in their mobilizing efforts. What is less obvious perhaps is that the institutional context will affect the very *choices* party members will make around mobilization, the causes they take up, the timing of their activities, and the strategies they pursue. Like the activists in Britain that Charles Tilly described (referred to above), parties operating within an institutional context will exercise choice within constraint. Their members will base their decisions on their passions and interpretations of what the best actions are to pursue, but these decisions are shaped by the very institutions they challenge.

Weber's concept of party power can help elucidate the ways political sociologists understand the place of state institutions in the contests that arise when people challenge existing power arrangements. On the one hand, these scholars are concerned with the *aims* and *tactics* employed by individuals that have come together to rally for change or recognition, that is, goal-seeking groups. As important to their investigation, however, is the institutional *context* in which these goal-seeking groups are operating and that they are often challenging, particularly the state-related components of that context. How state institutions configure, enhance, or delimit the aims, actions, and potential of these groups, and whether and how their actions in turn come to refashion existing state institutions, are key processes that these political sociologists seek to expose.

State Institutions and Claims to Citizenship

States govern who can and cannot make legitimate claims to **citizenship** and the benefits enjoyed by citizens. More correctly, the people who control states decide, through state institutions, who is a citizen of the territory and who is not. Not just anyone can vote in a Canadian election, get a provincial health card, or have access to all government welfare programs; they must provide proof of citizenship to do so. Furthermore, people who enjoy these privileges also have obligations they must fulfill, such as filing and paying taxes on time or answering the census questions when asked to do so by federal government officials. It also means that when citizens have grievances against the Canadian state, there are a set of institutional procedures they can follow: they can pursue a court case through the legal system (perhaps with reference to the Canadian Constitution), appeal to elected members of formal political parties, or try to influence the general public through VAs in civil society. Jane

Jenson says that the structures of state governance constitute a **citizenship regime** (Jenson and Phillips 1996; Jenson and Papillon 2000; Jenson and Phillips 2001; Jenson and Saint-Martin 2003). It encompasses the institutional arrangements that guide the decisions made by state officials about policy, expenditures, and governance of the populace. It influences what sorts of problems are seen as politically legitimate, that is, the kinds of claims citizens are permitted to make. It also has wrapped up in it certain notions of the nation and what kind of person is a 'proper' citizen of that nation.

Canada is a liberal-democratic state with a constitution that protects individual rights. That is why you will hear people say that 'everyone is equal' in Canada, implying that we all have the same citizenship rights. However, unique to Canada's governance structure is the constitutional recognition of multiculturalism and **nations within** Canada. So on the one hand, the *Constitution Act, 1982* enshrines individual rights. Thus, **s. 15** protects equality and prohibits discrimination on the basis of an individual's race, national or ethnic origin, colour, religion, sex, age, or mental or physical disability. On the other hand, it also protects the group rights of Canada's colonizing and colonized nations. For instance, **s. 16** protects the language rights of francophones and anglophones; **s. 25** protects past Aboriginal treaties; and **s. 35** defines Aboriginals as a national minority with 'special rights'. This means that, although Canada follows liberal-democratic principles by privileging the rights of individuals, it also attempts to move beyond them to accommodate its multicultural and multinational character. Sadly, few Canadians are aware of what this means, and even fewer understand how exceptional it is. Indeed, it is a 'gold-standard' document that has been used as a model by many other countries to re-vamp their own governance structures.

The groups that hold 'special' rights by the Canadian constitution can legitimately lay claim to these rights and have demanded that the federal government respect them. So, for instance, in the 1990s, women's groups, appealing under s. 15, lobbied the government to pass legislation ensuring women were given equal pay for doing substantially the same work as men in the civil service. Canadian Aboriginals have made claims to the Constitution, the Royal Proclamation of 1763, the *Indian Acts*, and past treaties to respect the rights they are guaranteed. And during the summer and fall of 2010, with partial reference to s. 16, francophone NGOs went to court to force the government to maintain as mandatory the language questions on the 2011 census. Their case was in reaction to a decision by the Conservative government to dismantle the previous mandatory long-form census, which asks such questions. The members of these organizations feared that not being officially 'counted' would limit their ability to operate and, even worse, erode their rights as citizens.

Making claims to institutionalized 'special' rights does not always ensure that those rights will be respected in the power contests in which they are employed. Although non-Aboriginal Canadians are increasingly sympathetic to the claims of First Nations peoples, many remain unaware of what Aboriginal rights entail (Ponting 2000). This lack of knowledge has led to some unfortunate incidents, such the monumental Oka crisis of 1990, which was triggered when disputed land was slated for development (York and Pindera 1991; Wilkes 2004, 2006); the destruction of traditional lands and the re-arrangement of citizenship without consent in the case of the James Bay Cree in Quebec (Niezen 2000); and the fining of Donald Marshall Jr. for fishing and selling eels, an event that ultimately sparked the Mi'kmaq lobster crisis in the fall of 1999 (Coates 2000; Ramos 2007). In each of these cases, Aboriginal peoples were making legitimate claims, based on rights enshrined in the Canadian Constitution, but which officials of the state had not respected. Despite being (constitutionally) legitimate grievances, they were handled by state officials as if they were debatable, and that affected not only how the contests were negotiated but also wider perceptions of the authenticity of First Nations demands.

What can an individual or group do if state leaders are unwilling to recognize the rights the state constitution is supposed to guarantee? Aggrieved groups have basically two routes of recourse. They can appeal to people within the state but also to people outside the sitting government, such as provincial officials, city representatives, groups of voters, members of other organizations, and even the media, to try to better their chances that their claims will be acknowledged and addressed. They can also appeal to alternative citizenship regimes—other states or international bodies that can hold sway or put pressure on the state that has blocked their demands. Jenson and Papillon (2000), for example, showed that the James Bay Cree made their grievances known to state governments in the US, like New York, that would be buying the electricity produced by Hydro Quebec's development of Cree land. They also appealed to international celebrities and other NGOs. Something similar happened when the results of the 1995 referendum on Quebec sovereignty looked close and the Cree faced possible annexation by a separate Quebec. The Cree appealed to the federal government and the international community to have their rights as 'Canadians' preserved to ensure they would not simply be transferred from one state to another without their consent. Such action—seeking redress from another citizenship regime when one's own has neglected or denied one's rights as a citizen—is not a new tactic, nor is it an isolated case. Ronald Niezen (2000) shows, for instance, that the Mohawk made appeals in the 1920s to the **League of Nations**, the precursor to the United Nations. The point is that state institutions play a significant role in shaping what are understood and handled as legitimate grievances about citizenship, who can lay claim to them, and how they will ultimately be settled.

Political Opportunities and Political Process Theory (PPT)

Clearly, state institutions are central to the formulation and acceptance of citizenship claims. But state institutions also influence other sorts of appeals and challenges to the existing social order. In previous chapters we have seen how material resources, as well as cultural and social capital, can be employed by groups wishing to confront or change existing power arrangements as well as their capacity to do so. Some political sociologists maintain, however, that such approaches do not pay enough attention to how the institutional context in which these contests take place influences the ability of groups to exploit any of these forms of capital. While these perspectives might shed light on *why* people come together to confront the prevailing power arrangements (because of interests pertaining to their material conditions or the cultural or social circumstances which they face), and *how* they manage to do so (through the mobilization of resources), they are not very good at explaining *when* social movements happen—that is, the timing of their appearance and its effect on a movement's aims, strategies, successes, and failures. These sorts of things, say political sociologists interested in institutions, are shaped, not only by factors internal to the movement, the grievances borne by its members, and the resources they have at their disposal, but also by processes external to it, that is, social forces in the wider social milieu. These scholars are most interested in the political processes surrounding mobilization, since social movements are typically concerned with revealing or confronting perceived inequalities or injustices embedded in state-related institutions and practices.

So what exactly are these 'political processes' that social movement researchers say can affect mobilization efforts? Early attempts to theorize the effects of the political climate on social movement activity focused on **political opportunities**. These are the changing conditions that 'open up' or 'close' the existing political order and provide people with the inspiration or grievance or 'space' to take action on an issue of importance to them. Peter Eisinger (1973) first used this term when he observed that American race riots of the 1960s were often in cities that generated conditions of grievance but did not repress dissenters. Charles Tilly (1978) expanded on these ideas by also considering the choices that challengers make when they face changing political conditions. In both instances, these scholars found that contention emerges when political institutions are closed or unresponsive enough to create dissatisfaction and dissent but open enough not to repress it.

In practice, many different measures have been used to examine political opportunity. In a review of political opportunity and political process literatures, David Meyer (2004) and David Meyer and Deborah Minkoff (2004) 'note that specifications include aspects of government structures (Kitschelt 1986), public policy (McAdam 1982; Tarrow 1988, 1989, 1998), geography (Boudreau 1996), and relations to other movements (Meyer and Staggenborg

1996); and this is just to name a few' (Ramos 2008b: 797). To consolidate these varied phenomena, they group different opportunities into *structural*, *signalling*, and *general* opportunities. Structural opportunities, which are the most formal include things such as changes in state policies and government expenditures. Signalling opportunities are more ephemeral changes in the political environment surrounding an issue, the news coverage it receives, for example, or changes in policy or shifts of political leanings. General opportunities are those that arise outside a specific issue, such as a new government or changes of key ministers.

Although these distinctions help us to get a sense of what political opportunities are, there is still some ambivalence in the field about how they operate. For example, if political opportunities can expand to facilitate mobilization, they can also contract to inhibit collective action. Jennifer Hadden and Sidney Tarrow (2007) ponder the decline of the Global Justice Movement (GJM) in the US since the famous 'Battle in Seattle'. This was a huge mobilization effort that brought together thousands of people in that city in 1999 to protest policies promoted by the ministers of the World Trade Organization, policies that the protesters believed exploited labour, degraded the environment, and deepened global inequality. After an initial period (of about two years) during which Seattle activism flourished, the GJM began to weaken, a response, say Hadden and Tarrow (2007: 369–70), to a 'shift in the domestic structure of political opportunities' in the US. The shift included two key developments, both of which emerged after the September 11th terrorist attacks in 2001: a change in the policing of protests, from a strategy of protest management to a strategy of 'incapacitation', or outright suppression of dissent; and President George W. Bush's linking of democracy to the 'war on terror', a tactic that presented the Iraq war as necessary to bring stability to a dangerous authoritarian state. The latter undermined activists' claims that the Iraq war was an act of imperialist expansion. Thus, Hadden and Tarrow point to a contraction of political opportunities available to the GJM in the US after 2001, a 'closing' of the political climate in that country that affected its progress independently of any changes internal to the movement. Others, in contrast, find that closing opportunities, the threat of repression, or loss of power and resources (or just the perception such threats or loss are imminent) in fact increases mobilization (Goldstone and Tilly 2001; Van Dyke and Soule 2002: 498). So although political opportunities have been an interesting and important addition to the tools employed by social movement scholars to understand challenges to power, there are a number of ambiguities about their definition and inconsistencies in their expected effects that remain problematic.

Although the term 'political opportunities' is still used extensively in the social movement literature, it is now employed less as a 'stand-alone' theory than as a component of the more comprehensive **political process** model, also known as political process theory (PPT). PPT pays attention to the interaction of the political opportunities confronting a movement with mobilizing structures, like organization, money, and access to elites, and the 'frames' its leadership employs in forwarding its aims. PPT includes a complex array of 'political' or power-related phenomena that operate together to affect social movement activities and outcomes (McAdam, McCarthy, and Zald 1996).

PPT has become the dominant approach to understanding social movements in North American political sociology these days. Led by the research of Sidney Tarrow, Doug McAdam, and Charles Tilly, and practised by acclaimed scholars of contention research such as Donatella della Porta, Bert Klandermans, David Meyer, Mayer Zald, William Gamson, and Sarah Soule, among many others, PPT places an emphasis on processes the authors identify as 'political', but not to the extent that other factors, both inside and outside the movement(s) in question, are neglected or ignored. Such analysis encompasses so many examples of mobilizing efforts that it is hard to summarize on the basis of place or even time period. That said, McAdam, Tarrow, and Tilly (2001) and Tarrow and Tilly (2006) have had some success in classifying this research under the general banner of **contentious politics**.

Probably the best-known work in the PPT tradition was also one of the first—Doug McAdam's (1982) analysis of the US civil rights movement. Wishing to respond to more voluntarist interpretations of mobilization that emphasized the grievances of movement membership, McAdam highlighted the political opportunities that created conditions more open to activists' aims. David Meyer (2004: 129) has listed these as including, '[f]avorable changes in policy and the political environment, including the collapse of the cotton economy in the South, African American migration to Northern cities, and a decline in the number of lynchings', which, according to McAdam 'lowered the cost and dangers of organizing for African Americans and increased their political value as an electoral constituency.' Other significant political occurrences were the decision by the US Supreme Court that segregated schooling was unconstitutional, a decision that increased political attention to the issue; public statements supportive of civil rights by Presidents John F. Kennedy and Lyndon Johnson; and the legitimacy and safety that such a political environment provided for civil rights activists to engage in and ramp up their mobilizing efforts (Meyer 2004: 129). But McAdam was careful to present these political opportunities as part of a mobilization process that also drew upon the very real passions of movement membership, as well as on existing organizing structures within the African-American community, like the church and fraternal organizations. His depiction of the movement recognized its progress as a very dynamic enterprise, one in which political opportunities were crucial to its outcome, but only with and through other processes operating within the movement itself (McAdam 1982).

Another key researcher in the PPT tradition is Suzanne Staggenborg. In addition to having published with some of the leaders in this field (e.g. Meyer and Staggenborg 1996; Klandermans and Staggenborg 2002), she has contributed a political process perspective to the study of the women's movement in North America and the abortion debate in the US and Canada. Her book on the pro-choice movement in the US (1994), for example, depicts the movement's progress as the outcome of a dynamic interplay of political opportunities and conditions (including the 'cycle of protest' underway in the 1960s and the legalization of abortion in 1973), organizational factors (especially the professionalization of the leadership and formalization of the organization after *Roe v. Wade*), and actions taken against a hostile counter-movement (the 'pro-life' movement of the late 1970s and 1980s). Like McAdam, Staggenborg stresses the importance of political conditions to mobilization efforts but not to the exclusion of the interactive effects of other key processes.

As popular as PPT is in social movement research, however, it has faced some serious criticism. Although almost everyone agrees that the political climate has to be considered when assessing social movement activities, what sorts of things constitute that climate and the degree and extent of its influence on mobilizing efforts have been hard to pin down. 'Political opportunity' and the other terms associated with PPT, 'mobilizing structures' and 'cultural frames', have been used so liberally and in reference to so many things that they are becoming virtually meaningless, say its critics. In a now famous exchange with leading PPT practitioners in the academic journal *Sociological Forum* (1999), Jeff Goodwin and James Jasper repeat what other PPT practitioners themselves had early on begun to realize, that 'the concept ...is in danger of becoming a sponge that soaks up virtually every aspect of the social movement environment—political institutions and culture, crises of various sorts, political alliances and policy shifts' (Gamson and Meyer 1996: 275). But if conceptual imprecision is a problem, more serious still are concerns about the structural bias of PPT. PPT scholars, say Goodwin and Jasper (1999), cannot seem to get away from the idea that the 'political' is 'structural' and more specifically, that it is bound in 'state structures' and that these assumptions are always limiting when it comes to social movement analysis. They point out that many social movements are not state-oriented but seek to affect and change cultural codes, so an analysis of political opportunities in these cases will not likely tell us much about them.

Goodwin and Jasper's critique is well taken, and in some respects, the criticisms levelled at PPT are mirrored in those directed toward institutionalist research more generally. That institutionalism has a structural bias is a somewhat empty charge given that institutionalism arose in explicit response to what its practitioners perceived to be an overemphasis in social science research on agency approaches to social phenomena. But the structuralism inherent in institutionalism does get the perspective into some trouble when it is talking about social change. The whole drift of the institutionalist argument is based on the notion that institutions impose limits on agency because of their stability. Institutions exhibit path dependency; that is where their power lies, in their capacity to direct the behaviour of others in certain ways in a relatively enduring fashion. For some critics, the reliance of institutionalists on critical junctures to shake and change otherwise stable institutions is not enough to explain institutional change, especially when those junctures seem to be visible only in hindsight (see Hira and Hira 2000). With respect to the imprecision of their key terms, there is no question that the notion of 'institution' can be fuzzy, especially when institutionalists move beyond formal institutions like bureaucracies to informal ones, such as guidelines or general 'rules of engagement' among political players.

Summary

Political sociologists continue to refine their approaches to institutions in their attempts to identify how they figure in contests over power. The 'state-centred' approach of the new institutionalist scholars comes the closest to granting state institutions an almost autonomous role in the negotiations that occur between social groupings around power. Because it is the institutions of the state that bestow power on their leaders, these scholars treat the state almost as an actor in itself, capable of 'action' insofar as the resources that it makes available to its controllers in power contests are available to no one else. These include territorial sovereignty or despotic power, its bureaucratic reach, or infrastructural power, and its capacity to use physical force. Other political sociologists are less concerned with establishing the autonomy of state institutions than with identifying the ways state and state-related institutions affect power contests by providing the container and general rule book for negotiations. Thus, scholars of nationalism ponder how the patterned interactions of modern states shaped the ways state leaders sought to consolidate their power and influenced the beliefs that people came to hold about themselves in relation to others within state territories. Others explore how the institutional isomorphism fostered by the expansion of the state has consequences for the relative power of social actors living and working outside the realm of the state as the non-state organizations that people deal with come to imitate the institutions, and hence the power relations, that characterize the state. And still others look at how state institutions delimit and enable power challengers, both directly, as when they dictate who can participate in power challenges and the means they can employ in those challenges, and indirectly, by shaping the wider political milieu in which power contests unfold.

Clearly, the state plays a key role in the research of political sociologists interested in how institutions shape power contests. From Skocpol to Mann to Gellner and Hall, these scholars look to the institutions of the state as having at least some causal influence on the outcomes of power negotiations in contemporary societies. But what do we make of the processes that some thinkers say are undermining the singular powers of the state? Increasingly, scholars are questioning the capacity of states to bestow *any* autonomous power on their leaders or to have any significant effect on power contests through their institutions or activities. Globalization, they say, is eroding the sovereignty of the state over its territory, that is, the capacity of its leaders to employ state institutions as an independent means of exercising power over its citizens or other states. Others have even questioned the privileging of people in the study of politics, advocating inclusion of non-human actors—animals, the environment, technology—in our investigations of how power works in contemporary societies. It is to these perspectives that we now turn.

Questions for Critical Thought

1. What are the institutions that shape your life?

2. Can the *Constitution Act, 1982* protect or expand your rights?

3. Which shifting political processes do you see as opportunities to generate social change?

4. How do you engage 'the state'?

Suggestions for Further Reading

Mann, Michael. 2004. *The Dark Side of Democracy: Explaining Ethnic Cleansing.* New York: Cambridge University Press. An examination of state violence and institutions in the use of violence and genocide. The analysis extends Mann's earlier observations on the 'sources' of social power.

Skocpol, Theda. 1979. *States and Social Revolutions: A Comparative Analysis of France, Russia, and China.* Cambridge, UK: Cambridge University Press. The work that has been credited with 'bringing the state back' into political sociological analysis and sparking much of the development of new-institutionalist perspectives.

Skocpol, Theda. 2004. *Diminished Democracy: From Membership to Management in American Civic Life.* Norman, OK: University of Oklahoma Press. This book examines how voluntary associations have developed in response to institutional pressures in contemporary America.

Websites

CIA World Factbook
www.cia.gov/library/publications/the-world-factbook

Brookings Institution
www.brookings.edu

Christian Davenport's Radical Information Project
www.bsos.umd.edu/gvpt/davenport/home.htm

Department of Justice (Canada): Constitution Acts 1867 to 1982
http://laws.justice.gc.ca/en/const/9.html

5 Emerging Trends in Political Sociology

Learning Objectives

- To become familiar with scholarship that questions the key assumptions of political sociology: Is its focus on human contests for power justified? Is the most important institution in such contests really the state?
- To encounter the work of Bruno Latour and Donna Haraway and the concepts of *actant* and *cyborg*
- To examine globalization as a new process that has altered material, cultural, social, and institutional processes traditionally understood as the bases of power, as well as the way that people challenge power
- To understand empire as a possible alternative to the state and globalization
- To re-examine citizenship in relation to charges of anthropocentricism and weakening states
- To understand transnationalism as another account of the changes being witnessed today

Introduction

Previous chapters introduced you to perspectives in political sociology that see power as negotiated and formed through material, cultural, social, and institutional forces. But these processes are usually not directly observable. Apart from sociologists telling us that they operate in this or that way, how do we know they actually exist? What about the privileging by political sociology of the state as *the* arena for politics? A number of social thinkers have said that global and transnational trends have eroded the state and that continuing to pay so much attention to what they see as a dying institution has undermined the capacity of political sociologists to deal with the new social realities of today. Others have gone even further by charging that sociology has continued to focus, not only on the wrong institutions, but on the wrong subject matter altogether! They say the discipline is too **anthropocentric**, that is, it pays too much attention to humans, and that for it to progress, sociology has to consider more seriously human interactions with non-human entities like animals, the environment, and technology. Yet other critics note that political sociology needs to account for the emergence of new sorts of political actions and social movements that demand different understandings of politics to match these changes. All of these critiques represent emerging trends within political sociology. Thus, in this chapter we move away from the Weberian frame that guided our discussions in Chapters 2, 3, and 4 and instead look at new means of seeing politics differently.

In this chapter we will begin by revisiting what is meant by **social forces**, the underlying patterns that sociologists believe shape human relations, and re-examine the assumptions sociologists use to understand the social world and power. We then introduce the work of Bruno Latour and Donna Haraway, who are key theorists that challenge how sociologists look at the social world and who both contemplate looking at new realms of social relations. We also consider globalization by looking at what it means and then examining empirically how it is or is not transforming existing material, cultural and social, and institutional relationships. Additionally we look at other arguments on empire and transnationalism as alternative explanations for the social changes currently being witnessed by Canadians and others around the world.

Social Forces and the Assumptions of Sociologists

Most people have not taken a social science course, and many rarely think about social forces, that is, the underlying patterns of interaction between individuals and groups which shape societies. Perhaps this even included you before you began reading this book. As outlined in previous chapters, such forces reportedly unfold through material, cultural and social, and institutional processes that shape the social world. They are the key tools of political sociologists. Yet, like gravity, those processes are not seen. Instead, we experience them through their **proxies**. We see and experience the symbols of these social forces, such as currencies, that reflect underlying material value; knowledge of codes and cultural markers that reflect status power; and states and organizations that reflect institutional forces. However, unlike gravity, which most people accept as existing, all these proxies of social forces are contested, debated, and challenged—not only by everyday people but also by political sociologists. There is in fact, little agreement, even among scholars, on how these are patterned, how they influence or respond to individuals and groups, and how they are associated with one another. This has led some sociologists to question whether social scientists in fact have it wrong. Perhaps there really aren't any 'social' processes at all, and those identified are tainted by the faulty assumptions of sociologists and their need to justify them in order to maintain themselves as members of a distinct discipline.

A key assumption of sociology is that it studies interactions among *people* and the social processes that they create, sustain, and respond to. As we have seen, political sociology is specifically aimed at understanding how those processes shape access to, control over, and challenges to power. But underlying these assumptions is the belief that sociologists should not be concerned with other *things*, like objects or animals, for example, or our genes, molecules, and so forth. The lens of sociology is that of the social, not the internal, the psychological, or the biological, and certainly not the physical or the techno-logical. Indeed, many leading social scientists have spent much of their careers trying to enforce such distinctions. Thirty years ago, sociologist Richard Sennett (1977) lamented the increasing move of the discipline to psycho-logical analysis at the cost of social explanations. Others vehemently argued against trends toward **sociobiology**, which is a perspective that understands social behaviour as having biological origins (see Sahlins 1978 or Ruse 1985 for a summary and critique of the debate). If political sociologists engage with such factors at all, they tend to approach them as representations of under-lying social processes.

But what if these assumptions are wrong? What if the social world is actually shaped, not exclusively by humans and their interactions, but by the *things* that we are made of, the things that we use and interact with, and the things that structure the world we experience? If such is the case, maybe those things actually make us interact the way we do, and not the other way around. Perhaps political sociologists have narrowed their focus too much and in doing so have failed to account for a wide range of interactions that shape power relationships. Maybe instead of asking *who* holds and challenges power, we should be asking *what* shapes power.

Recent attention to **automobility**, for instance, shows that many North American lives are shaped by physical infrastructure designed to accommodate cars as the main means of transportation (Norton 2008; Conley 2010; Conley and Tigar McLaren 2009). Urban planners have witnessed the decay of many urban centres as a cost of suburban expansion and the demand to provide convenient infrastructure for automobiles. North America has seen the build-ing of highways instead of subways and rapid mass transit. Some even pes-simistically believe that the need to secure fuel motivated the American invasion of Iraq in 2003. Alan Greenspan, former Chairman of the US Federal Reserve, is one among many to make such claims (Paterson 2007; Beaumont and Walters 2007). Car culture, others argue, has also contributed to the rise of fast-food drive-through restaurants, which has changed how North Americans socialize around and relate to food. Whereas many political sociologists would argue that individuals make decisions to act in this way and the rise of these trends are a product of their actions, some recent thinkers have asked whether it is actually automobiles, or other non-human entities, that compel individuals to act rather than the other way around. Ultimately this line of thought denies the primacy of humans in understanding social relations or networks and chal-lenges sociology's focus on underlying processes instead of what is actually seen and experienced. It questions the evidence used by political sociologists to justify their observations, claims, and conclusions.

While some criticize the attention sociology has given to people, others have questioned the discipline's focus on *the state* as the primary arena that houses political processes. Many of the political sociologists we have discussed in this book wrote about trends that emerged in response to large-scale social changes originating well over a century ago, those associated with the Industrial Revolution and the progress of modernity, and especially the rise of states. Others have concentrated on the aftermath of those changes and how they shape contemporary societies. Yet, as the first decade of the twenty-first century ended, a number of social thinkers began to question whether contemporary societies are still configured by these same factors. Can the 'old' ideas, conceived at a time when modern states were still emerging, explain politics in a world where it seems the bounds of states are becoming more and more irrelevant?

For example, when the American subprime mortgages crisis emerged around 2007 economic shocks were experienced in North America, Western Europe, and the top economies of Asia (China, India, and Japan). Even though the crisis originated in the US, it spawned an economic meltdown felt by citizens of many states around the world. Occurrences like these suggest that state leaders in individual countries have less control over their national economies than they once did. If countries have become less independent economically, they also appear to be becoming less culturally distinct. The emergence of English as the dominant language of commerce and science has facilitated the spread of American pop culture and consumerism across borders, resulting in what some scholars see as cultural homogenization. The rise of social networking sites (SNS) and use of the Internet have also challenged the bounds of how we interact. In fact, about 80 per cent of Canadians now use the Internet for personal reasons (Statistics Canada 2010). What once seemed like science fiction has become a matter of everyday interaction. We can easily use Skype to keep in touch with far-flung siblings, or collaborate in writing books with colleagues at different institutions, or use Google to find out obscure 'facts' almost instantaneously. Knowledge production, some claim, is no longer the exclusive prerogative of intellectuals in 'ivory towers' but instead is open to all that can use the new technologies. Social movements have engaged in border crossing too. In recent years international organizations have popped up around the world to raise funds for mosquito netting in Kenya, agitate against the use of land mines in Cambodia, and collect aid for earthquake victims in Haiti. The scope of their actions cross state borders as do the activities and decisions of international institutions like the United Nations. All this has led some political sociologists to question whether the state, as a sovereign and autonomous, territorially bounded political entity, is indeed as important as is once was.

Even formal politics has changed. Voter turnout for elections in industrial countries has continued to decline, yet the campaigns of populist leaders and candidates, such as Howard Dean or Barack Obama in the US, attracted many thousands of small donations from average citizens rather than tapping the deep pockets of elites. Challenges to citizenship regimes have become complex, with contention happening both within states, in the form of nationalist movements for example, and also beyond states, as groups appeal to international organizations and institutions to pressure states to change their practices. For example, the Zapatistas used the Internet and activist networks to challenge the Mexican state in the mid-1990s, with some claiming that they sparked a new form of politics through their actions—a 'politics from below' (see Khasnabish 2008).

Let us examine each of these challenges to more established ways of doing political sociology in more detail.

Who—or What—Is a Social Actor?

Although much of our book has focused on introducing the key perspectives in political sociology, less attention has been paid to *how* those works draw their conclusions. For instance, we have shown that a number of scholars look to descriptions of material, cultural and social, and institutional relations to account for how power is distributed in a society. We have also introduced you to many technical terms used by political sociologists looking at these different sources of social power. But we have spent much less time talking about *why* different accounts are more salient than others. To do so requires some thought about the assumptions that form the bases of the different perspectives and the evidence that is used to support them.

One of the most established social thinkers to consider such questions is Bruno Latour (2007), who takes issue with sociology's reliance on **technical accounts**. These are explanations that 'combine cause-effect explanation . . . with grounding in some systematic specialized discipline' (Tilly 2006: 130). Latour believes that too much of sociology, including that which looks at power and politics, is focused on describing **aggregates** of social behaviour and creating specialized terms, or **jargon**, to describe the everyday world instead of looking at the actual processes that shape it. He fears that too much attention is paid to establishing and maintaining the legitimacy of the discipline rather than looking at what really configures our interactions, relationships, networks, and power.

Latour is not the first to make such claims. Several years ago, Thomas Kuhn (1962) argued that even the natural sciences are political. He showed that scientists who are members of established disciplines that subscribe to a given **paradigm** of thought have a vested interest in maintaining the dominance of their account over other explanations. Much like the members of John Porter's charter groups, the scientists who helped to establish the prevailing paradigm come to set the norms for the discipline and then continue to enjoy an advantage over latecomers offering alternative views. Robert Merton (1968) described this tendency as a **Matthew effect**, in reference to the Biblical verse (Matthew 25: 29), which says, 'For to all those who have, more will be given, and they will have an abundance; but from those who have nothing, even what they have will be taken away.' The result, says Kuhn, is '**normal science**', science that simply reproduces or at most only tweaks, the existing paradigm. True innovation in science is rare because of all the factors discouraging its cultivation and acceptance.

We can see much similarity between these observations and those of Latour. He laments that the politics of knowledge in the social sciences, in particular sociology, prevent people from offering strong and creative accounts of what shapes the social world. More specifically, Latour asks whether sociologists observe the world the way they do because it exists or because those observations justify their positions as sociologists. In an attempt to unearth better conclusions, he turns the social puzzle on its head, so to speak. He does this in two ways, first by asking how a discipline like sociology can be founded on the investigation of latent social forces, the underlying process we have been describing in earlier chapters, instead of on visible interactions. Secondly, he does this by asking why sociology bases its core assumption on the view that humans influence or 'act' upon things, instead of the other way around. He encourages social scientists to begin thinking about whether *things* can be social and in turn whether they can act and in turn wield **agency**.

You might think it is strange to consider how computers influence you or whether the ocean can actively structure social relationships. But, in several chapters, we have been telling you that underlying social processes associated with people's possession of material or cultural and social or institutional resources shape the power contests in which they are continually engaged. Yet, when is the last time you *saw* those social processes in action? At least computers and oceans are things that you can observe directly, and there are indications that we sometimes even perceive them as possessing some agency. In fact, others like Abbott (2001) observe that social scientists often talk about the actions of 'variables' rather than people. For instance, a scholar might conclude that 'the state structures material and organizational relations', as if 'the state' and 'material and organizational relations' were somehow actors themselves, rather than composed of human beings. Some, such as Scott (1998), even talk about 'seeing like a state'. So perhaps these non-human institutions do have agency; otherwise why would so many people talk about them in that way? Academics are not the only ones to talk about non-humans having agency. The business sections of international newspapers were littered with reference to Japan's 'idle' robots during an international economic recession. The *New York Times* even carried a story on the 'problem' (Tabuchi 2009). Poor robots! The article used language that one would expect to see in reference to the plight of human workers in previous recessions. It is clear that technology is a component of contemporary economies and that it influences material production, so why not think of it as actively engaged in shaping relations, rather than just something that enables or reflects them?

Donna Haraway (1985, 1991) believes this is a good idea and uses the notion of the **cyborg** as a metaphor for the theorization of human-thing relationships in contemporary societies. She finds that in a postmodern world, humans interact with and thus negotiate relationships with many non-human entities. In many cases, we rely on technology to do everyday tasks. We use eyeglasses to help us read, we use cars to help us get around, we use computers to help us calculate astronomical equations and write our essays and e-mails. The distinction between technology and people is often blurred, and this is what Haraway means by cyborg. If technology, such as robots, can shape human social relations then perhaps other non-human entities can shape social relationships too.

Haraway's more recent work extends the notions of non-human negotiations to animals (2008; 2006). Humans interact not only with technology or machines but also with animals and other species—pets in particular. In Haraway's analysis, she contends that pets, which she calls **companion species**, are subjects of social interaction and so require means of communication, etiquette, and protocol for that interaction. Pets are thus real agents in human-pet relations, says Haraway, and because they are agents they can exercise power in those relationships. Granted, they hold less power than the humans with whom they interact, and Haraway (2008) considers the negotiation of ethics and responsibility between humans and non-humans with this in mind (Peterson 2008: 610). But the notion that pets influence people will come as no surprise to pet owners. Have you ever gone home early from work or school to feed or care for your cat or dog, or woken up in the middle of the night to let them out to do 'their business'? Have you ever engaged in political action for or with them, like lobbying for a dog park, or changes to animal cruelty legislation? Do you love your pet like a family member? In all these situations, it is worth considering whether you hold power outright in the relationship, or whether your pet dictates your actions and emotions too. Such considerations are important, say thinkers like Haraway, because they help political sociologists understand what the boundaries of the social and political world are and help us gain a better understanding of the dynamics of power—which are the primary foci of political sociology.

Pets are one thing; they are like small children in a way, and so the idea that they act and exercise some power may not be so hard to grasp. But how are we to think about inanimate objects 'acting' or exercising agency? Latour offers a way of considering this through **actor-network theory**. He argues that sociologists should shift their **units of analysis** from just human interactions to the networks of relationships among **actants**, entities that include humans, non-humans, and human–non-human arrangements ('driver-car', for example, or 'rider-horse') in a social setting. Such a perspective, he believes, is better than traditional human-only approaches to understanding agency and social relations, because paying attention to actants does not limit or pre-determine the observations and outcomes that might be expected from the work. The researcher does not look for bourgeoisie or proletarians in the crowd; she does not seek out indications of the use and impact of cultural capital or the 'unseen' influence of institutions on the interactions she observes. Thus, to Latour's mind a method of observing the world that limits sociologists' pre-determined assumptions about the interactions they wish to learn more about leads to a better understanding of how social processes really operate.

Latour's and Haraway's ideas have been very influential over the last two decades and have been taken up in many social analyses. Raymond Murphy (2004, 2009), among others, has shown how disasters caused by weather can be understood as actants in contemporary societies. In an investigation of the ice storm that crippled parts of the northeastern US, eastern Ontario, and western Quebec and Montreal in January of 1998, he found that the storm radically influenced how people interacted and how they saw the environment. Murphy (2004) shows how the storm changed the way the authorities, politicians, the military, and others moved from openness to secrecy in managing the results of the storm. The storm acted and influenced those who held power. Thus, not only are environmental disasters used by human power holders as a reason to restructure social relations, but they can themselves play an independent role in shaping social interactions. His analysis is one among many to transcend the divide between nature, culture, and society. Mark Stoddart (forthcoming) follows this perspective by investigating how weather shapes the discourses of skiers, their understanding of their sport, and even their political activism. Stoddart, who asked skiers in British Columbia about their experiences on the slopes, found that weather plays a large role. Not surprisingly, many skiers talked about how weather affects their ability to do their sport, going into much detail about snow quality, weather reports, storms, and avalanches. In many instances, however, they personified the weather and talked about it as sort of partner or collaborator in what they do. In another work, Stoddart (2011) shows that skiers' and environmentalists' perceptions of and relationship with nature affect their political advocacy. Nature comes to influence the wills, or power, of skiers and environmentalists. In his research on the discourse and mobilization around the development of a proposed ski resort in British Columbia, Stoddart found that some of the most salient debates by environmentalists, journalists, and others were about the protection of grizzly bears and their 'rights'. Who would have thought that bears could be actors in political debates over the development of a ski resort?

Overall, the inclusion of non-human entities and processes in their analyses changes how sociologists see politics. As Haluza-Delay and Davison (2008: 649) note, these trends offer 'conceptual innovations to address "interactionality of society-nature" and are radical innovations because they challenge the modernist principles that underlie much social science. In other words, asking *what* exercises power along with *who* exercises it is important for helping define and justify the foundational assumptions of much of sociological analysis and how we see politics.

Globalization?

While some scholars ponder how sociology's focus on humans has impeded the discipline's understandings of power, others argue that sociologists are looking at the wrong institutions as containers of power. In the case of political sociology specifically, these researchers wonder whether the state is as important as political sociologists make it out to be, especially these days. With the spread of global capitalism and the fall of the Soviet Union, a number of thinkers claim that we have entered a new era where old notions of time and social space are collapsing (for example, Anthony King 1995; Alberto Melucci 1996a; Manuel Castells 2000; John Urry 2000; Arjun Appadurai 1990). Some go so far as to say that we have reached the 'end of history' (Fukuyama 1992), where capitalism has won out over alternative systems such as communism, and the dictates of global capitalism will now and indefinitely reign supreme. As the world becomes increasingly integrated into the American or Northern sphere of influence, and the economies and politics of individual countries become more and more interdependent, societies are undergoing what these scholars maintain is a massive restructuring that rivals the changes of the Industrial Revolution and the emergence of modernity. As part of that restructuring, say some, states are losing their status as the dominant institutions in the world. **Globalization**, they say, is changing the relationships that shape power and in turn the ways in which sociologists should examine it.

You have probably heard the term 'globalization', but have you ever thought about what it means? Most social thinkers define it as a new social process where the constraints of geographic, economic, cultural, and social arrangements have receded and been replaced with processes that extend beyond state boundaries (Waters 1995). Globalization scholars say that the old ways of understanding social processes and politics are of little help today considering that economies have become increasingly integrated, cultures homogenized, networks broadened, and state institutions challenged. Such developments potentially undermine, or at least introduce new and problematic twists to, traditional perspectives on political processes.

With respect to material resources, those who adhere to globalization perspectives point out that economies have become increasingly integrated, in part because of shrinking geographies and the rise of new technologies. These trends have had repercussions for national elites and for workers challenging exploitive labour practices within their states (see Albrow 1997; Chase-Dunn and Boswell 1999; Boswell and Chase-Dunn 1996, 2000; Castells 2000;

TABLE 5.1 Foreign Direct Investment (Stocks) in Canada by Region, 2009

Region	Millions of Dollars	%
North America	292,541	53.2
Europe	186,966	34.0
Asia, Oceania	52,720	9.6
South and Central America	15,324	2.8
Africa	1,849	0.3
Total of regions		100.0

Source: Adapted from CANSIM Table 376–0051 (April 2010).

TABLE 5.2 Top 10 Countries with Foreign Direct Investment (Stocks) in Canada, 2009

Country	Millions of Dollars	Rank	%
United States	288,287	1	52.5
United Kingdom	63,469	2	11.6
Netherlands	46,529	3	8.5
Switzerland	21,191	4	3.9
France	18,218	5	3.3
Brazil	14,845	6	2.7
Germany	13,892	7	2.5
Japan	13,122	8	2.4
Luxembourg	9,856	9	1.8
People's Republic of China	8,854	10	1.6
Total of Top 10 Countries	498,263		90.7

Source: Adapted from CANSIM Table 376–0051 (April 2010).

Hardt and Negri 2001). Often cited by those who defend such claims are examples of increasing **foreign direct investment (FDI)** across states, new international flows of material production, and the rise of new labour practices, such as the creation of **export processing zones**, that circumvent the ability of national workers to unionize and challenge the power holders in their countries.

Examples of FDI can be seen in Table 5.1, which shows that regions from all over the world invest in Canada. North America invested about 292.5 billion dollars in FDI (stocks) in 2009; European countries invested approximately 187 billion dollars in the Canadian economy that year; Asian countries and Oceania invested almost another 53 billion dollars.

When the top ten countries investing in Canada are examined in Table 5.2, we see that the US, the UK, and the Netherlands account for 72.5 per cent of foreign direct investment (stocks). Clearly the Canadian economy is influenced by foreign business.

Canada also depends greatly on trade with other countries to maintain its power in the international system of states and the wealth of its elite (see Table 5.3). In 2010 the country had a trade deficit. In other words, the value of goods that Canada imported from other countries was greater than the value of what it exported to other countries. Over time, Canada has exported more,

TABLE 5.3 Imports, Exports, and Trade Balance of Goods on a Balance-of-Payments Basis, by Country or Country Grouping

	2005	2006	2007	2008	2009	2010
	\$ millions					
Exports	450,210.00	453,951.90	463,120.40	489,995.40	369,528.80	404,581.70
United States[1]	368,278.90	361,442.10	355,731.50	370,015.30	271,173.80	296,441.90
Japan	10,172.80	10,278.10	10,026.80	11,871.70	8,865.00	9,715.50
United Kingdom	9,360.50	11,282.20	14,152.30	14,168.10	13,036.90	16,983.30
Other European Union[2]	18,643.80	20,903.70	24,392.70	25,383.30	19,034.00	19,470.80
Other OECD[3]	14,545.60	16,808.10	19,743.60	21,077.20	16,699.30	17,904.00
All other countries	29,208.50	33,237.60	39,073.50	47,479.80	40,719.60	44,066.10
Imports	387,837.80	404,345.40	415,683.10	443,751.70	374,096.80	413,648.20
United States[1]	259,332.90	265,088.30	270,066.90	281,555.40	236,288.90	259,831.50
Japan	11,213.10	11,849.90	11,967.10	11,670.40	9,327.40	10,029.60
United Kingdom	9,066.50	9,547.10	9,962.90	11,323.70	8,533.60	9,562.20
Other European Union[2]	29,487.30	32,547.50	32,403.70	35,347.00	30,238.60	30,784.70
Other OECD[3]	24,282.10	23,680.10	25,159.80	27,408.40	25,973.00	29,010.80
All other countries	54,455.90	61,632.40	66,122.70	76,447.00	63,735.40	74,429.30
Balance	62,372.20	49,606.50	47,437.30	46,243.70	−4,568.00	−9,066.50
United States[1]	108,946.00	96,353.80	85,664.60	88,459.90	34,884.90	36,610.40
Japan	−1,040.30	−1,571.80	−1,940.30	201.30	−462.40	−314.10
United Kingdom	294.00	1,735.10	4,189.40	2,844.40	4,503.30	7,421.10
Other European Union[2]	−10,843.50	−11,643.80	−8,011.00	−9,963.70	−11,204.60	−11,313.90
Other OECD[3]	−9,736.50	−6,872.00	−5,416.20	−6,331.20	−9,273.70	−11,106.80
All other countries	−25,247.40	−28,394.80	−27,049.20	−28,967.20	−23,015.80	−30,363.20

1. Also includes Puerto Rico and Virgin Islands

2. Other European Union includes Austria, Belgium, Bulgaria, Cyprus, Czech Republic, Denmark, Estonia, Finland, France, Germany, Greece, Hungary, Ireland, Italy, Latvia, Lithuania, Luxembourg, Malta, Netherlands, Poland, Portugal, Romania, Slovakia, Slovenia, Spain, and Sweden.

3. Other countries in the Organisation for Economic Co-operation and Development (OECD) includes Australia, Canada, Iceland, Mexico, New Zealand, Norway, South Korea, Switzerland, and Turkey.

Source: Statistics Canada CANSIM database http://cansim2.statcan.gc.ca, table 228-0003.

but this relationship with other countries has clearly changed. Both FDI and import and export statistics show that the Canadian state is dependent on other states for the success of its economy.

This dependence can also be seen in labour practices. John Peters (2002: 17) notes that '[b]etween 1992 and 2000, union membership dropped overall by some 100,000, and while over the past few years 1.5 million jobs have been created, only 180,000 new union members have been added—an effective new unionization rate of 8%.' He concludes that because of an increasingly competitive global economy, state leaders have resisted supporting the expansion of labour rights. As a result, unions have been caught in a 'catch-22' between demanding better conditions for their members and facing the threat of plant closures and the moving of production to states more well-disposed to business interests. In fact, recent years have seen unprecedented willingness to compromise on the part of unions in the auto industry, which traditionally has been a site of union strength. As the 'big three' North American automakers faced bankruptcy and forced restructuring not long ago, their directors blamed high labour costs, including too generous worker benefits for their lack of competitiveness. In turn they pressured the unions to accept wage cuts, and in the US the **United Auto Workers** union, one of the largest in that country, agreed to a delay in company contributions to their medical fund and to the suspension of a program that paid laid-off workers (Ramsey 2008). These trends—the growing proportion of the Canadian economy in the hands of foreign elites, and the linking of labour wages and rights to forces in the global rather than the national economy—signal changes to the way that material resources are distributed between social classes, and the ways such resources can be utilized by these groups in their struggles for power.

Other globalization scholars add that a hegemonic consumer culture has begun to undermine the diversity of local cultures. They claim that cultures around the world are becoming increasingly Americanized, Westernized, or at the very least similar to the most powerful countries in the world system. As Hollywood films gain prominence in international movie theatres (Barber 1995), for instance, and fast-food culture spreads to all parts of the globe (Watson 1997), these fears are strengthened. When *Business Week* and the branding firm Interbrand examined the top international brands in 2009, they found that eight out of the top ten were American. Their list, ranked from one to ten in order of importance, consisted of Coca-Cola, IBM, Microsoft, GE, Nokia, McDonald's, Google, Toyota, Intel, and Disney (Businessweek 2009). Westernized global consumer culture, say some, has even become accepted as local culture to such an extent that people often have a false consciousness about who exactly produced what they are consuming (Robertson 1995). These trends, among others such as the rise of English as the dominant 'world language' are signs that cultural power is no longer controlled by local and national interests, but instead by global trends.

Others look to increased mobility and communication as signs of the rise of a global society. John Urry (2002, 2007), for instance, notes that today people travel more than in the past. Here, he does not mean just physical travel. For Urry, travel comes in many forms, imaginative and virtual as well as corporeal, and it is undertaken through communication technologies like the Internet, television, or movies, as well as by physical movement. He goes so far as to say that travel has become 'a way of life for many' (Urry 2000: Chapter 3), and he argues that sociologists should adopt **mobilities** as their prime focus of social relationships. Long gone, it seems, are the days when people were constrained to specific geographical locations, ignored what was going on in other countries, or never left their place of birth. As the United Nations' development report notes, 'More people are travelling than ever before, with 590 million going abroad in 1996, compared to about 260 million in 1980.' Likewise, '[more people are making international telephone calls than ever before, and are paying less. A three minute phone call from New York to London cost $245 in 1930—in 1990 it cost just $3' (United Nations 2010a).

Alberto Melucci (1989, 1996b), who observed such trends, declared that people have become 'nomads'. Others such as Zygmunt Bauman (2000) say this phenomenon is representative of our era of 'liquid modernity', where old boundaries are collapsing and new relationships are being negotiated. Manuel Castells (2007) even argues that the new communication-network technologies through which people can now 'travel' change the way power is established, especially over the production of knowledge. Castells says new communications technologies allow for interaction among people in an essentially boundless communications space, which counters the traditional vertical or top-down ways of thinking about and structuring power. No longer is power held by elites that control the means of communication that are faced by challengers within their localities or regions or countries. Now, both elites and challengers travel and communicate across borders, with the result that there are new and innovative repertoires of contention.

Not only are economies, cultures, and societies seen to be globalizing, but so too are institutions. The past thirty years have witnessed a proliferation of international agreements that challenge the sovereignty of existing states. One can readily point to the rise of the European Union, which effectively integrated most of the economies of Western Europe, or the implementation of NAFTA in Canada, Mexico, and the US. The prominence of the United Nations and other international institutions has led some scholars to postulate the rise of a **world society** or **world polity** where the practices and procedures structuring people's lives and actions are becoming increasingly homogeneous. If such is the case, then individual states may not be the primary institutions or arenas that shape political processes any more.

Internationalism seems to characterize Canadian international relations these days. Table 5.4 shows that Canada has trade agreements or formal trade relations with states around the world. It is also apparent that since the late 1980s, the number of bilateral agreements that Canada has negotiated and signed with other countries has increased, as have more ambitious **multilateral** agreements. Perhaps the most important of these agreements is NAFTA, which integrated the Canadian, Mexican, and US economies and entailed the standardization of economic policies, labour practices, and the production of goods and services across these countries. Such developments have limited the capacity of labour and capital alike to press their own states for changes, and the power of the leaders of individual states to address (or deny) them. Another venue for promoting internationalism, if not globalization, has been the United Nations (UN). Since its founding after the Second World War, the number of member states has almost quadrupled. At its first session in January 1946, fifty-one nations were represented (UN 2005: E.04.1.7). Just sixty-five

Table 5.4 International Trade Negotiations and Agreements by Region and Country

Region	Participating Countries	'In Force' Date/Status
Sub-Saharan Africa		
Canada – South Africa Foreign Investment Protection and Promotion (FIPA)	South Africa	signed: 27-Nov-95
Republic of South Africa Trade and Investment Cooperation Arrangement (TICA)	Republic of South Africa	signed: 24-Sep-98
Asia		
Canada – China Foreign Investment Protection and Promotion (FIPA) – updated	China	Pending
Canada – India Foreign Investment Protection and Promotion (FIPA)	India	Negotiations concluded
Canada – Japan Economic Framework and Joint Study	Japan	
Canada – Korea Free Trade Agreement Negotiations	Korea	Pending
Canada – Mongolia Foreign Investment Promotion and Protection (FIPA)	Mongolia	Pending
Canada – Philippines Foreign Investment Protection and Promotion (FIPA)	Philippines	13-Nov-96
Canada – Singapore Free Trade Agreement Negotiations	Singapore	Pending
Canada – Thailand Foreign Investment Protection and Promotion (FIPA)	Thailand	24-Sep-98
Canada – Vietnam Foreign Investment Protection and Promotion (FIPA)	Vietnam	Pending
Australia		
Australia Trade and Economic Cooperation Arrangement (TECA)	Australia	15-Nov-95
Europe and European Union		
Canada – Armenia Foreign Investment Protection and Promotion (FIPA)	Armenia	29-Mar-99
Canada – Croatia Foreign Investment Protection and Promotion (FIPA)	Croatia	30-Jan-01
Canada – Czech and Slovak Federal Republic Foreign Investment Protection and Promotion (FIPA)	Czech and Slovak Federal Republic	9-Mar-92
Canada – European Free Trade Association (EFTA)	Europe	Negotiations concluded
Canada – European Union Trade and Investment Enhancement Agreement (TIEA)	EU countries	Pending
Canada – Hungary Foreign Investment Protection and Promotion (FIPA)	Hungary	21-Nov-93
Canada – Latvia Foreign Investment Protection and Promotion (FIPA)	Latvia	27-Jul-95
Canada – Poland Foreign Investment Protection and Promotion (FIPA)	Poland	22-Nov-90
Canada – Romania Foreign Investment Protection and Promotion (FIPA)	Romania	11-Feb-97
Confederation of Switzerland Trade and Economic Cooperation Arrangement (TECA)	Switzerland	signed: 9-Dec-97
Canada – USSR Foreign Investment Protection and Promotion (FIPA)	USSR	27-Jun-91
Canada – Ukraine Foreign Investment Protection and Promotion (FIPA)	Ukraine	24-Jul-95
Kingdom of Norway Trade and Economic Cooperation Arrangement (TECA)	Norway	signed: 3-Dec-97
Republic of Iceland Trade and Economic Cooperation Arrangement (TECA)	Iceland	signed: 24-Mar-98
Middle East and North Africa		
Canada – Egypt Foreign Investment Protection and Promotion (FIPA)	Egypt	3-Nov-97
Canada – Israel Free Trade Agreement (CIFTA)	Israel	1-Jan-97
Canada – Jordan Foreign Investment Protection and Promotion (FIPA)	Jordan	Pending
Canada – Lebanon Foreign Investment Protection and Promotion (FIPA)	Lebanon	19-Jun-99

TABLE 5.4 Continued

Region	Participating Countries	'In Force' Date/Status
North America		
Canada – US Free Trade Agreement (CUSFTA) *now NAFTA	United States	12-Oct-1987 (superseded by NAFTA, which includes Mexico)
North American Free Trade Agreement (NAFTA), Canada and the North America Free Trade Agreement	United States, Mexico	1-Jan-94
Legal Text of the Canada-US Softwood Lumber Agreement (pdf)	Canada	12-Sep-06
Amendments to the Softwood Lumber Agreement 2006 (pdf)	United States	12-Oct-06
Canada – US Agreement on Government Procurement	United States	16-Feb-10
Central America and the Caribbean		
Canada – Barbados Foreign Investment Protection and Promotion (FIPA)	Barbados	17-Jan-97
Canada – Caribbean Community Free Trade Negotiations (CARICOM)	Antigua and Barbuda, The Bahamas, Barbados, Belize, Dominica, Grenada, Guyana, Haiti, Jamaica, Montserrat, Saint Lucia, St. Kitts and Nevis, St. Vincent and the Grenadines, Suriname, Trinidad and Tobago.	Pending
Canada – Central America Four (CA4)	El Salvador, Guatemala, Honduras, Nicaragua	Pending
Canada – Costa Rica Foreign Investment Protection and Promotion (FIPA)	Costa Rica	29-Sep-99
Canada – Costa Rica Free Trade Agreement (CCRFTA)	Costa Rica	1-Nov-02
Canada – Dominican Republic Free Trade Agreement Negotiations	Dominican	Pending
Canada – Panama Free Trade Agreement (FTA)	Panama	Signed 14-May-10
Canada – Panama Foreign Investment Protection and Promotion (FIPA)	Panama	13-Feb-98
Canada – El Salvador Foreign Investment Protection and Promotion (FIPA)	El Salvador	signed: 31-May-99
Canada – Trinidad and Tobago Foreign Investment Protection and Promotion (FIPA)	Trinidad and Tobago	8-Jul-96
Central America Memorandum of Understanding on Trade and Investment (MOUTI)	Costa Rica, El Salvador, Guatemala, Honduras and Nicaragua	signed: 18-Mar-98
South America (with Andean Community)		
Andean Community Trade and Investment Cooperation Arrangement (TICA)	Bolivia, Colombia, Ecuador, Peru and Venezuela	signed: 31-May-99
Canada – Andean Community Countries Free Trade Discussions	Bolivia, Columbia, Ecuador, Peru, Venezuela	Pending
Canada – Argentina Foreign Investment Protection and Promotion (FIPA)	Argentina	29-Apr-93
Canada – Chile Free Trade Agreement (CCFTA)	Chile	5-Jul-97
Canada – Colombia Free Trade Agreement (FTA)	Colombia	signed: 21-Nov-2008
Canada – Ecuador Foreign Investment Protection and Promotion (FIPA)	Ecuador	6-Jun-97
Canada – Peru Foreign Investment Protection and Promotion (FIPA)	Peru	20-Jun-07
Canada – Uruguay Foreign Investment Protection and Promotion (FIPA)	Uruguay	2-Jun-99
Canada – Venezuela Foreign Investment Protection and Promotion (FIPA)	Venezuela	28-Jan-98
Southern Cone Common Market (MERCOSUR) Trade and Investment Cooperation Arrangements (TICA)	Brazil, Argentina, Paraguay and Uruguay	signed: 16-Jun-98

Source: Adapted from: www.international.gc.ca/trade-agreements-accords-commerciaux/agr-acc/neg_country-pays_region.aspx?lang=en.

years later, in 2010, it had 192 member nations and a number of non-nation organizations (UN 2010b). Right from the outset, the UN promoted humanitarianism and international understanding. It founded, for example, **UNESCO (United Nations Educational, Scientific and Cultural Organization)**, which 'was established to promote peace and security through the application of education, science and culture to international understanding and human welfare' (Valderrama 1995: 25). The UN also created the 1948 **Universal Declaration of Human Rights**, which recognizes rights that transcend individuals and communities, and the **WHO (World Health Organization)** to coordinate public-health promotion. The UN has been front and centre in the recognition of ethnic and cultural minorities, establishing the **Working Group on Indigenous Populations** in 1982, coordinating military personnel in peacekeeping missions around the world, and founding the **International Court of Justice** in The Hague, which settles disputes among states and tries war criminals. More recently the push of internationalism has been evident in the **Millennium Development Goals** set by the organization, one of which is to try to 'eradicate extreme poverty and hunger' globally by 2015 (UN 2010c). Clearly the UN and its supporting member states have made a commitment to internationalism that transcends the powers of any one state.

The notion that the decisions and actions of state leaders, indeed even the actions of non-governmental organizations and citizens within these states, can be restricted by institutions operating at the global level lies at the heart of the **world polity**, **world culture**, or **world society** approaches in political sociology (see Boli and Thomas 1997; Meyer et al. 1997). Researchers who take this perspective have elaborated on the ways that global institutions, such as those affiliated with the UN, influence many activities more commonly understood to be driven by personal initiatives and group agency or by state leaders responding to uniquely national concerns. These activities include the development and content of constitutions, national human rights declarations and discourse, welfare programs, women's suffrage (Ramirez, Soysal, and Shanahan 1997), and even university curricula (Meyer, Ramirez, and Soysal 1992).

Central to the observations of world polity scholars is that a growing focus on international human rights and the reduction in the capacity of state leaders to ignore these rights have advanced the notion of 'individual personhood' and demands to protect it as features central to the culture of the emerging world society (Frank and Meyer 2002). In this global environment, state leaders cannot oppress their citizens indiscriminately. Everyone, including people in previously disadvantaged groups, such as women, ethnic minorities, or indigenous populations, have 'person rights' to which they can appeal in the international realm if those rights are abused or not recognized by their own countries. The result can be a weakening of the legitimacy of the very state that denies them. Personhood, say these researchers, has become a central feature of citizenship, a feature that can undermine the authority of individual states over their own citizens.

Scholars who subscribe to the world polity perspective also believe that international organizations and membership in them dictate standardization on a number of fronts in the name of modernization, development, and social progress. For example, which rights will and will not be recognized by emerging states, how public health will be administered and which epidemics will be tackled, and what types of institutions emerge. As we noted in Chapter 4, the state is the primary unit of membership in the international community. To become a recognized state often means that a country cannot act in ways that diverge from the principles of the dominant world polity. As a result, states are forced to meet a minimum set of criteria—such as recognition of individual rights, a commitment to meet the basic subsistence needs of its citizens, and open and non-aggressive relations with other states. Countries that do not follow these basic tenets are quickly excluded from the world polity and are perhaps even labelled as 'rogue' by the leaders of states at the core of the world polity. Iran, Iraq, and North Korea are only a few countries that have suffered such labelling, which clearly has consequences for both national elites and the masses of citizens they oversee.

Lastly, like scholars of nationalism and nation building before them, world polity scholars see educational institutions as central to maintaining the legitimacy of the emerging polity and global culture. They argue that education links the ideologies of human rights and of social progress (Meyer 2000; Meyer and Ramirez 2000; Meyer et al. 1992). The rise of formal mass education around the world has facilitated the spread of encoded and scripted humanism in school curricula everywhere. As a result, not only do individual states have less control over the knowledge and information communicated through their school systems, but the information their citizens are receiving has the potential to challenge the authority of the very states that are delivering it.

Challenges to Citizenship

Central to both critiques of anthropocentrism and to the role of states in politics is the way in which citizenship is defined and who gets to legitimize it, that is, *who* or *what* is entitled to rights, *which* institutions grant them, and *what* privileges or rights are protected. These are obviously important questions for political sociologists because, as established in Chapter 4, rights bearers possess a greater capacity to realize their wills or hold more power, generally speaking, than those who have no or fewer rights. Here we will examine more closely how globalization and anthropocentrism affect them.

Over the last century, citizenship debates have increasingly come to be framed in the language of human rights. These days, to be a citizen of a country means that you enjoy, or should enjoy, certain privileges to which you are entitled, not only as a Canadian, or German, or South African, but also as a member of the *human species*. Some of the most important rights in this regard are freedom of choice and equality. That all humans should have the liberty to make their own choices and should be treated the same as everyone else are principles that are central to **liberalism**, the political ideology that draws from and protects these rights. Liberal rights celebrate and protect the individual and are enshrined in the constitutions of most democratic countries.

So what's the debate about? Well, some scholars, for instance Makau Mutua (2001, 2002), argue that the depiction of human rights that powerful liberal societies uphold, and that has come to dominate the international rights discourse, promotes a model of citizenship that is excessively Westernized. By declaring that liberal or individual rights are rights of the species, powerful countries have succeeded in enshrining a conception of rights that is specific to Western culture but may not work so well with other cultural understandings of rights. As a result, human rights, argues Mutua, have become tools in the processes of colonization and homogenization of cultures by the West. These thinkers say that individual-centred human rights fail to defend ethnic and religious minorities, may even be detrimental to diversity, and could promote human rights at the cost of social, environmental, or other rights that are necessary for social existence.

Let's think about this. In Canada, section 15 of the Constitution says that all citizens are free and equal, which allows each of us to exist as an individual with liberal rights. But can it also ensure the freedom of individual citizens to privilege their group? What happens if your language, religion, or dress is different than those of the dominant culture, but the individual-centred rights of that culture impede your ability to practise your preferred social practices? In January 2010, for example, the state senate in France introduced legislation forbidding people to conceal their faces in public. The decision effectively makes it illegal for women adhering to the Muslim faith to wear the face-covering *burqa* or *niqab*. Supporters justified the legislation by saying that these garments restrict the freedoms and liberties of women and thus are contrary to the long-held commitment of the French government and its people to *égalité* (equality), or individual rights. But how does this square with the individual rights of these women to choose to wear the *niqab* and pursue their lives freely? Such cases form the basis of charges that human rights are colonizing.

The question now becomes whether liberalism is only capable of promoting individual rights to the exclusion of group rights or whether it can encompass a wider range of possibilities. It is around this point that many of the most recent debates on citizenship revolve. It is true that the liberal rights discourse understands the maintenance and reproduction of groups only as outgrowths of the free choices of individuals (Kymlicka 1998: 73) and that groups should not necessarily be protected by legislation or other institutions. But as Will Kymlicka argues, if one accepts that liberalism is predicated on recognizing and embracing the rights of the individual, then one must recognize that those same rights should also protect individuals who adhere to the beliefs and practices of subdominant cultures or minority groups in a state or of national groups that transcend states. For this reason, Kymlicka (1995) argues that recognition of minority rights is not a contradiction of liberal traditions, but rather a fuller adaptation of them. For Kymlicka, multicultural citizenship is one that recognizes not only the rights of individuals but also the rights of individuals to belong to and engage in the practices and beliefs of subdominant or multiple cultures. It allows for citizenship in the dominant state but also recognizes that individual freedom and equal opportunity are achieved only when people can exercise their own group rights within a larger shared institutional frame.

However, this debate is less than clear-cut. As Rhoda Howard(-Hassmann) (1991, 2000) shows with respect to Quebec language rights, privileging group rights over individual rights always comes at a cost. For instance, what happens to the rights of minorities within minorities? This was a question asked by many First Nations people living in Quebec in 1995. They did not wish to be forced to join an independent Quebec if that year's referendum resulted in the province's seceding from Canada. Or what about majorities that are minorities among majorities of minorities? Anglophone Quebecers in the Eastern Townships of western Quebec wondered what would happen to their rights if the same referendum succeeded. In his later work Kymlicka (2003) acknowledges that individuals need more than multicultural citizenship rights alone. He notes that such rights might protect individuals' freedom and equality to exist in subgroups, they might also promote understanding of subgroups, and they might even promote loyalty to a single set of (state) institutions in order to promote the interests of all groups. But guaranteeing the rights of multiple cultures may not promote diversity, understanding, compassion, or true **multiculturalism** (Kymlicka 2003: 156). It is one thing to tolerate one another and respect abstract notions of rights; it is quite another for people to get to know, love, and respect one another.

Although group rights may or may not contradict the notion of individual human rights, others have wondered why certain rights have been enshrined over others. Some scholars have been critical of the fact that the original human rights agenda of the 1940s, which was advocated by Latin American and Soviet Bloc countries and which recognized self-determination of peoples and economic and social rights, was lost (Cmeil 2004). Instead the agenda was shrunk by human rights organizations, which focused on liberal, individual, civil liberty rights. Ignored were people's rights to work and social-welfare protections (Alston 1994). Also lost was any consideration of people's rights to health and other non-liberal aspects of life. Some would argue that the loss of focus has limited the discourse on rights and has delegitimized claims to rights that extend beyond individuals.

At the core of debates on human rights are the humanist and anthropocentric tendencies of those rights. Proponents of liberal rights prize certain definitions of 'human' over others, and in turn imply that those who do not fit those definitions are of lesser value or non-human. Indeed, they deny some people and things any rights at all. Not everyone, not even in Canada, has access to the full list of rights offered by the Constitution. For example, children are not given the same rights and freedoms, nor are subject to the same obligations, as adult Canadians. They do not have the right to vote or to participate in important decisions, even in areas that affect them directly, such as education or urban planning. They are not alone. Individuals deemed so mentally challenged or disabled that their competence is questioned, or who have had to sign over their power of consent to others, also have fewer rights. In a world that prizes human rights and respects the capacity of people to use those rights, such distinctions can be detrimental to the well-being and legitimacy of those that are not recognized. It is not our intention here to engage in a debate on the rights of children or the specially-abled, but rather to highlight how important rights have become in our contemporary world. Essentially those without full human rights have less power to realize their wills in many aspects of daily life.

While you might agree that children and other people that have fewer rights should have more, what about animals, the environment, or non-human entities? You might not think that they need rights comparable to those that humans have; however, in contemporary societies that prize the protection of rights, perhaps they do need them in order to avoid extinction, exploitation, and cruel treatment. Animals already do have rights in many industrialized countries, including Canada, where people can be prosecuted if they neglect animals in their care. In fact, the president of the Toronto Humane Society and four of its staff were charged with cruelty to animals in 2009. The charges were later dropped when brought to court (CBC 2010c). They, however, signal the degree to which animals do have rights and the lengths to which people will go to ensure they are protected. John Sorenson (2010) takes up these issues by looking at the economic, environmental, and health costs that are incurred when animals' rights are not protected. He also reminds us that animal rights do not come at the cost of other rights, such as those of humans, but are instead part of a larger societal commitment to social justice (2010: 12). Similar arguments can be made about the environment or any other aspect of the world we inhabit. Insights into the dominance of liberal rights and critical questioning of whether they should privilege 'competent' individual humans alone is an emerging trend in political sociology and one that affects anyone (or anything) striving to have their rights recognized in a world of changing citizenship regimes.

Empire

While some claim that globalization and the rise of international institutions have cast doubt on political sociologists' use of the state as a centrepiece of their analyses, others have argued that the changes being witnessed are evidence of the rise of a new form of **empire**. Among the proponents of this argument are **autonomist Marxist** philosophers Michael Hardt and Antonio Negri (2001). In their widely cited work, *Empire*, they argue that the world has become a postmodern de-coupled polity dominated by the elite in the US and wealthy **G8** countries. Moreover, the power of the elite is facilitated by powerful multinational corporations and the ideology of democracy. Hardt and Negri thus articulate a new form of empire, an empire more massive than the empires of the past and one that is nothing less than the 'centerless, deterritorialized global capitalist system itself' (Steinmetz 2005: 361). Like Marxists before them, they argue that it is important to imagine a new world and resist the hegemonic system. To do so, however, may require new ways of seeing the world, politics, and activism.

Perhaps the real changes to international relations are not engendering the withering of states, but instead fostering the emergence of a powerful American empire (Nye 2003). Such an observation differs from claims by Hardt and Negri that a centreless global capitalist empire has taken root; yet it is based in the same language of empire. It is true that if you look back on the history of **nation-states**, they are a relatively recent phenomenon. In contrast, empires, those containers of political processes comprising large-scale institutions and more fluid forms of governance, can be traced to the earliest moments of recorded human history. Scholars such as Colomer (2008), who look at how international relations are changing, ponder whether it is time to 'bring the empire back in' much in the same way that Theda Skocpol once led a movement in political sociology to 'bring the state back in'. Maybe it would be more helpful to look at the multifarious politics of today through the lens of empire rather than the modern state, which is a more delimited structure.

However, George Steinmetz (2005) notes that the term 'empire' is often invoked in these debates with a lack of precision. He argues that the current discourse around empire is ahistorical. Contemporary social analysts have lost track of its meaning and use it in disparate and often ambiguous ways. To enhance the historical accuracy of this account, Steinmetz develops a typology of empires that have existed throughout history and considers the place of the purported US empire in comparison to past empires. He concludes that the US is indeed imperialist, but that its form of empire is *non-territorial*, making it different from the colonial powers of the past that were so committed to territorial expansion. Instead, he observes that the US has exported neo-liberalism and post-Fordist approaches to governance and organization but has been reluctant to maintain overseas colonies—an argument that squares well with some of the claims of world polity theorists. Unfortunately, as Steinmetz notes, much of the recent analysis of empire has been by critical leftists, political scientists, and historians and has been largely avoided by the political sociologists who could best elaborate and scrutinize this approach. Regardless, what seems clear from a review of recent claims about globalization and states is that whatever the changes being experienced by international institutions, they are not necessarily global, nor are they distinct from older historical processes.

Hardt and Negri (2001), however, also challenge us to imagine new possibilities to match the new processes of the social world. In part they do this for some of the same reasons why we have challenged you to think about whether you can *really* be 'not that into politics': because contemporary societies, particularly those in the privileged North, are seeing unprecedented declines in the number of citizens participating in formal politics. Democratic countries, one after another, report declining voter turnouts, particularly among young people who appear to be choosing to opt out of formal politics. In Canada, for instance, in the 2011 federal election only about 61 per cent of Canadians voted, and in Nunavut that figure was even lower, at approximately 49 per cent (see Figure 5.1).

This compared to the record turnout in 1958, when almost 80 per cent of Canadians voted (CBC 2008). The growing tendency for people not to vote, say some, contributed to the election of minority governments in the 2000s and the concomitant search by some individuals for alternative forms of politics, a pursuit that has been linked to the rise of new political parties, such as the Greens or Québec solidaire.

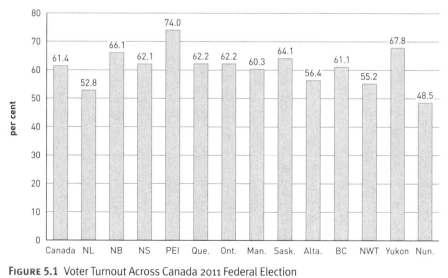

FIGURE 5.1 Voter Turnout Across Canada 2011 Federal Election

Source: www.cbc.ca/news/politics/canadavotes2011/story/2011/05/03/cv-election-voter-turnout-1029.html# [03/05/2011 12:40:54].

Note: preliminary estimates May 3, 2011 – day after election.

Yet, to conclude from these trends that people are 'not that into politics' or are politically apathetic would be wrong. As we've been arguing throughout this book, politics is relational and is linked to the contestation of power. If that is the case, one cannot escape it. Likewise, just because people are not voting in the same way they used to does not mean that they are not political. In fact, if you consider the rise of populists using innovative political tactics through the Internet and other means, such as Howard Dean and Barack Obama or the figures aligned with the Tea Party or Occupy Movement, you find that people are very much into politics, just not the formal politics of the status quo.

Is a New World Possible?

New forms of politics seem to be emerging. Scholars who study political movements have begun to look at global processes and are concerned with whether and how globalization has shaped political contention. The so-called 'Battle in Seattle' in 1999 saw thousands of individuals and groups, from many regions of the world, and nurturing a wide range of grievances, come together in opposition to the economic policies being promoted by delegates to the World Trade Organization. The protesters believed that the organization's policies were at the foundation of a myriad of ecological, economic, cultural, and social ills they wished to correct. Similar large mobilization efforts occurred throughout the first decade of the twenty-first century, as seen in a similar protest against the third summit of the Americas in Quebec City in 2001. Social movement scholar Donatella della Porta and her colleagues (2006) ponder whether traditional social movement perspectives can account for these seemingly novel challenges to globalization. They maintain that contention against global capitalism consists of organizational structures, identities, strategies, and interactions with power holders that are distinct from old ways of protest and they in turn foster 'democracy from below'.

Continuing on the subject of social movements, other scholars seek to show how politics has changed by looking at the use of **transnational activist networks**, or TANs. These are composed of people 'working internationally on an issue, who are bound together by shared values, a common discourse, and dense exchanges of information and services'. Such networks 'are most prevalent in issue areas characterized by high value content and informational uncertainty' (Keck and Sikkink 1998: 2), such as those concerned with indigenous rights, human rights, women's rights, or the environment. In such cases, aggrieved groups seeking recognition of their rights, claims, and legitimacy may appeal to the citizenship regime of their own state, but if it ignores them they might make claims through international networks. This was the case with the James Bay Cree, for instance, in their fight against Hydro Quebec's development of their traditional lands (Jenson

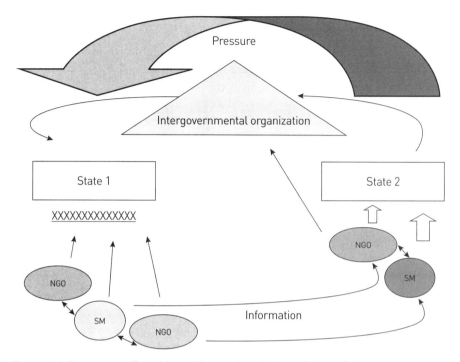

FIGURE 5.2 Boomerang effect: Adapted from Keck and Sikkink (1998: 13)

and Papillon 2000; Niezen 2000). When the Quebec government ignored their grievances, they appealed to NGOs in the environmental movement and lobbied the state of New York and the UN to pressure Canada and Quebec to respect their rights. Margaret Keck and Kathryn Sikkink (1998) argue that such pressure is a boomerang effect of transnational activism (see figure 5.2). Essentially, when social movement NGOs face 'blockage' in their appeals to leaders of a given state, they share information through TANs of like-minded NGOs and movements around the world, whose members in turn put pressure on their own governments and international organizations to recognize the plight of the original NGOs and movements that cannot be heard in their own country. As was the case with the James Bay Cree, such international pressure often leads to changes in other states. For instance, as briefly noted in Chapter 4, state leaders in New York reconsidered their purchasing of electricity from Hydro Quebec until the Quebec government negotiated settlements with the Cree whose land would be destroyed to produce the electricity. Such innovation in contentious action and politics is far from apathetic, though it might not appear on the radar of those seeking to look at formal forms of politics alone.

Transnationalism?

As convincing as some of the declarations about globalization appear to be, some scholars find them overstated and disputable. At the very core of the argument of emerging globalization is that it is a new process, distinctly different from the processes of industrialization, modernization, and the emergence of the state that preceded it. However, throughout recorded human history there have been many examples of international, if not global, exchanges of material, cultural and social, and political resources. Just think about the spice trade. It involved interaction by regions and empires of the ancient world to facilitate the commercial exchange of spices and other commodities. The modern Olympics has for generations brought the world together to promote global co-operation through sport. And international agreements among states have been taking place at least since 1648 and the Treaty of Westphalia, when, for the first time, warring countries in Europe agreed to respect the 'advantage of the other' as a means of securing their own interests. Internationalism and global exchange may not be as novel as some claim.

It is also debatable that the world is witnessing a shift in material relations from a national to a global focus. Recall that Table 5.2 showed that foreign investment in the Canadian economy has increased over time. If you look at the table more closely, however, you will see that the US accounts for about 53 per cent of that investment. That is over half of all foreign FDI (in stocks) in Canada. This is far from the multi-country investment and ownership that is often implied by globalization theorists.

Peter Urmetzer (2005), who offers a detailed analysis of the extent to which foreign direct investment is globalized, questions whether states have lost control of their economies to the extent that some globalization thinkers suggest. If we return to Table 5.4, we also see that most of Canada's international agreements and negotiations are **bilateral**, that is, between just two states. Such negotiation is not global by any means. Furthermore, Canada's international agreements are almost all with countries in the western (that is, American) hemisphere. In fact, as we are writing this book, Canada has only two agreements among the many countries in sub-Saharan Africa. Canadian firms have also experienced trouble doing business in many parts of the world, as evidenced in the 2010–11 dispute between Research in Motion, which is based in Waterloo, Ontario, and India over its BlackBerry technology. Such trouble has discouraged Canadian businesses from integrating more closely with the economies of other countries. If we turn to labour rights, again we find that individual states and their citizens still exert much pressure on labour conditions and on how companies treat their employees. As Naomi Klein (2000) shows in her book *No Logo*, consumers in the global North can and do shape the labour standards for the production of products that companies sell to them.

Even the claims about global communication can be overstated. It is, of course, indisputable that we live in an era of unprecedented technological innovation, and for those with material wealth, increased travel and communication is indeed an option. However, 'Despite all the talk of globalization, the bulk of the world remains largely untouched by it. It is estimated that half the world's population has never even made or received a telephone call' (UN 2000). This is not to mention the vast 'digital divide' that exists in the world. Figure 5.3 shows the number of computers per 100 people around the world. When you look at it, the image is striking. North America, Europe, Japan, South Korea, and Australia are heavily equipped, whereas in countries in most of Africa a computer is hard to come by. The thirty or so richest countries of the world may be experiencing the network society talked about by Castells (1996), but much of the world remains unplugged. Additionally, in a post-September 11th era, the securitization and monitoring of communication and travel have been unprecedentedly limiting, even for the most privileged populations. Christopher Murphy (2007), for instance, examines the broadening police mandate, expanding role of police forces, and increasing police power and resources in Canada since that fateful day.

Contentions that world cultures are homogenizing around a Western model are also questionable. It is true that a lot of cultural and social exchange occurs among wealthy states, particularly among the wealthy people within them, but not everyone participates. If culture is becoming so homogeneous,

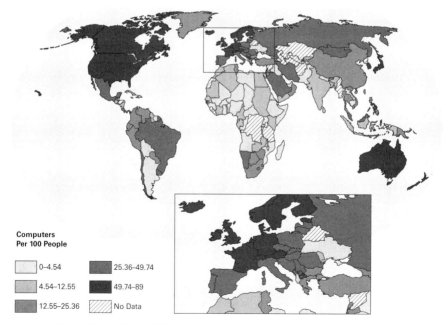

Computers Per 100 People

0–4.54	25.36–49.74
4.54–12.55	49.74–89
12.55–25.36	No Data

Figure 5.3 The Global Digital Divide

as Benjamin Barber (1995) noted, then why do we at the same time see rising radicalism and the continued formation of nationalist groups seeking political and cultural independence from, rather than integration into, the international community? Likewise as Arjun Appadurai (1990) notes, international migration has meant that Western culture itself is becoming more diversified. The Americanization of the world is not happening in the straightforward way that some alarmists claim.

Finally, when David Brady and his colleagues (2005) examined whether economic globalization was enfeebling the welfare state, they found little evidence that it was. Instead, states appear to be rather resilient. For instance, although the number of international institutions, such as the UN, has grown considerably since the Second World War, few have the power to challenge the will of powerful states. Take for example the US's practice of continually ignoring UN resolutions when they do not fit that state's agenda, and its leaders' refusal to pay UN dues during the 1990s (Nye 2002). So influential is the American state that in 1998, the then Secretary General of the organization, Kofi Annan, wrote in the *New York Times* that 'the United Nations, for all practical purposes, remains in a state of bankruptcy. Our doors are kept open only because other countries in essence provide interest-free loans to cover largely American-created shortfalls' in financial support (Annan 1998). Subsequently the US did make contributions aiding the organization, but it has continued to use its economic and financial power to influence it. As recently as 2007, the failure of the US to pay its back funds to the UN created a budget shortfall that hampered the organization from launching peacekeeping efforts during the Darfur crisis in Sudan. If the power of states is in jeopardy, then why is the biggest symbol of the world polity so dependent on them?

For all these reasons, many scholars would say that the world has witnessed the rise of **transnational** processes, or **transnationalization**. The key difference between globalization and transnationalization is the scale of the process. The former theory claims that the entire world is involved, whereas the latter makes a lesser claim, that only more than one state is involved in an interaction with at least one other state. As Tarrow (2005: 2–3) rightly cautions, it is still states that uphold international norms and implement laws, not international organizations. Moreover, as Clifford Bob (2005) and Margaret Keck and Kathryn Sikkink (1998) note, there are indeed 'activists beyond borders'; however, they still work largely within and against states as the main containers of power. Maybe the ways in which state leaders exercise power, the issues with which they are concerned, and the institutions through which they work have changed, but states are by no means withering away.

Summary

Throughout this chapter we have introduced you to some new trends in political sociology and their critiques of existing perspectives. We engaged two core assumptions of political sociology: (1) that individuals alone possess power and act upon others and things, and (2) that the state is the most dominant institution housing other political processes. We first looked at critiques of anthropocentrism by introducing the ideas of Latour and Haraway. We then considered the claim that globalization is a new phenomenon and examined the extent to which material, cultural and social, and institutional processes are now unfolding on a global scale. We also introduced the concept of empire, through the works of Hardt and Negri and of Steinmetz, as well as the notion of 'democracy from below' articulated by della Porta and others as elaborations of globalization research. We ended by looking at transnationalism as an alternative explanation of the emerging internationalism witnessed over the last few decades.

Questions for Critical Thought

1. What are your assumptions about who or what exercises power over you? Is it just other people who you think impose their wills on you, or would you include *things* like animals, technology, or nature on that list?

2. Why are 'rights' so important in contemporary societies?

3. What are the similarities and differences between states, empires, global institutions, and transnational institutions?

4. How do you 'see' and 'do' politics?

Suggestions for Further Reading

Latour, Bruno. 2007. *Reassembling the Social: An Introduction to Actor-Network Theory*. New York: Oxford University Press. A collection of writings by Bruno Latour and a synthesis of his work on the actor-network theory and critique of sociology.

Steinmetz, George (ed). Forthcoming. *Sociology and Empire: Colonial Studies and the Imperial Entanglements of a Discipline*. Chapel Hill, NC: Duke. A cross-section of scholarship on empires and those studying them. The collection looks at a number of cases from around the world.

Tarrow, Sidney. 2005. *The New Transnational Activism*. New York: Cambridge University Press. This book offers a systematic analysis of recent trends in mobilization and considers whether new patterns of contention are emerging.

Urmetzer, Peter. 2005. *Globalization Unplugged: Sovereignty and the Canadian State in the Twenty-First Century*. Toronto: University of Toronto Press. An introduction to claims made in the literature dealing with globalization and a systematic analysis of whether they are applicable to a Canadian context.

Websites ....

United Nations
www.un.org

YaleGlobal online
http://yaleglobal.yale.edu

World Bank Development Indicators
http://data.worldbank.org

World Social Forum
http://fsm2011.org

6　Conclusion

Learning Objectives

- ⊛ To re-examine the definition of political sociology
- ⊛ To recognize political sociology as a field that seeks to identify the social forces that shape and challenge power relations, especially as they interrelate with the state
- ⊛ To understand how political sociologists look at underlying processes of power that apply across cases, periods, and contexts
- ⊛ To enhance your social literacy by demonstrating how political sociology provides you with conceptual tools that can help you to understand how processes of power shape social relations and societies
- ⊛ To see how you can use a political sociological perspective to engage in and understand power contests outside of academia

Introduction

The political sociologists introduced in the preceding chapters approach politics in many different ways, highlighting the processes that they believe are crucial to understanding how power is negotiated in human societies. We grouped their insights around Weber's understanding of power as stemming from class, status, and party—that is, material, cultural and social, and institutional processes. Along the way, we engaged with some of the emerging debates in political sociology.

Recall that materialists generally say that differential access to and control over material resources ultimately determines who exercises power and who is best able to resist it; cultural and social theorists emphasize the power-wielding capacities embedded in symbolic markers, knowledge, and networks; and institutionalists examine how social institutions, especially those associated with the state, shape the maintenance of and challenges to the status quo. Recall also some of the new 'lenses' through which political sociologists are examining contemporary societies and power, perspectives that see power and political processes as being affected by non-humans, new institutions, and new units of analysis. Clearly, the study of political sociology is wide-ranging, its subject areas broad, and its conclusions varied—all signs of a vigorous discipline engaged in academic, social, and political debate.

Having introduced you to the major approaches taken up by political sociologists in their study of power, we would now like to return to some of the points we made in the introduction to refine them in light of your newly acquired knowledge of the field. Specifically, we will revisit our definition of political sociology and re-examine what we mean by *seeing politics differently* by highlighting key insights from researchers introduced in earlier chapters. As you have learned, political sociologists are eclectic in their subject matter and the ways in which they apply the different perspectives. You will see, however, that much of the strength of their scholarship stems not from its variety, although that is impressive too, but rather from the applicability of their insights to a wide range of social and political situations. We will then go on to argue that because of its breadth, political sociology offers conceptual tools that can enhance your **social literacy**, that is, your ability to engage critically with social relations and phenomena. We conclude by providing examples of how you can use political sociological perspectives to become more aware of and understand power contests, not only as they pertain to academic settings, but also in your everyday life.

Political Sociology Is . . .

We began this book by telling you what political sociology is not. It is not a field of study dedicated to researching the institutions and mechanisms of the state. That task has been ably performed by political scientists for a long time. Neither is it only and always concerned with 'politics' in the sense that most of us understand that term, the goings-on of politicians and other political interests. Rather, political sociologists are interested in exploring the continual contestation and negotiation of *power* in human societies. They are interested in formal politics to be sure but primarily as they interrelate with the ways power is wielded and challenged in wider society and experienced in everyday lives.

But power is a broad concept, one that, it could be argued, every other sociologist engages as well. Even if we restrict our definition of political sociologists, as we have done in this book, to those who study the forms of power that derive primarily from material, cultural and social, and institutional sources, this still encompasses a wide range of sociological concerns. Moreover, political sociologists obviously take up an extraordinary array of subjects— from class and the economy to media and education; from inequalities among ethnicities, nations, and 'races' to the interactions of humans with technology; and from the dynamics of the family to social revolutions. If all this is political sociology, then what in sociology is not included in its purview?

A very good question! It is true that most, if not all, of the sociologists we know, regardless of whether they study tourism or post-Soviet economies or the social construction of pigeons as urban pests, are ultimately concerned with how and why power is held and exercised asymmetrically and what, if anything, should be done about it. But political sociologists are distinguishable from the crowd for their focus on the *processes* affecting the negotiation of power more than on particular manifestations of power. In other words, the politics of the case are more important than the case itself. And what is most interesting to many political sociologists are *patterns* in those politics, consistencies or differences across situations that might say something beyond the particulars of each case and about the nature and negotiation of power more generally.

Now, this does not mean that political sociologists don't care about the details of the circumstances they are interested in. They need to know a lot about the cases they explore in order to best understand how the politics that characterize them play out. Thus a researcher needs to become an expert in eighteenth century Irish history if she wishes to use the case of Ireland in her examination of how state institutions shape religious policy (Stanbridge 2003). A political sociologist has to familiarize himself with Estonian culture, and maybe even learn the Estonian language, if he wants to include Estonia in his comparative study of how countries' rates of membership in voluntary associations affect citizens' participation in formal politics (Alapuro 2008). Likewise, it does not mean that political sociologists don't care about the children or minority groups or countries they use as the subjects of their research. Their primary focus may be on political phenomena, but the subject matter they use to highlight those phenomena is important to them too.

It does, however, mean that political sociologists conduct research for reasons other than just describing the power differentials unique to a particular case. Most wish to explore deeper ends and are thus interested in what different cases can tell about how the bases of power are established and maintained. They are interested in how differential control over social and political resources affects the capacity of some groups to exercise their wills more readily than others or how groups tend to go about challenging established power arrangements. Thus, a political sociologist might study the life and times of an influential king, a fascist dictator, and a religious leader but not only because he is interested in how and over whom that king, dictator, and religious leader exercised power. He likely also wishes to see how those manifestations of power compare, perhaps make some observations as to why those patterns exist, and ideally formulate concepts that could be useful to analyzing power in other contexts.

Max Weber did this kind of comparative work to answer the broader question of why people allow others to dominate them or tell them what to do. After studying many different authority figures in a variety of times and places, he concluded that people obey others if those others hold *rational-legal authority*, that is, if they occupy positions of power in a bureaucracy; hold *traditional authority* and appeal to history and precedent; or hold *charismatic authority*, that is, if they possess an indefinable something that compels others to follow them. Domination that was exercised on the basis of any other sort of means, coercion for example, or fear, Weber said was illegitimate and would eventually fail (Weber 1946: 78–9). Notice that it was not Weber's ultimate aim to reveal the particulars of monarchical authority or to detail the abilities and charms of 'natural' leaders, although he did become familiar with such cases and many more. Rather, he sought deeper conclusions than what were immediately evident, namely, the mechanics of domination that could be identified irrespective of era, style of governance, or scale of institutions.

We can see the same approach to politics and history in Karl Marx's work. As we discovered in Chapter 2, Marx understood power as stemming from people's access to and control over material resources and, more specifically, the means of production. From this initial observation he theorized, among other things, that the power enjoyed by feudal lords was not eternal, nor was the subservience of peasants in any way natural. Although their respective dominance and subordination in feudal society may have been perceived as essential and timeless, and the institutions that supported this unequal power relationship may have looked as if they were inevitable, they were just the outward manifestations of the conditions of ownership on which the entire system was based. Marx likewise showed that workers in the modern capital- ist era are not indentured to a life of hard work nor are the owners of factories set to rule the world for ever, regardless of how entrenched these conditions seem or how unimaginable an alternative situation appears. He *saw politics*, the negotiations around power, *differently*, and showed that we cannot just look at the end positions of power to explain power inequities, but rather we must examine the processes that have given rise to them. From such a per- spective, Marx was able to argue that the social relations and institutions of the modern capitalist period were not fixed and unchangeable and that cap- italism too would eventually go the way of feudalism, owing to the material relations that configure the key social groupings, institutions, and ideologies of capitalist societies.

Thanks to the extraordinary ability of Weber and Marx to look past the most obvious manifestations of power and grasp the political processes that configure them, they were able to formulate conceptual tools that could be used to make sense of a wide array of power inequalities. The strength of these tools is evident, not only from how well they accounted for the distribution of power in their day, but from the fact that present-day political sociologists still use and build on these tools to help make sense of power negotiations in post-modern societies.

Of course, Weber and Marx are not the only ones to have shaped the disci- pline through their insights. More recent scholars have theorized conceptual tools that have proven useful to political sociologists too. Pierre Bourdieu's characterization of social and cultural markers, practices, beliefs, and so forth as forms of capital that can be acquired and wielded in power negotiations in ways similar to material resources was a watershed in political sociological analyses of power. This is because it offered a powerful tool to researchers seeking ways to conceptualize how people and groups exercise and challenge power through means that are not obviously of a material nature. Like Weber and Marx, Bourdieu was able to look beyond conventional explanations for power inequalities among different groups, such as accounts that claimed that some social or cultural groups were simply less talented or able than the members of dominant groups, for example, or that certain ethnic or cultural practices somehow predisposed some people to be more successful than others. Instead he observed that all these groups had in common certain social and cultural characteristics that were less valued than those possessed by individuals belonging to the more powerful groups in a society. Notice again that Bourdieu's formulation, although its theorization was possible only after intense study of many individual cases, still holds regardless of the specific social and cultural factors characterizing a particular group, or even the geographical or historical context in which they are present. Theda Skocpol and Michael Mann do the same thing with conventional accounts of revolution and genocide. They challenge typical interpretations that consider these acts to be driven by the discontent or bloody-mindedness of particular individuals or groups bent on refashioning their societies, and show instead that the institutions configuring social action play a big role in how such events unfold. These statements have to be grounded in the careful and detailed study of cases of political upheaval and mass killing, of course. But their conclusions can be applied to power negotiations in other circumstances, as evidenced by Skocpol's use of her institutionalist perspective to help illuminate 'revolutions' of different sorts, like the development of social welfare policies in the US (Skocpol 1995) and what many see as a worrying decline in membership in voluntary associations (Skocpol 2004).

Political sociologists' impulse to reveal the latent processes shaping power contests has prompted some to claim that the hidden processes that are usually evoked as explanations for power inequities are themselves based on hidden processes. In Chapter 5, we introduced you to scholars who argue that materialists, social and cultural theorists, and institutionalists may purport to reveal the 'real' processes underlying power negotiations, but that they employ methods which make assumptions about the nature of power negotiations that do not necessarily hold true. People like Bruno Latour, Donna Haraway, and globalization scholars say that these tools unproductively privilege humans over things and animals, and individual states over global and transnational forces. As a consequence, they produce incomplete, indeed incorrect, representations of how power is distributed, exercised, and challenged. These scholars have formulated alternative concepts, like actants and cyborgs, that provide other ways of understanding power negotiations across cases. These, they say, rectify the veiled assumptions of older more established ways of addressing power inequities.

Perhaps it is this drive to identify and make statements about the more general mechanisms shaping politics that inspires many political sociologists to take up study of so many specific cases. They can be quite eclectic when it comes to the subjects they pursue. Charles Tilly was a prolific political sociologist with an encyclopedic knowledge of incidents of contentious politics in history. In his early work he focused on historical France (Tilly 1964, 1986) and then Great Britain (1995), and then turned to exploring contentious politics and social movements across time periods and states (2004, 2007, 2008). He also dealt with issues of inequality, historical and social movement methods, and even how people offer explanations for *why* things occur (2006). In the process, he identified common mechanisms that shape power relations and their negotiation. Even when cases did not fit, they offered insight and opportunities for Tilly to theorize new concepts to fill the gaps in existing knowledge.

Indeed, most political sociologists end up engaging with an assortment of subject matters during their careers in their pursuit of a better understanding of the power-related processes that interest them. John Porter may have been primarily concerned with identifying mechanisms of inequality in Canada, but his analyses mostly tried to use standard sociological methods and insights to account for inequalities in different spheres of the social world, more generally: the economic, the social, the political institutional (Porter 1965), and the educational (Porter, Porter, and Blishen 1979). He used the same insights to understand inequalities among class, linguistic, ethnic, and gender groups. The same can be said of Robert Brym, whose work spans topics as diverse as the mobilization of Newfoundland fishermen (Brym and Neis 1978), the dynamics of class power, economic development, and politics (Brym and Sacouman 1979; Brym, Gillespie, and Lenton 1989), the minds and nature of intellectuals, politics and Canadian sociology (Brym 1980; Brym and Fox 1989), online dating (Brym and Lenton 2001), and even suicide bombing (Brym and Araj 2006, 2008). Others include Edward Grabb, who has reviewed civic engagement (Andersen, Curtis, and Grabb 2006), how class shapes political attitudes and power (Grabb 1981), and social inequality more generally (Grabb 2007); Douglas Baer, who examined how education affects people's support of the dominant ideology (Baer and Lambert 1982), how family factors shape delinquent behaviour (Kierkus and Baer 2002), and claims about the decline of social capital (Baer, Curtis, and Grabb 2001); William Carroll, who specialized in understanding the activities of the corporate elite (2004, 2007) but has also undertaken investigations of the media (Hackett and Carroll 2006), social movements (Carroll and Ratner 1996a, 1996b, 2001), and higher education (Carroll and Beaton 2000); and Patricia Marchak, who, like Carroll, examined the corporatization of higher education (Marchak 1996) but also explored the fishing and forestry industries in British Columbia (Marchak 1983; Marchak, Guppy, and McMullan 1987) and state terrorism in Argentina (Marchak 1999).

But for all the variety in their subject matter, political sociologists are alike in their inclination to view the world through a political lens. As a result, they see politics everywhere, recognize most social actions as political acts, and interpret social outcomes as results of power contests, understanding that individuals and groups use different means to seek or maintain their positions of power or challenge the existing state of affairs. They then take those observations and inclinations and ponder how they help explain outcomes in different social contexts, such as families, voluntary associations, social movements, and business organizations; across time and place, in different countries and cultures and across different time periods; and among different social configurations, including religious, state, and educational and judicial systems. Political sociologists—even those who subscribe to the new perspectives in the field—are thus always striving to look past immediate, especially individualistic, explanations of social processes and outcomes to see how they are configured by the differential power held by the human, and sometimes nonhuman, actors they consider to be the principal players in those interactions.

Remind Me Again Where the State Fits In

Political sociologists are concerned with identifying the underlying patterns in the ways power relations are constituted and play out, but they also care about identifying the primary containers of that power, that is, the main sites at which power is negotiated. In our contemporary world those containers are human individuals and states: humans are understood to be the principal holders and exercisers of power through individual and group actions, and states are seen as the places where the most significant power contests are played out. It is for this reason that so much of political sociology concentrates on issues such as citizenship, human rights, and the way people exercise power and use institutions to maintain power or challenge it. It is also why political sociologists pay so much attention to states, which remain the most prominent and arguably the most important institutions in societies today. As we have seen, states influence to a large degree the powers to which individuals have access, *who* is permitted to exercise power in their territories (for example by setting the requirements of and rights affiliated with citizenship), and *how* those powers can be legitimately negotiated (such as through the courts or in the streets). Let us hasten to add that, in privileging human actors and states as the primary units of power, political sociologists do not repeat the conventional wisdom that individuals are atomized unrelated beings or that the state exists and operates in a realm separate from the people and groups that constitute 'civil society'. Rather, they view individuals and their actions as bounded by their relationships to other individuals, and the state as just one (albeit critical) institution that enshrines them.

By approaching the state as only one of many *interrelated* institutions and political processes that structure social relations, political sociologists are always aware that the state, like other social institutions, is an entity staffed by people, maintained by people, and constructed and negotiated by people. States, like other manifestations of political processes, are constituted by the interactions of individuals and groups who engage them. For this reason, we would say that political sociologists are less likely to reify the state, that is, to approach and study it as a stand-alone entity, separate from the people who occupy its positions and 'the rest' of society.

We say 'less likely' because even political sociologists, at times, talk about the state as if it existed apart from people. Institutionalists, in their efforts to expose how institutionalized patterns of interaction affect the decisions and actions of the individuals and groups who operate within their bounds, have been accused of exaggerating the capacity of the state to act monolithically and independently of the interests of others in a society. Materialists likewise have faced charges that the functional nature of their argument, that is, that the state ultimately functions in the direct or indirect interests of the most materially advantaged, presents the state as artificially and unrealistically cohesive. Even the 'new' perspectives have been accused of underrepresenting the multiplicity of state activities and the areas in which state officials can exercise power when recent scholars make unilateral statements concerning the declining power of the state in the global era. Nevertheless, there is less tendency among political sociologists to understand the state as an entity separate from the rest of society. Instead, they recognize that the power of a state is necessarily interrelated with the distribution of power evident in areas not directly related to governing activities. Like other social institutions and political processes, it will reflect and affect power relations in a wider society.

Perhaps the best way to clarify the role the state plays in political sociological analysis is by way of some examples. Throughout the book we have made reference to a number of Canadian experiences with which political sociologists have concerned themselves, such as: the advance of women's rights, the Quebec nationalist movement, issues pertaining to First Nations peoples, and the environment. Each of these has involved direct and public involvement of the state in many ways, through challenges to federal divorce laws in the 1970s that sought more equitable treatment of women, for example; by the referenda that have been held in Quebec to gauge support for greater provincial autonomy; by the imposition of martial law by the federal government during the October Crisis in 1970; by the striking of the Truth and Reconciliation Commission by the Canadian government to investigate the history of abuses suffered by First Nations peoples in residential schools that attempted to assimilate them and destroy their culture; and through recent meetings held between Canadian and US government officials concerning the benefits and environmental hazards of the Alberta oil sands projects. Whether you know or have even heard of these examples of how Canadian state officials have shaped and contributed to the unfolding of these issues has likely more to do with whether you have learned or kept up with the formal politics pertaining to these matters than whether you are familiar with a political sociological perspective.

But a political sociological perspective illuminates a host of other ways in which the state has been involved in the development of these affairs by encouraging us to look deeper and more closely at how they came about, by exploring the social forces and factors that determined how they were framed, how they proceeded, and what their outcomes were or will be. These can differ depending on the perspective or combination of perspectives that political sociologists adopt. We have already seen how materialist feminists have interpreted the unequal treatment of women as an outgrowth of a system that privileges material and economic contributions to society over the non-material production in which women have traditionally been engaged. They say the state plays a role in maintaining this unequal treatment by formulating and implementing policies that are billed as good for everyone but end up maintaining women's 'natural' dependent position in the household. A federal child care program that provides a small, taxable cash payment to families rather than access to a system of government-funded child care may be defended by state officials as enhancing parents' 'choice' of care for their children since they can use the money for any sort of care they wish. But critics say it hardly covers the cost of full-time child care and so compels families to absorb the costs themselves or decide that one member must stay home as the primary care provider. The reality that this one family member is nearly always a woman demonstrates, these researchers would argue, how a seemingly neutral state policy actually helps maintain women's dependent position in the home (Adkin and Abu-Laban 2008). This sort of understanding of state action, in this case a gendered reading of child care policy, can be considered only if we look beyond immediate representations and justifications of state policy toward the way policy reflects, sustains, or modifies the ways power is distributed in families and in wider society.

We have also seen how political sociologists understand and analyze the practice of colonization in Canada and elsewhere. The Canadian state's long history of denying the cultural and collective identities of minority groups has been linked to the emergence of Quebec nationalism, as well as to attempts by First Nations people to attain official recognition from the state, from other Canadians, and from the international community. In these cases, political sociologists highlight the unintended political consequences of state policies. For example, when Canada announced a proposal to eliminate Aboriginal status in a 1969 White Paper on Indian policy, as a means of offering full citizenship to marginalized indigenous peoples, it was met with heavy opposition and may have even sparked the rise of modern Canadian Aboriginal activism

(Long 1992; Wilkes 2006; Ramos 2008a). The White Paper was followed by a decade of increased mobilization and legal disputes over contested land. In these cases, formal politics, unfolding in social circumstances characterized by discrimination toward minority group members, cultivated conditions that ended by fostering the emergence of counter-state movements.

Recall too that, according to some political sociologists, cultural trends and habits affect the way people identify with environmentalism (Haluza-Delay 2008) and that the framing of those issues influences whether and how individuals participate in the movement. An important part of framing research is an analysis of how messages are received, modified, or countered by the state. That is because the decisions made by politicians about environmental matters and the justifications or frames for those decisions can affect whether a movement will survive and succeed, or lose momentum and dissolve (Tindall 2003; Cormier and Tindall 2005). In addition to these more direct decisions of state officials about the environment, other state-related actions, including the pressure state leaders are receiving from other powerful groups in the country and in the international community, the state's response, if any, to the social movements more generally, and the ideological stance of the government, will affect the nature of environmentalist challenges. A government whose political ideology is committed to ensuring that the pursuit of economic ends proceeds unfettered will likely respond unfavourably to a movement lobbying for an environmental tax on big polluters. It may, however, be more amenable to a group calling for tax credits to businesses that exhibit environmentally responsible behaviour. Whatever decisions are made will of course affect the movement, its legitimacy, and its ability to attract and keep members, and will thus further affect the way power contests unfold.

Notice that formal politics is present in all these investigations but acts only as the most obvious manifestations of issues arising from these experiences. Political sociologists dig deeper to understand how these representations came about as a result of the differential utilization of material, cultural and social, institutional, and other resources in power negotiations.

Political Sociology Can Enhance Your Social Literacy

Admittedly, people like Weber, Marx, Bourdieu, and Latour, were and are exceptional in their ability to look past the obvious manifestations of power imbalances and to theorize concepts that counter conventional interpretations of their outcomes. That's why they have become leaders in the field. But we would argue that all of us are capable of doing much the same thing in our day-to-day lives. Indeed, we believe that your ability and willingness to see politics the way that these and other political sociologists do is essential to developing and enhancing your social literacy. This is your ability to 'read' and understand the social world in ways that grasp some of the deeper, less obvious factors that shape your actions and experiences and those of other people. Let us explain.

Almost all sociologists seek to understand the grammar of societies. One of sociology's most esteemed voices, C. Wright Mills (1959), recognized this years ago. He characterized sociology's task as looking at the links between 'personal troubles' and 'public issues' by developing what he called a **sociological imagination**. He recognized that most people, especially North Americans, view their own and other people's circumstances in individualistic terms or as personal troubles. Many consider their fate, as well as the fate of those around them, to be determined by individual efforts and talents. Others argue that individual outcomes are 'the luck of the draw' or happen because it's 'just the way things are', and they may express frustration and despair at the hand they have been dealt. Mills argued that both views are wrong because both fail to capture how people's places in societies are established: not through individual decisions or by natural and inalterable forces, but through the continuous interactions among individuals, social groups, and broader social and historical trends.

To clarify, Mills used the case of unemployment. We can examine unemployment as a personal trouble, the result of an individual's lack of effective social capital, for example, or of her laziness or unwillingness to find work. If, however, we observe that thousands of people are unemployed, the situation can no longer be understood entirely as a personal trouble, it is also a public issue. Unemployment is not about the bad luck or indolence of each unemployed individual, but is instead also about the social forces and factors that shape work and the labour market. For instance, you saw in Chapters 2 and 3 that women in Canada perform more unpaid labour, tend to work in specific occupations, and earn less on average then men. Is this because each individual woman out of the millions that make up the female labour force chooses to put in a double or triple workday, just happens to prefer nursing, teaching, and service work over construction or engineering, and asks for, or is satisfied with receiving, a lower salary than her male counterparts? Well, no, that would be ridiculous. But that is how interpreting these statistics in terms of the personal troubles of each woman in Canada would explain them. On the contrary, there are systemic reasons related to women's unequal access to and control over material, social and cultural, and institutional resources that contribute to many of these differences. Mills argued that an astute observer of society can distinguish between personal troubles and public issues by identifying contradictions or inconsistencies such as these. That is, by taking situations that look like individual problems and seeing how they manifest themselves in broader patterns or trends.

More recently, Michael Schwalbe (2004) has used the notion of **sociological mindfulness** to express ideas similar to Mills's. Schwalbe argues that being mindful is a process of 'tuning in' to the world in a way that helps make sense of it. This requires that people continually engage in internal conversation and reflection, activities that help them see past the typical explanations of what is taking place. Like Mills, Schwalbe says the way to sustain this conversation is by looking for disputes over meanings and accounts of why things are the way they are. The scholars we introduced you to in Chapter 5 certainly engage in such conversations, which have revealed how important it is for people to ask, not only who exercises agency, holds rights, or enjoys citizenship, but what things and animals possess those qualities as well. The questioning of assumptions by recent political sociologists has allowed for novel and fuller ways of understanding how the social world operates. Schwalbe's mindfulness is a personal process that everyone can and should engage in.

Drawing on the spirit of Mills's and Schwalbe's work, we use the term social literacy to explain what you can gain from *seeing politics differently* or from adopting a political sociological perspective on the world. We are by no means the first to use the metaphor of literacy to describe the capacity to 'read' and understand social processes. In fact, it has been used extensively in media and technology studies (see Livingstone 2007; Lewis and Jhally 1998) in the field of education (see Haste 2003; Street 1995; Crick and Porter 1978), and even in analyses of politics and power (see Gale 1994; Janks 2010). But we think it is particularly applicable to political sociology too. Let us explain why.

To be literate in the usual sense means that you can read and write. More specifically, it means that you understand that particular combinations of symbols, for example, letters and words, have certain and sometimes competing meanings that you can use to communicate with others. When you are literate, what would otherwise appear as just squiggly lines on a page are transformed into meaningful communication that you can then reflect upon, accept or reject, and even respond to by composing your own meaningful collection of squiggly lines and even new meanings of your own. To be *socially* literate, we argue, involves a similar process: that you can 'read' or map the symbols and representations that constitute the social world; interpret the meaning(s) underlying that map and distinguish between conventional and competing readings; and make use of those same symbols and representations to construct your own meanings. The 'squiggly lines' of the social world become the material, social and cultural, and institutional processes that make up the many events that constitute that world and that you may have previously taken for granted. The more ways that you can read and engage the social world, the more socially literate you will be. Staying with the literacy comparison for a moment longer, we know that the more words you are familiar with, the firmer your grasp of grammar, and the more deeply and widely you have read, the more skilled you will be at discerning the meanings communicated in the written word. You will be in a much better position to critique and respond to its message, as well as to write your *own* messages. A literate person can certainly enjoy nineteenth century Romantic poetry, but an expert trained in the analysis of Romantic poetry who has read and studied the canon and reflected on various analyses and criticisms of its poets will read and respond to such poetry very differently. He may even create his own poetry using influences of the nineteenth century, perhaps mixing them with other genres. Indeed, the ability to do this consciously is the very essence of literacy. Similarly, the more skills and tools you have at hand to map and analyze the social world, the more comprehensive and balanced you will be when assessing its operations and engaging it in established and potentially new ways.

This is where political sociology comes in. Because of its overarching concern with identifying and analyzing social relationships as *power* relationships, political sociology provides a lens through which all manner of social phenomena can be examined. Furthermore, it offers a wide range of tools, or concepts, that you can then apply to these relationships to help you make sense of their operation and outcomes and even create or challenge them.

Ordinarily, most people make use of maybe one or two 'tools' to help grasp social reality: personal experience, or the experiences of people close to them, and a strong belief in individualism, that is, the certainty that people end up where they are because of their individual efforts. The result is the risk of conflating, as Mills warned, personal troubles with public issues. Thus, a person may come to believe that all people on social assistance are out to take advantage of the system because she has heard of a neighbour who has a child every year to continue to qualify for it. The other danger is that we attribute success and failure strictly to individual effort or indolence, we do so without acknowledging the many other things that can shape a person's outcomes to a significant degree. Thus, we might attribute the poverty of people in developing countries to their lack of ambition or ingenuity, perhaps comparing the hardships that we ourselves or people we know have overcome as evidence of their apathy.

With the conceptual tools that political sociology provides, however, we are able to see these and other social phenomena in different ways. When we understand these situations as manifestations of underlying processes related to the negotiation and distribution of power, then alternative readings present themselves. If we wish to make some observations on welfare recipients or poverty in developing countries, we first recognize, following Mills, the fallacy of equating personal experiences and observations with a grasp of public issues. A *person* on social assistance cannot be used to represent the social *phenomena* of millions of people on social assistance, nor can you compare your hardships directly to those faced by people in circumstances entirely different from yours. We can then begin to reflect on the public issue as an outcome of the unequal distribution of and access to material, social and cultural, or institutional resources among different groups. Suddenly, a whole range of other possibilities suggest themselves.

Perhaps an increase in the number of people on social assistance could be attributable to more people losing their jobs, not because they were fired or didn't show up for work, but because of economic forces beyond their control. That this might be the case is suggested, for example, by a recent report by Citizens for Public Justice, which found that the poverty rate in Canada increased from 9.2 to 11.7 per cent between 2007 and 2009, when most of the world experienced an economic recession (Pasma 2010: 2). Such figures raise further questions of a political sociological nature.

Were the people who lost their jobs more likely to have been poor before the recession? A materialist would predict so, since the low pay and precarious conditions under which many of the working class labour mean that they are more likely to be laid off when employers face financial difficulties. Did a disproportionate number of the people turning to social assistance belong to identifiable groups? Were many of them women, for example, or disabled, immigrants, or elderly? If they were, political sociologists who examine how social and cultural factors affect people's relative power would not be surprised, given that these groups have been shown to hold less power because they display cultural and social markers that are less valued in Canadian society than those of dominant groups. What were some of the institutional responses to the recession? Did these responses do anything to reduce the impact of the recession on the people most affected by it? The governments of Canada and other countries spent trillions of tax dollars to try to prevent the recession from becoming deeper and more widespread. However, that money, for the most part, was not spent on social programs to help the unemployed, but instead to secure the bad loans that had been made by world banks and financial institutions that had led to the recession in the first place. The decision by state leaders to respond to the economic crisis in one way (by propping up the global financial system) rather than another (by mitigating the hardships wrought by the downturn on the most vulnerable) would interest institutionalists examining how state leaders shape the nature of power inequities. As you can see, a political sociological perspective makes an issue that, from a conventional view, may seem straightforward—'A greater demand for social assistance means that it's too easy to get'—much more complicated to be sure! But it also encourages a more comprehensive, and realistic, approach to public issues.

Regarding poverty in the developing world, it doesn't take a political sociologist to notice that many of these places were former colonies of Britain, France, Germany, the US, and other privileged countries. But a political sociologist knows that she must acknowledge and consider the repercussions of that history when trying to make sense of poverty there. Can it be understood as a corollary of the long history of power imbalances stemming from the material inequalities sustained between the colonizer and the colonized? Can it be the outcome of the undervaluing or oppression of some ethnic groups over others? Does it stem from state policies that encourage foreign investment in these countries over national development, or that favour production for the global rather than the domestic economy? Such questions have to be asked to get at a truer picture of the complex forces that contribute to the inequalities among countries.

But there is more to social literacy. As most advocates of different forms of literacy would contend, just stopping at seeing and reading, while essential, would not in fact fulfill the goals of literacy (Arthur and Davison 2000: 9; Livingstone 2007: 4; Haste 2003: 10; Janks 2010). Instead, a literate person is one that can also be critical of and assess dominant and alternative understandings of the world. And again, political sociology offers the conceptual tools to help you do so. For example, materialists have taught us to be wary of alienation and false consciousness; cultural and social thinkers have shown us to distinguish among dominant, negotiated, and oppositional readings of the world; institutionalists have taught us to beware of incrementalism and to look to structural opportunities to challenge existing power relationships. More recent political sociologists have given us concepts like the actant for considering how people relate not only to one another but also to the rest of the world; and debates over globalization, empire, and transnationalism have helped us assess whether the institutions that shape power are changing. In other words, the social forces and political processes identified by political sociologists allow us, not only to understand power relations but also to ask why they exist and even to challenge them.

Put simply, social literacy enhances your capacity to engage with the social world in a more informed way. Having only personal experience and the ideology of individualism to draw upon as tools to interpret social phenomena limits dramatically the range of responses to these phenomena one can formulate. Because those responses tend to ignore or understate the impact that access to resources that serve as the bases of power have on social outcomes, they can take on an overly personal, sometimes even hostile character, as when 'welfare mothers' are blamed for their own poverty, or destitute farmers in Ethiopia are faulted for not having specialized in the right crop and thus having caused the country's underdevelopment. The social literacy acquired from adopting a political sociological perspective permits a more informed and comprehensive view of these situations.

Political sociologists' identification of different political processes and sites of power, as well as the conceptual tools they identify, thus provides a grammar for understanding the social world and its power arrangements. With this grammar, people are not only better able to notice and be critical of what they see, but they can participate actively in the re-negotiation, production, and contestation of power. They become true and active political players, individuals who can spot the power imbalances operating in social relations, ponder their origins, and commit to changing those imbalances if they so choose.

But Where Do I Start?

Forty years ago, Carol Hanisch (1970), a radical proponent of what came to be known as second-wave feminism, wrote an article entitled 'The personal is political.' The phrase, besides becoming one of the defining statements of the women's movement, expressed feminists' belief that women's lives and issues, including housework and child care, sex and appearance, and their relationships with their partners, must be considered and analyzed through a political lens. Hanisch said that these 'personal' matters cannot be properly understood and addressed unless they are recognized as reflections or extensions of 'politics' or wider power relations, especially between women and men. We would agree wholeheartedly with Hanisch's representation of the relationship between the personal and the political, as would most sociologists. But since our aim is to convince you that a political sociological perspective is a particularly useful one to have on the world, we might turn Hanisch's phrase on its head to make the point that the political is also personal or, more succinctly, *politics is personal*. In other words, and as we have tried to show you, politics is not something that happens 'out there' and that we can choose to ignore or 'be into' or not. Rather, politics always shapes our personal lives. Because of this, it is important that we be aware of it and be capable of seeing and reflecting upon the ways in which the lives of people, groups, and institutions possessing different levels and types of power are affected by political processes.

What about when we go shopping with our friends? Can an afternoon at the mall be understood in political terms? Yes, it can. One way involves becoming more aware that most of the clothing and other things you look at and buy in Canadian stores are made in China or other parts of the developing world. You would think that things produced so far away would be more expensive than they are, considering the distances they have to travel to get to St John's or Timmins or Regina. How is it even possible for stores to sell radios for four dollars or shirts for five dollars or DVD players for forty dollars? They can, in part, because the system of global production supported by national and international state institutions enables manufacturers to employ people in developing states for very low wages and in less healthy work conditions than in North America. Low labour and manufacturing costs in much of the world enable us to buy cheap consumer goods here, goods that are often unaffordable to the very people who make them. The cost of manufacturing has to be borne by someone somewhere. In the case of most consumer goods, it is borne to a large degree by people in faraway countries whom we rarely if ever think about, even though they have forged, handled, sewn, and touched the things we use or wear every day. Indeed, companies spend a lot of money to help us forget or just not think about where the products we use originate and concentrate instead on how their acquisition will benefit us as individuals. And all of this goes on through the mechanisms of the state that regulate production, collect taxes from their manufacture and purchase, monitor the use or abuse of labour, and so on. Thus, something as innocuous as an afternoon shopping trip becomes an overtly political act when you consider where your personal consumption decisions fit in the wider network of power relationships defining global production.

Suppose, then, that you just sit in a coffee shop and text your friends? Even that is a political act. The shop you choose (Tim's or Starbucks), the coffee you order (a double-double or a latte), the clothes you're wearing (a parka and tuque, or a Brooks Brothers suit) and the texting device you employ (Android or iPhone) are cultural markers that you display unconsciously or deliberately and that broadcast your status power. But more than this, just the fact that the coffee shop exists and that you have the freedom and leisure time to sit there in almost complete safety is an indication that you live in a privileged society, one whose members enjoy far more material, cultural, and institutional advantages than many others people around the world. Unless the coffee you are drinking is certified as **fair-trade**, the beans it is made from were probably grown and picked in places where labour laws are not as stringent as in Canada, nor wages as good, which is part of the reason you are able to drink it in the first place, not to mention pay an inexpensive price for it. The technological device that you are using to text your friends, although it seems as if everyone has one, is, as we have seen, available to only a small proportion of the world's population, many of whom nevertheless labour to manufacture it on behalf of large corporations, which sell them to you. Few, if any, of the children in the Democratic Republic of Congo, who mine the coltan that is used in such devices and work in the factories of suppliers to some of the major companies that market them (Robertson 2010), will ever possess the devices they help to produce. And if you happen to be drinking your coffee from a disposable cup, it will likely end up in a nearby landfill, where it will take many thousands of years to decompose, or be burned in an incinerator that can release harmful pollutants into the air. And all of these processes, in Canada and elsewhere, are regulated, monitored, administered, and framed by the state and state-related entities. So in many ways a visit to the coffee shop can indeed be understood politically.

Suppose then that you just sit in your room and read a book. Surely that can't be seen through a political lens. Well, yes it can. That you have a room to retreat to, that you have ready access to books, and that you are literate is not only because you paid the rent this month, went to the public library yesterday, and studied hard in school—it is because of your privileged position within your society. In other words, your circumstances have depended on your individual actions, but they are also possible only because you are able to find a job or obtain loans that others have made available to you, because municipal and provincial governments maintain a free library system through tax dollars, and because the law restricts the employment of children—indeed forbids it in the case of the youngest children, and instead requires them to attend school. And all these things are there because of past and ongoing power contests between groups supportive of and opposed to the state's role in providing money to help fund public libraries and deliver a (relatively high) minimal level of education to all its citizens.

This kind of noticing of things that normally go unnoticed and that are taken for granted but nevertheless enable you to 'be yourself' and pursue your individual desires takes practice. As we discussed in the introduction and a number of times throughout this chapter, most of us are accustomed to observing and understanding social relationships in terms of the characteristics of the individuals involved rather than the powers they possess. So when we see people who enjoy material advantage, we see that advantage as stemming from their hard work and risk taking. Groups that are disadvantaged in Canada and in the rest of the world are often considered to be that way because they don't have the ambition to improve themselves. And social movements that do not bring about the changes they desire are often blamed for failing because of the incompetence of their leaders and membership.

What a political sociological perspective does, however, is encourage you to look past the individual and assess the conditions and contexts outside the individual that may be shaping her ability or inability to do what she wishes or, as Weber would say, exercise her will despite the resistance of others. We have tried to give you some of the tools for doing this so that you can think about how material, cultural and social, and institutional advantage (or disadvantage) can shape the power of individuals and groups, both in Canada and beyond. We do not mean that you should abandon individual accounts of differential power entirely, but instead should also begin to consider more seriously the social determinants of power. We have also tried to highlight the crucial role of the state in all this as the container of power contests, as the place where many of the rules on how individuals and groups are permitted to exercise power are made, and as the institution whose officials themselves hold significant power to shape and even determine outright how power is distributed and plays out in contemporary societies. Government officials and formal politics should be something that you pay attention to, not only because your vote determines who will be able to set the rules of the game, although that's significant enough. It is also important because developing a sociological perspective on power that recognizes and takes it seriously is an essential part of becoming socially literate. We hope that in gaining this literacy you try to formulate your *own* interpretations of the social world *you* inhabit and the politics *you* engage in during *your* everyday life. To do this in an informed way requires being critical of the assumptions you hold about yourself and others, as well as of the accounts and institutions that are normally understood to determine the world or govern your life. The 'you' that you will become as a result will be better informed and therefore better able to make decisions and take actions that will benefit you, your family and friends, and the people around you. And those are things that all of us, not only political sociologists, strive to do.

Summary

The next time someone asks if you are into politics, look them in the eye and say, 'Of course I am! And so are you!' Draw upon your own experiences of having access to and control over material resources, like fashionable clothes or personal investments, and think about how they offer you some advantage over others in enabling you to realize your will. Listen to the language you employ with ease and the accent you may have, and ponder how these markers enhance or detract from your status vis-à-vis others. Consider the ways the clubs you belong to contribute to social networks that expand or limit the number and kind of people you meet and affect your position in disputes or negotiations with others and in the institutions in which you participate. And notice the ways that these same institutions—the dynamics of your family and friendship circle, the routines and rules governing your school and workplace, and the structures making up your municipal, provincial, and federal governments—configure your actions and decisions either by enabling you and others to make real choices about how you wish to live your lives or by erecting barriers against your ability to do so. We hope that with time you develop an instinct to see beyond the conventional, more obvious explanations for power inequities, and to see politics differently—like a political sociologist.

Questions for Critical Thought

1. What is political sociology?
2. Are there any core insights of political sociology that can be applied irrespective of context, case, or time frame?
3. What roles do individual people and the state play in political processes?
4. Can someone decide *not* to be 'into politics'?

Suggested Reading

Helmes-Hayes, Rick, and James Curtis (eds). 1998. *The Vertical Mosaic Revisited.* Toronto: University of Toronto Press. Examines the importance of John Porter's vertical mosaic thirty years after its original publication. It includes commentaries by key Canadian political sociologists on the vertical-mosaic thesis and reformulations for the contemporary era.

Nash, Kate, and Alan Scott (eds). 2001. *Blackwell Companion to Political Sociology*. Malden, Mass.: Blackwell. An encyclopaedia of North American political sociology. It is a one-stop resource that covers the main debates and innovations in this area of sociology.

Staggenborg, Suzanne. 2011. *Social Movements*. 2nd edn. Don Mills, Ont: Oxford University Press. Examines a broad range of social movement perspectives and uses Canadian cases to illustrate them. A concise reader that is accessible, yet sophisticated, in its presentation of material.

Websites

Alternet
www.alternet.org

Canadian Sociological Association
www.csa-scs.ca

Department of Justice Canada (Charter of Rights and Freedoms)
http://laws.justice.gc.ca/en/charter/1.html

Rabble magazine
www.rabble.ca

Story of Stuff Project
www.storyofstuff.com

TEDIdeas Worth Spreading
www.ted.com

The Onion
www.theonion.com

Huffington Post
www.huffingtonpost.com

Glossary

actant Anything that influences the actions of another thing. A term used by actor-network theorists to recognize that non-humans can act and in turn shape or influence negotiations with other things.

actor-network theory A theory that proposes looking at the interactions and influences of all things and the networks that are generated, maintained, and changed by those interactions. The theory, which was proposed by Bruno Latour, among others, encourages researchers to question their own assumptions about the social world and anthropocentricity.

agency The ability to act independently and influence power. The ability to exert one's will. In sociology this has traditionally been seen in contrast to social structures.

agent A person or group that is able to act and influence power. More loosely, something that can influence or cause effect.

aggregate A grouping or category. It is a term often used by researchers who employ social statistics.

alienated Restricted in one's capacity to negotiate power relations and from engaging in politics. A term that is associated with Marxist perspectives.

anthropocentric Paying too much attention to humans at the cost of looking at other possible factors.

ascribed Inherent in someone (in reference to a characteristic or trait). A characteristic that cannot be changed and demarks difference. Racial and sexual traits are often said to be ascribed because people are born with them and they are difficult, if not impossible, to change.

automobility The study of the relationships and social processes that are shaped by, and are extensions of, auto culture and the rise of cars and highways as the main means of transportation in most contemporary societies.

autonomist Marxist Pertaining to a branch of Marxism that was prominent in Italy and which has later inspired anarchist thinkers. It is a perspective that is also linked to the works of Michael Hardt and Antonio Negri, who promote the creation of 'new imaginaries', or ways of seeing the world.

back stage The space where people let down their guard, act normally, or even feel safe enough to breach expected norms. It is a term associated with the dramaturgical approach theorized by Erving Goffman. In this approach people act out their everyday life on different stages. (The front stage is where people act into the roles and expectations of the broader society.) *See also* front stage.

back-to-the-land A movement that saw many people move to rural areas in an effort to forge a simpler and more sustainable lifestyle. It originated in the 1920s and 1930s and was witnessed in the 1960s and 1970s. The movement sought a way of living in which people could live off their land and could avoid engaging in the destructive aspects of capitalist and industrial societies.

bilateral Having two sides. Refers to direct agreements or negotiation between two states or power holders.

black box Something whose inner workings are opaque or less than evident.

bonding social capital A type of capital that consists of the mutual trust and obligation that can be generated within a group and that can be exchanged or drawn upon. In other words attachment, value, and belonging to a group. A term associated with Robert Putnam's work on social capital and civil society.

bourgeoisie Those who own and control the means of material production in capitalist societies. A term used by Karl Marx and Friedrich Engels to distinguish the elite from the masses.

bridging social capital A type of capital that refers to the bonds and relationships that can be generated between people of different groups, and which in turn leads to the production of trust and obligation. A term associated with Robert Putnam's work on social capital and civil society.

bureaucracy An organizational form that is ordered by criteria independent of the personal qualities of the people who hold positions of power. It is a system that is rationalized and associated with states and the post–Industrial Revolution period.

Canadian Auto Workers (CAW) One of the most prominent unions in Canada, representing workers of subsidiaries of the 'big three' US automakers and other workers in the auto and other employment sectors.

capital The unseen shared value that is placed on symbols that can be exchanged and drawn upon by others, including economic, cultural, and social forms.

catch-22 A situation in which the outcome is equally unfavourable no matter what is done. A term coined by Joseph Heller, in his novel bearing the same name.

CCF (Co-operative Commonwealth Federation) A left-leaning social democratic political party that was the precursor to the current NDP (New Democratic Party) and was pivotal in the launching of Canadian health care and populist politics on the Prairies.

charter group The first group to found or colonize a state, which has a political and economic advantage over others that immigrate or arrive later. The term is associated with John Porter's work on the vertical mosaic. In Canada, Charter Groups can also refer to anglophone, francophone, Aboriginal, or other groups that are recognized in the *Constitution Act, 1982*.

cinq à sept French for 'five to seven'. A term used in Quebec to refer to 'happy hour' at pubs or bars. It is the period between 5 and 7 p.m., during which licensed establishments usually offer specially priced drinks and food.

citizenship Rights and privileges that people are granted by a recognized state in exchange for their support and loyalty to it.

citizenship regime The institutional arrangements that guide the decisions of power holders and which recognize who is and is not a citizen and what issues and claims are treated as politically legitimate.

civil society Institutions, such as voluntary or non-governmental organizations, that are independent of states.

claims making The practice of making public statements on an issue to raise awareness of it or influence how it is understood and perceived. The term is also linked to a literature in political science and sociology known as agenda-setting or arena models.

class A social group of people that share the same material circumstances. In the Marxist tradition this is understood also in terms of people sharing the same relationship to the means of production.

Cold War A period in the mid-to-late twentieth century when the Soviet Union and the US were the two world superpowers competing in international relations and world politics. During this period, many observed that neither superpower could act unchecked because of the dominance of the other.

collective behaviour (1) Group action, such as a social movement. (2) An early perspective in the social movement literature (collective behaviour theory) that is often associated with contagion models of mobilization.

collective identity A common sense of belonging to a group. It is also a perspective in the social movement literature that has emerged out of the New Social Movement tradition.

colonialism The policy of acquiring or maintaining colonies.

communism A social system that aims to eliminate private ownership and abolish differences among classes. It is a system that was advocated by Karl Marx and Friedrich Engels.

companion species A species of animal that shares a social and emotional relationship with humans. Was coined by Judith Butler, in recognition of the mutual interaction that occurs between humans and other animals.

comparative historical analysis A method of social analysis that compares a number of historical cases in order to illustrate different or similar processes. It is a term popularized by Charles Ragin as well as the work of historical sociology.

con man (confidence man) A person who deceives others by playing roles or making claims to status that he or she does not have in order to gain an advantage or steal from others.

contagion The rapid spread of something like a fashion, mob mentality, or riot. It is associated with classic collective behaviour accounts of social movement action.

contentious politics A range of politics that exist outside of formal institutions and against dominant power holders. A term that was popularized by Charles Tilly and that is associated with social movement perspectives.

Co-operative Commonwealth Federation *See* CCF.

core, semi-peripheral, and peripheral countries The three categories of states recognized by Immanuel Wallerstein's world systems theory. **Core** countries are those that are industrialized and rely on the importing of raw resources and exporting of goods to other countries. **Peripheral** countries are those that are underdeveloped and that depend on the core countries, to which they export primary commodities and resources for processing. **Semi-peripheral** countries are those that fall between the two.

counter-hegemony The ability to launch oppositional views that challenge existing power holders. An alternative ideology and cultural understanding that challenges the existing and dominant power holders. A term associated with Antonio Gramsci's writings. *See also* hegemony.

critical junctures Moments that resist organizational trends and inertia and that contribute to institutional change. A term linked to institutionalist accounts of power and politics.

cultural and social capital The value that is embedded in cultural and social resources that can be exchanged and drawn upon. It facilitates exchanges between people, understandings of the world, social networks, trust, and obligations.

culture The norms, meanings, values, mores, and knowledge of a society. Often used in reference to art, literature, scholarship, and other forms of knowledge but also includes everyday practices and customs.

culture industry The political economy involved in the production of norms, meanings, values, mores, knowledge, and customs of a society through media, art, literature, and entertainment. A term that is associated with the work of Max Horkheimer and Theodor Adorno. They argued that the culture industry was a total power that led to standardization and homogenization of culture and the disempowerment of the mass public.

culture shift The transition by industrial societies to post-materialist lifestyles in which citizens begin to structure politics around culture and lifestyle needs. A term popularized by Ronald Inglehart.

cyborg Hybrid adaptation between humans and technology. For instance the use of eyeglasses as a part of a person or car and driver. It is a metaphor used by Donna Haraway in her analysis of human and non-human relations.

decoding A process of searching for the latent or underlying meanings that imbue cultural and social symbols. The opposite of encoding.

deconstruct To look for underlying meanings in order to understand how the social world works. A term linked to post-modern perspectives and cultural studies.

decolonization A process of ridding foreign states of their power over overseas territories. A process linked with independence movements that emerged in the mid-twentieth century.

democracy A governance structure that is associated with majority rule and individual citizenship or civil rights. Variations of this system are found in North America, Western Europe and most industrial countries. It should not be confused with capitalism, which is an economic system.

dependency theory An explanation of global inequality that emerged in the 1950s and 1960s. It saw that poorer resource rich countries are largely dependent on exporting their resources to rich industrial countries and this leads to their continued under-development. Theorists of this approach, such as Andre Gunder Frank, believed this was the result of colonization and the international relations created in its aftermath.

discrimination The act of distinguishing differences among people or things. It can also be linked with prejudice, where people not only make distinctions but also exercise hierarchical and predetermined bias toward members of various groups.

dominant An advantaged position in hierarchical relationships. A person in such a position tends to hold more power than those in subordinate social positions.

dominant meaning or reading The interpretation of a text that was intended by the author and that fits with dominant norms and understandings. One of three forms of encoding and decoding meanings of cultural and social texts identified by Stuart Hall.

double ghetto The marginalization of women's work in both the public and private spheres. A term coined by Pat and Hugh Armstrong to highlight the obstacles women face in both spheres.

dramaturgy The practice of understanding the social world as a stage where roles and interactions take place. A sociological perspective that is linked to Erving Goffman and symbolic interactionism.

Ebonics A dialect of American English spoken by many African Americans. In the 1990s some schools and school boards in the US considered whether to adopt it as the language of instruction in regions where it was used by the majority of students.

empire A political unit that extends across a number of territories and predates the modern state as a container of politics by many centuries. A term that has increasingly been applied to the American sphere of influence since the fall of the Soviet Union left the US as the sole superpower.

encoding The act of imbuing a cultural or social text with meaning. The opposite of decoding. A term that is common among those who do cultural studies and interpretive analyses of societies.

esprit de corps A French expression that means common spirit of morale, camaraderie, and loyalty to a group.

ethnic competition (model) The notion that when an ethnic group gains control of greater material resources and access to better education, it becomes more able to make claims and demands on behalf of the group. Some have theorized that this is linked with rise of contentious action and conflict.

export processing zone (EPZ) Special area within a state where its tariff restrictions, laws, and labour practices are not fully enforced and goods are produced for export to other countries. Such zones usually house foreign companies that exploit local workers. The *maquiladoras* along the northern Mexican border with the US is an example of an EPZ.

fair-trade movement A consumer movement that aims to establish fairer exchange value or pricing for various goods, such as coffee, chocolate, sugar, cotton, hemp, and so forth.

false consciousness Misunderstanding by a person of his or her lot in life and the wider social structure and relationships that shape power and politics. A term that was coined by Karl Marx.

Fascism A governance structure that promotes authoritarian, nationalist, and hierarchical government structures.

feminist Someone who promotes the interests and study of issues relating to women. It is both a term to refer to a member of a political movement and a stream of academic analysis that emphasizes the concerns of women.

feudal period (feudalism) A social system and form of governance between about 700 and 1600 CE, predating the Industrial Revolution. It was based on a set of reciprocal legal and military obligations due to a weak monarchy and was caste-like in its distinction between elites and land owners versus peasants.

field In sociological analysis, a setting that is defined by a range of underlying relationships and processes. It is associated with the work of Pierre Bourdieu.

foreign direct investment (FDI) An investment in enterprises outside of the state economy of the investor. It is often cited by globalization theorists as a sign of changing material relationships because it represents the flow of capital across national borders.

Frankfurt School A school of critical neo-Marxist social theory. Some of its main figures were Theodor Adorno, Max Horkheimer, Herbert Marcuse, and Jurgen Habermas.

front stage The place where people act the roles and expectations of the broader society. A term associated with the dramaturgical approach theorized by Erving Goffman. In this approach people negotiate their everyday life through different stages. *See also* back stage.

G8 Group of eight. A forum for the discussion of primarily international trade and other economic matters by rich countries. Its members are Canada, France, Germany, Italy, Japan, Russia, the United Kingdom, and the United States.

gay pride The celebration of LGBT identities and orientations.

genocide The purposeful and systematic elimination, by murder or other means, of a group of people considered by perpetrators to be somehow distinct.

glass ceiling An invisible barrier that prevents the upward mobility of subordinate groups. It is often used to refer to barriers to promotion and wage increases. It is a concept that has been theorized and applied at length by a number of feminist scholars as well as those contesting racial and ethnic discrimination.

globalization A social process in which the constraints of geographic, economic, cultural, and social arrangements have receded and have been replaced with processes that extend beyond state boundaries to a global scale.

governmentality A state of experience where people regulate and limit their own behaviour without formal enforcement by institutions of power, such as the state. A term coined by Michel Foucault.

hegemony the dominance of ideology and culture by an elite group to the point that few alternatives exist or can be imagined. *See also* counter-hegemony.

high culture Norms, meanings, values, mores, and knowledge of an elite. Often it is represented through obscure art, literature, or scholarship that requires detailed knowledge and is often treated as being more authentic, specialized, organic, experiential, and active than popular or mass culture.

human capital The value associated with a person's skills, education, knowledge and capabilities. A term that is often used in the sociology of labour markets and economy.

ideal type A tool for social analysis promoted by Max Weber. It is a model against which sociologists can compare social observations in order to understand variations in different institutions and organizations.

imagined communities Shared collective identities generated by nations through the creation of new symbols of cultural and social attachment, such as languages, newspapers, flags, maps, or other artefacts that define a nation. The concept was coined by Benedict Anderson.

imperialism Unequal economic, political, cultural, social and territorial relationships based on empires that extend across states.

income distribution The range of earnings by the members of a nation or other entity, from the lowest to the highest.

Indian Acts A series of Canadian Acts that govern the affairs of status Indians and specifies the formal relationship and responsibilities of the Canadian state to them.

Industrial Revolution A period of rapid social, political, and economic change first occurring in Western Europe roughly from 1750 to 1850. It was associated with a major shift from agricultural and ruralbased production of goods to mechanized and urban production. Much of early sociology responds to the social consequences of these changes.

inertia The tendency of a body or organization to maintain itself unless extreme external forces alter it. The term is often used by organizational theorists to help account for path dependency of bureaucratic organizations.

institutions durable patterns of behaviour that order people's lives in relatively predictable ways. Institutions are composed of norms and social practices that have calcified to the extent that they create predictable patterns or maps of behaviour that people will usually follow.

institutional completeness The ability of an ethnic community to establish all the institutions needed to satisfy the community's needs so that a member does not have to interact with institutions outside of it. The term was coined by Raymond Breton.

institutional isomorphic change The tendency for organizations outside the state to come into alignment with the ordering of state agencies to facilitate communication and exchange with it.

(new) institutionalists Those who focus on the operation of formal organizations, networks, and states as the primary locus of power relations and political processes.

instrumental (In reference to a person's actions) serving to maximize outcomes to his or her benefit; treated as useful for exercising one's will or attaining a goal. Instrumentality is often an assumption of exchange theory, game theory, and rational choice theory.

International Court of Justice (ICJ) Also known as the World Court. A judicial court that is supported by the United Nations to settle legal disputes among states.

iron cage The limiting effects of increased rationalization and bureaucratization of a social system on individuals and groups within it. A term coined by Max Weber.

jargon Technical and specialized terms of a particular profession or group that most other people do not know. They are learned terms that are a mark specialized knowledge.

joual The dialect of French spoken by working-class Quebecers.

latent Underlying, observed indirectly, or hidden. It is the opposite of manifest. Political sociology engages latent processes that shape the contestation of power.

League of Nations An international organization that pre-dates the United Nations. It existed between 1920 and 1946 and at its peak it had fifty-eight member states. It was largely deemed a failure because of its inability to resolve the conflicts that led to the Second World War.

LGBT An abbreviation for lesbian, gay, bisexual, and transgender. It is increasingly used to refer to members of those communities.

liberal democracy Government structure that combines democratic practices with the philosophy of individual rights and freedoms. Such governance structures are associated with the US, Western European, and many industrial countries of the world.

liberalism A political doctrine that prizes the rights of individuals and civil liberties or freedom. It can be paired with the support of individual citizenship and civil rights, often to counter the power of formal institutions.

liberté, égalité, fraternité French for 'liberty, equality, brotherhood'. The slogan of the French Revolution. It is often associated with the initial principles of liberalism and individual-based human rights.

life chances The opportunities a person has as a result of his or her position in relation to material, cultural and social, and institution sources of power. It is a concept that was coined by Max Weber.

manifest Seen, directly observed, or apparent. The opposite of latent. Political sociology uses manifest evidence to engage the latent processes that shape the contestation of power.

manufacturing consent The title of an influential book by Edward S. Herman and Noam Chomsky on how media reflect elite interests and how they are used to elicit compliance and acquiescence by everyday people. In their book they articulate a 'propaganda model' consisting of five filters: size and concentration of ownership, advertising as a means making money, reliance on experts, the use of flak to discredit critics, and ideology (specifically anti-communist). The book should not be confused with Michael Burawoy's work of the same name.

market worth The value of something, such as labour or a product, determined by what people are willing to pay for it. The term is often used in the sociology of labour markets to talk about wages and by those adopting a political economic perspective.

Matthew effect The observation that those who hold power often generate disproportionately more power and that as a result it is difficult for those in subordinate positions to achieve upward mobility or status. Named by Robert K. Merton after biblical verse, Matthew 25: 29, which says, 'For to all those who have, more will be given, and they will have an abundance; but from those who have nothing, even what they have will be taken away.'

means of production The material resources with which humans engage to produce their material needs. Karl Marx recognized that those who control these resources hold more power and advantage over others who do not. This is because those that do not control the means of production are dependent on those that control it to produce a livelihood.

meritocratic The principle that everyone should and does have equal life chances or opportunities and that reward and achievement are based on individual merit. It is a concept that is often paired with tenets of liberal thought.

Millennium Development Goals An agenda endorsed by the United Nations to fight global poverty and improve human existence.

minimum wage The lowest hourly pay that is legal, which is set by provincial and territorial governments in Canada. At the time of publication, adult minimum wages across Canada were $8.75 (British Columbia), $8.80 (Alberta), $9.00 Yukon, $9.25 (Saskatchewan), $9.30 (Prince Edward Island), $9.50 (Manitoba and New Brunswick), $9.65 (Nova Scotia and Quebec), $10.00 (Newfoundland and Northwest Territories), $10.25 (Ontario), and $11.00 (Nunavut). Some differences in rates exist in some provinces for different specialized industries and workers under the age of 18.

mobilities A term used by John Urry to reflect the study of the movement of people and things. He argues that the contemporary world has seen both an increase in movement and the speed by which it occurs. He encourages social scientists to begin looking at movement as a social process shaping relationships.

mobility *See* social mobility.

mobilization A generic term that refers to collective behaviour. It is often used by scholars of social movements to mean contentious action, such as protest, and or the formation of organizations to sustain it.

modernist, modernism, modernity Refers to a movement toward rationality, systematicity, and progress and is often associated with the pursuit of scientific knowledge. It is also linked with twentieth-century societies, though many have argued that by the mid-1970s the most developed societies have entered into a new period of late-modernity or even globalization.

multiculturalism The existence of several cultures, ethnicities, and races within one country or entity. In Canada, it is also an official policy.

multilateral Agreements or negotiations between three or more states or power holders.

NAFTA *See* North American Free Trade Agreement.

nationalism The feeling and/or promotion of solidarity and identification with a single nation, at times in opposition to other nations or ethnic groups. It is also associated with the move of other nations to seek sovereignty from colonizers and for nations to seek statehood.

nation-state The pairing of a single nation, or national identity, with the governance of a territory and set of institutions. A type of state that governs and is constituted by a single nation.

nations within A term used by many Aboriginal peoples to distinguish nations that have been colonized within a nation-state but that do not necessarily seek their own state.

negotiated meaning or reading One of three forms of encoding and decoding meanings of cultural and social texts identified by Stuart Hall. It is a mix of the author's intended interpretation of his or her texts, which fits with more dominant norms and understandings, and unintended interpretations by audiences that in essence change how texts are constructed.

New Left A social movement of the 1960s and 1970s that sought to broaden leftist politics away from traditional class- and material-based mobilization to include social and cultural goals. It was also associated with democratic and non-hierarchical values and with the hippie movement of the same era.

newly industrializing country A state that has begun to make a transition from peripheral or semi-peripheral status to core status. These include former underdeveloped states that industrialized rapidly in the 1970s to become some of the world's manufacturing powerhouses. Examples include Korean and Taiwan.

new social movements (NSM) Movements that are based on the pursuit of collective identity and lifestyle goals rather than more traditional union or class-based movements. Often the goal of these movements is the very act of mobilizing and gaining recognition. These movements are associated with the politics of the 1960s and 1970s and the emergence of post-industrial societies. It is also a branch of social movement theory that focuses on identity based mobilization.

NGO (non-governmental organization) An organization that is independent of the state and business and is a part of civil society.

noble(s) Member of a privileged class that is associated with monarchical rule. It is often hereditary and can be understood as the aristocracy of a society.

normal science The routine work of scientists that subscribe to a given paradigm, theory, set of understandings, or assumptions. Thomas Kuhn coined the term to illustrate why established scientific norms face few challenges against their underlying assumptions.

North American Free Trade Agreement (NAFTA) A multilateral trade agreement that lifts most trade restrictions among Canada, Mexico, and the United States. It came into effect in January of 1994.

nouveau riche (French for 'new rich'). A person who has acquired his or her wealth recently (as opposed to inheriting it) but who does not necessarily have the status and cultural and social capital of more established elites.

oligopoly Control of a society by a small number of individuals, groups, organizations, or institutions. This situation is often disadvantageous to those who do not belong to the small group and who seek to gain or challenge its power.

oppositional meaning or reading An unintended interpretation of a text by audiences, which in essence changes how meaning is constructed and read. One of three forms of encoding and decoding meanings of cultural and social texts identified by Stuart Hall.

organic intellectual An academic that appeals to the mass public and uses accessible and relevant language and experiences in doing so. It is a term coined by Antonio Gramsci, who advocated the use of education and commentary in creating working-class and counter-hegemonic culture. It is similar to the notion of public intellectual advanced by Michael Burawoy.

Orientalism A term used by Edward Said to refer to Western exoticization and misinterpretation of Middle Eastern and North African cultures. Commonly used in post-colonial literatures and cultural studies to highlight unequal power relations in the construction of cultural and social understandings.

paradigm A common body of knowledge and set of scientific assumptions that drive the research of a scientific community. A term used by Thomas Kuhn.

part-time work Job where an employee works less than thirty hours per week in the paid labour force and therefore is often not entitled to the benefits, pensions, and other 'perks' of full-time work.

party power The type of power found in having access to and control of formal politics and institutions. One of the three forms of power that Weber identifies in addition to class and status.

path dependency The way in which current and future decisions or opportunities are limited by past circumstances. A form of inertia in organizational politics and mobilization.

patriarchy A society where governance and culture are dominated by men. It can also refer to a male-headed family structure.

peasants (peasantry) A social class of people who work the land in agricultural societies but do not own it. Because of this they lack access to and control of material resources and power.

performance (performing) Metaphors used to refer to the negotiation of social processes.

periphery *See* core.

pluralism A governance structure that has more than one centre of power and which allows for competition among groups to affect government policy and the state. Such forms of governance can exist with or without democratic practices. In political science the 'pluralist' tradition understands the state and its operations as the manifestation of the will of groups in civil society freely and 'voluntarily' competing to affect government policy.

political economy A sociological tradition that emerged out of Marxist and Weberian understandings of societies. It tends to emphasize the analysis of material resources, institutions, and power relations and their influence on various social processes.

political opportunities Changes in social structures and relations of power that signal when it is advantageous or disadvantageous to mobilize or act politically. It is also a perspective in the social movement literature that emphasizes the importance of shifting structures of power.

political process The dynamic contestation of power among dominant elites and subordinate challengers. It is also associated with a branch of social movement theory.

popular culture, mass culture Norms, meanings, values, mores, and knowledge of everyday people. Often it is represented through commercial art and literature that requires little specialized knowledge and is at times considered less authentic, specialized, organic, experiential, and active than traditional or high culture.

post-colonialism A paradigm that looks at experiences of the colonized and the after-effects of colonialism. It is associated with scholars writing in the post–Second World War era and with the rise of nationalist and independence movements.

power resource theory (PRT) A theory that the distribution of power between classes affects the nature of a society's governing and other institutions. Increased working-class power is seen as producing more egalitarian institutions and societies.

preferred meaning or reading *See* dominant meaning or reading.

prejudice A conclusions drawn before seeing evidence that might challenge it. It is often associated with negative views of people that rely on stereotypes.

proletariat The masses of workers who do not have access to or control over the means of production. They are in an subservient, oppositional, and dialectic relationship with the bourgeoisie, who do control the modes and means of production. A term coined by Karl Marx.

propaganda model *See* manufacturing consent.

proxy A thing that represents something or someone else. Often in social science there are no direct measures of latent processes, so researchers rely on observable representations of them in order to advance theirclaims. For example, theoretically one might think of poverty; practically is can be seen when people have less money. In this example, money is a proxy used to measure poverty.

public sociology A type of sociology that focuses on engaging everyday people and on using sociology in everyday life. One of four types introduced by Michael Burawoy to describe the work of sociologists. It is similar to the earlier notion of organic intellectual advocated by Antonio Gramsci.

Quiet Revolution The massive and rapid transition in the mid-twentieth century that marked the rise of the Quebec state, the decline of the Catholic Church in the province, the rise in levels of education, the lowering of birth rates, and a move from agricultural to industrial production.

racialize, racialization The process of categorizing, labelling, and stereotyping people on the basis of ascribed biological, or 'racial' characteristics.

rational choice theory A sociological perspective advocated by James Coleman, which uses applied mathematics to help determine the decision and choices people will make in different social situations. It is similar to exchange theory and game theory and assumes that people are instrumental.

reductionist Describes the practice of offering an explanation of a complex social process or solution to a complex problem that simplifies the process or problem. Many argue that this occurs at the cost of seeing important processes that might offer better accounts.

relative deprivation theory A perspective that sees mobilization as related to the lack of control of resources that one feels entitled to.

repertoire The range of options, tactics, and actions that contentious actors use in their politics. It is a concept that was popularized by the work of Charles Tilly.

resource mobilization theory (RMT) A social movement perspective that looks at the material, human capital, and organizational resources needed to mobilize contentious actors. It is also an account that sees mobilization as rational and instrumental.

role The expected ways of engaging in social situations and the expectations associated with different markers and status.

schema, schemata A mental picture, understanding, or ontology of the world that influences how a person interprets it.

section 15 (s. 15) The equality clause of the Charter of Rights and Freedoms that is part of the Canadian Constitution. It states:

> **15.** (1) Every individual is equal before and under the law and has the right to the equal protection and equal benefit of the law without discrimination and, in particular, without discrimination based on race, national or ethnic origin, colour, religion, sex, age, or mental or physical disability.
> (2) Subsection (1) does not preclude any law, program or activity that has as its object the amelioration of conditions of disadvantaged individuals or groups including those that are disadvantaged because of race, national or ethnic origin, colour, religion, sex, age, or mental or physical disability

section 16 (s. 16) The official-languages clause of the Charter of Rights and Freedoms and Canadian Constitution. It states:

> **16.** (1) English and French are the official languages of Canada and have equality of status and equal rights and privileges as to their use in all institutions of the Parliament and government of Canada.
> (2) English and French are the official languages of New Brunswick and have equality of status and equal rights and privileges as to the use in all institutions of the legislature and government of New Brunswick.
> (3) Nothing in this Charter limits the authority of Parliament or a legislature to advance the equality of status or use of English and French.
> **16.1** (1) The English linguistic community and the French linguistic community in New Brunswick have equality of status and equal rights and privileges, including the right to distinct educational institutions and such distinct cultural institutions as are necessary for the preservation and promotion of those communities.
> (2) The role of the legislature and the government of New Brunswick to preserve and promote the status, rights and privileges referred to in subsection (1) is affirmed.

section 25 (s. 25) A 'general' part of the Charter of Rights and Freedoms and Canadian Constitution that deals with aboriginal rights. It states:

> **25.** The guarantee in this Charter of certain rights and freedoms shall not be construed so as to abrogate or derogate from any aboriginal, treaty or other rights or freedoms that pertain to the aboriginal peoples of Canada including
> *(a)* any rights or freedoms that have been recognized by the Royal Proclamation of October 7, 1763; and
> *(b)* any rights or freedoms that now exist by way of land claims agreements or may be so acquired.

section 35 (s. 35) The rights of Aboriginal peoples of Canada clause of the Canadian Constitution. It states:

> **35.** (1) The existing aboriginal and treaty rights of the aboriginal peoples of Canada are hereby recognized and affirmed.
> (2) In this Act, "aboriginal peoples of Canada" includes the Indian, Inuit, and Métis peoples of Canada.
> (3) For greater certainty, in subsection (1) "treaty rights" includes rights that now exist by way of land claims agreements or may be so acquired.
> (4) Notwithstanding any other provision of this Act, the aboriginal and treaty rights referred to in subsection (1) are guaranteed equally to male and female persons.
> **35.1** The government of Canada and the provincial governments are committed to the principal that, before any amendment is made to Class 24 of section 91 of the "Constitution Act, 1867", to section 25 of this Act or to this Part,
> *(a)* a constitutional conference that includes in its agenda an item relating to the proposed amendment, composed of the Prime Minister of Canada and the first ministers of the provinces, will be convened by the Prime Minister of Canada; and

(b) the Prime Minister of Canada will invite representatives of the aboriginal peoples of Canada to participate in the discussions on that item.

semiotics A branch of applied structural linguistics which studies the signs and symbols used in communication and their warrant to underlying meanings.

semi-periphery *See* core.

social Pertaining to the relationships among humans and what is otherwise represented in group interactions and behaviour.

social actor A person or group of people that influences and is influenced by interactions with others.

social capital The underlying value that is associated with human and group relationships and interactions. It is one of the three forms of capital identified by Pierre Bourdieu and has been popularized in North America by the works of James Coleman and Robert Putnam.

social democracy, social democratic A mode of governance that prizes the pursuit of social justice, equity, and the use of the welfare state to promote them. It is a hybrid form of governance that embraces ideals both of traditional leftist systems and those of liberal democracy.

social forces Underlying processes that shape and affect social interactions and collective behaviour. It is also the title of one of the most prominent academic journals dealing with political sociology.

social literacy The ability to identify and understand latent social processes, but also the ability to engage, influence, and change them; that is, one's capacity to read and understand the social world, including some of the deeper, less obvious, factors that shape one's actions and experiences.

social mobility The ability to pursue opportunities and life chances that improve a person's access to and control of material, cultural and social, and institutional resources.

sociobiology A perspective in sociology that theorizes a link between innate human characteristics and social processes. It is based on evolutionary biology and has been the centre of heated debates in the social sciences.

socio-economic status (SES) The prestige that one gains as a result of one's access to and control of material resources.

sociological imagination The ability to discriminate between individual experiences and broader social trends in order to understand social relations. Some sociologists believe that this ability should be the goal of sociology. It is a term that was developed by C. Wright Mills in his book of the same name.

sociological mindfulness The ability to see the world in sociological terms. A continual reflexive conversation that helps people make sense of the world by looking for disputes over explanations and meanings for social phenomena. It is a term coined by Michael Schwalbe.

split labour market A situation in which two or more distinct groups, often ethnic or racial, compete for the same opportunities. This offers an advantage to employers and dominant power holders because it allows them to play the competing groups against one another to drive down labour costs. The split labour market theory is associated with the work of Edna Bonacich.

staples thesis An account that links a region's political and economic development to the extraction and export of raw materials or resources to more powerful states. It is a perspective that was popularized by Harold Innis in his account of the development of the Canadian state and regional differences within it.

state The primary institution and container of power in the contemporary world. It is characterized by a formal bureaucracy that largely shapes material, cultural and social, and institutional political processes.

state-centred approach A political sociological perspective that prizes the importance of states rather than other institutions in the explanation of political processes. It is associated with Theda Skocpol's call to 'bring the state back' into social analysis.

status group An aggregate of people that have the same degree of social prestige and honour. It is a concept that was introduced by Max Weber.

stereotype A cartoon, caricature or representation of a person or people that is largely inaccurate.

stratified Hierarchically ordered, arranged in layers. In relation to power this occurs when some groups control more material, cultural and social, and institutional resources than others and block others from challenging their control or gaining access to them.

strong ties Bonds between people that result in small but dense social networks. It is the opposite of weak ties, which result in large and loose networks. Together these were concepts used by Mark Granovetter to understand success in the labour market and the ability to relate to others. He found that people with weak ties were more successful in finding a job because they were better able to engage people outside of their primary social networks. These concepts contributed to latter concepts such as bonding and bridging social capital.

structure and agency (debate) A long-standing problem in sociology. Many perspectives prize the influence of social systems and institutions as determinants of social processes. Other accounts look to the role of individual choice and innovation. It was a key theoretical concern during the 1980s and 1990s and led to hybrid approaches that try to account for social forces without valuing one set of explanations over the other.

subordinate A person who is in a disadvantaged position in a hierarchical relationship. Such a person has less power than those in more dominant social positions.

superstructure The overarching culture and institutions comprising a society, the nature of which are constituted by class relations. The term was coined by Karl Marx.

technical account Explanation that is highly specialized, is based on the logic of a given academic perspective, and is often inaccessible to those that have not been trained in it. It is a term used by Charles Tilly.

third-wave feminism The first wave of the women's movement was largely associated with suffrage or acquiring voting rights for women during the early twentieth century. The second wave of the movement began to fight for equality rights more broadly in the public sphere from the 1950s to the 1970s. Once gains had been achieved on that front, the movement in the third wave began to engage issues around diversity of experience and the definition of womanhood itself. This began in the mid-1980s and continues today.

total power An entity that infringes upon every aspect of people's negotiation of social processes or power.

transnational Extending beyond the borders of a single state or country.

transnational activist network (TAN) NGOs and social movement activists that are linked by communication, travel, and exchange across the borders of a single state. The term was coined by Margaret Keck and Kathryn Sikkink.

transnationalization A process of extending economic, cultural, social, and political spheres beyond a single state or country.

UN *See* United Nations.

UNESCO (United Nations Educational, Scientific and Cultural Organization) A branch of the United Nations that is mandated with promoting international understanding, knowledge, and respect for diverse cultures.

United Auto Workers (UAW) Union representing the workers at the largest American automakers. One of the largest and most influential unions in America, if not the world. It has a long history of representing workers' rights and has largely been successful in its efforts.

United Nations (UN) An international organization that was founded after the Second World War in an attempt to promote international co-operation and resolve international conflicts through peaceful means and negotiation. It currently has 193 member states.

unit of analysis The measurement that is defined in order to offer evidence of an underlying concept.

Universal Declaration of Human Rights A thirty-article declaration endorsed by the members of the UN in 1948 to protect the interests and rights of all people. The preamble reads:

Whereas recognition of the inherent dignity and of the equal and inalienable rights of all members of the human family is the foundation of freedom, justice and peace in the world,

Whereas disregard and contempt for human rights have resulted in barbarous acts which have outraged the conscience of mankind, and the advent of a world in which human beings shall enjoy freedom of speech and belief and freedom from fear and want has been proclaimed as the highest aspiration of the common people,

Whereas it is essential, if man is not to be compelled to have recourse, as a last resort, to rebellion against tyranny and oppression, that human rights should be protected by the rule of law,

Whereas it is essential to promote the development of friendly relations between nations,

Whereas the peoples of the United Nations have in the Charter reaffirmed their faith in fundamental human rights, in the dignity and worth of the human person and in the equal rights of men and women and have determined to promote social progress and better standards of life in larger freedom,

Whereas Member States have pledged themselves to achieve, in co-operation with the United Nations, the promotion of universal respect for and observance of human rights and fundamental freedoms,

Whereas a common understanding of these rights and freedoms is of the greatest importance for the full realization of this pledge,

Now, Therefore THE GENERAL ASSEMBLY proclaims THIS UNIVERSAL DECLARATION OF HUMAN RIGHTS as a common standard of achievement for all peoples and all nations, to the end that every individual and every organ of society, keeping this Declaration constantly in mind, shall strive by teaching and education to promote respect for these rights and freedoms and by progressive measures, national and international, to secure their universal and effective recognition and observance, both among the peoples of Member States themselves and among the peoples of territories under their jurisdiction.

utopia The ideal or perfect state. It is also used to mean imaginary potential. It is a term associated with Marx's scholarship and advocacy of communism.

VAs (voluntary associations) Organizations or NGOs that rely on voluntary labour.

vertical mosaic Term used to refer to the class and ethnic stratification of Canadian society based on material, educational, social, and political resources. A term coined by John Porter.

vertical ties Strong bonds within a social group or network, as opposed to relationships between groups and networks. Similar to strong ties and bonding social capital.

wage gap The difference in wages between groups of people. Often this is represented as the difference between average wages of a dominant group and those of subordinate groups.

warlord A person who has military and civil power in a region that is not effectively governed by a state.

Wasase movement An indigenous-based strategy to mobilize Aboriginal peoples in their struggles for social justice. It is also a book by Taiaiake Alfred.

weak ties *See* strong ties.

welfare state A country that prizes social justice and redistribution of wealth and develops institutions to promote equality among their citizens. Often such a state promotes public health care, housing, and other national state-run programs.

WHO (World Health Organization) The branch of the United Nations that offers leadership on health standards, research, and practices.

work disruption Time spent out of the labour force because of a person's life course. It is often associated with women and child rearing or the periods of unemployment when people migrate to new countries. It is also linked with lower returns to human capital.

Working Group on Indigenous Populations A group setup up by the United Nations in 1982 to engage issues related to indigenous populations.

working poor Those who work at paid wage labour but still earn livelihoods that are substandard and even at or below the poverty line.

world culture (*also*** world polity, world society)** The emerging global society that is promoted by international institutions, which dictate the homogenization of cultural and social practices and knowledge.

world polity *See* world culture.

world society *See* world culture.

world-systems theory First advocated by Immanuel Wallerstein to understand inequality among states in a capitalist global economic system. He generally categorizes states into one of three groupings core, periphery and semi-periphery. *See* core.

xenophobia Dislike, or fear of, or hostility toward foreigners and people of different ethnic, racial, or national origins as well as that which is perceived as unknown.

zero-sum game A situation in which losses and gains offset each other. The term is associated with game theory.

Bibliography

Abbott, Andrew. 2001. *Time Matters: On Theory and Method*. Chicago: University of Chicago Press.

Adams, Howard. 1995. *Tortured People: The Politics of Colonization*. Penticton, BC: Theytus Books.

Adkin, Laurie, and Yasmeen Abu Laban. 2008. 'The challenge of care: Early childhood education and care in Canada and Quebec'. *Studies in Political Economy* 81 (Spring): 49–76.

Aizlewood, Amanda, and Ravi Pendakur. 2005. 'Ethnicity and social capital in Canada'. *Canadian Ethnic Studies* 37 (2): 77–102.

Alapuro, Risto. 2008. 'Russian and Estonian civil society discourses compared'. In *Media, Culture and Society in Putin's Russia*, edited by S. White. New York: Palgrave Macmillan.

Albrow, Martin. 1997. *The Global Age: State and Society Beyond Modernity*. Standford, Calif.: Stanford University Press.

Alfred, Taiaiake. 2005. *Wasase: Indigenous Pathways of Action and Freedom*. Peterborough, Ont.: Broadview Press.

Almey, Marcia. 2007. *Women in Canada: Work Chapter Updates*. Cat. 89F0133XIE. Ottawa: Statistics Canada.

Alston, Philip. 1994. 'The best interest principle: Towards a reconciliation of culture and human rights'. *International Journal of Law and the Family* 8 (1): 1–25.

Anderson, Benedict. [1983] 1991. *Imagined Communities: Reflections on the Origin and Spread of Nationalism*. New York: Verso.

Andersen, Robert, James Curtis, and Edward Grabb. 2006. 'Trends in civic association activity in four democracies: The special case of women in the United States'. *American Sociological Review*. 71 (3): 376–400.

Annan, Kofi. 1998. 'The unpaid bill that's crippling the UN'. *New York Times*, 9 Mar. www.nytimes.com/1998/03/09/opinion/the-unpaid-bill-that-s-crippling-the-un.html. Accessed 23 Oct., 2011.

Appadurai, Arjun. 1990. 'Disjuncture and difference in the global cultural economy.' *Theory, Culture and Society* 7 (2): 295–310. Durham, NC: Duke University Press.

Applebome, Peter. 1996. 'Scholl district elevates status of Black English'. *New York Times*, Dec. 20. http://www.nytimes.com/1996/12/20/us/school-district-elevates-status-of-black-english.html. Accessed 4 April, 2011.

Armstrong, Pat and Hugh Armstrong. 2010. *The Double Ghetto: Canadian Women and Their Segregated Work*. 3rd edn. Don Mills, Ont.: Oxford University Press.

Arthur, James, and Jon Davison. 2000. 'Social literacy and citizenship education in the school curriculum'. *Curriculum Journal* 11 (1): 9–23.

Avery, Donald. 1975. 'Continental European immigrant workers in Canada 1896–1919: From "stalwart peasants" to radical proletariat'. *Canadian Review of Sociology and Anthropology* 12 (1): 53–64.

Bacon, Francis. [1597] 1613. *The Essaies of Sir Francis Bacon*. London: Laggard. Book contributor: University of Toronto (Thomas Fisher Rare Book Library). http://www.archive.org/details/essaiesofsfranc00baco. Accessed 2 Sept., 2011.

Baer, Douglas, and Ronald D. Lambert. 1982. 'Education and support for dominant ideology'. *Canadian Review of Sociology and Anthropology* 19 (2): 173–95.

Baer, Douglas, Edward Grabb, and William A. Johnston. 1990. 'The values of Canadians and Americans: A critical analysis and reassessment'. *Social Forces* 68 (3): 693–713.

Baer, Douglas, Edward Grabb, and William A. Johnston. 1991. 'Economic dissatisfaction, potential unionism and attitudes toward unions in Canada'. *Canadian Review of Sociology and Anthropology* 28 (1): 67–83.

Baer, Douglas, Edward Grabb and William Johnston. 1993. 'National character, regional culture, and the values of Canadians and Americans'. *Canadian Review of Sociology and Anthropology* 30 (1): 13–36.

Baer, Douglas, James Curtis, and Edward Grabb. 2001. 'Has volunteer activity declined? Cross-national analyses for fifteen countries'. *Canadian Review of Sociology and Anthropology* 38 (3): 249–74.

Bannerji, Himani. 1995. *Thinking Through: Essays on Feminism, Marxism and Anti-Racism*. Toronto: Women's Press.

Bannerji, Himani. 2000. *The Dark Side of the Nation: Essays on Multiculturalism, Nationalism and Gender*. Toronto: Canadian Scholars' Press.

Bannerji, Himani. 2005. 'Building from Marx: Reflections on class and race'. *Social Justice* 32 (4): 144–60.

Barber, Benjamin. 1995. *Jihad vs McWorld: How Globalization and Tribalism are Reshaping the World*. New York: Times.

Barnes, Andre. 2010. *Youth Voter Turnout in Canada: 1. Trends and Issues*. Publication no. 2010-19E. Parliamentary Information and Research Service. Ottawa: Library of Parliament. http://www.parl.gc.ca/Content/LOP/ResearchPublications/2010-19-e.htm#a5. Accessed 28 April, 2011.

Barrett, Michèle. 1980. *Women's Oppression Today: Problems in Marxist Feminist Analysis*. New York: Verso.

Barthes, Roland. 1977. *Elements of Semiology*. New York: Hill and Wang.

Bauman, Zygmunt. 2000. *Liquid Modernity*. Malden, Mass.: Blackwell.

Beaumont, Peter, and Joanna Walters. 2007. 'Greenspan Admits Iraq was about oil, as deaths put at 1.2m'. *Observer*, 16 September. http://www.guardian.co.uk/world/2007/sep/16/iraq.iraqtimeline. Accessed 31 Oct., 2010.

Béland, Daniel. 2005. 'Ideas and social policy: An institutionalist perspective'. *Social Policy and Administration* 39 (1): 1–18.

Béland, Daniel. 2006. 'The politics of social learning: Finance, institutions, and pension reform in the United States and Canada'. *Governance* 19 (4): 559–83.

Béland, Daniel, and André Lecours. 2008. *Nationalism and Social Policy: The Politics of Territorial Solidarity*. New York: Oxford University Press.

Benston, Margaret. 1969. 'The political economy of women's liberation'. *Monthly Review* 21 (4): 13–27.

Berman, Sheri. 1997. 'Civil Society and the Collapse of the Weimar Republic'. *World Politics* 49 (3): 401–29.

Bezanson, Kate. 2006. 'Gender and the limits of social capital'. *Canadian Review of Sociology and Anthropology* 43 (4): 427–43.

Bhabha, Jacqueline. 2004. 'The "mere fortuity" of birth? Are children citizens?' *Differences* 15 (2): 91–117.

Bianco, Anthony. 2006. 'No union please, we're Wal-Mart.' *Bloomberg Businessweek* http://www.businessweek.com/magazine/content/06_07/b3971115.htm. Accessed 22 Oct., 2011.

Black, Don, and John Myles. 1986. 'Dependent industrialization and the Canadian class structure: A comparative analysis of Canada, the United States, and Sweden.'

Canadian Review of Sociology and Anthropology 23 (2): 157–81.

Bloomberg Businessweek. 2009. '100 Best Brands'. http://www.businessweek.com/interactive_reports/best_global_brands_2009.html. Accessed 9 Aug., 2011.

Bob, Clifford. 2005. *The Marketing of Rebellion: Insurgents, Media, and International Activism*. New York: Cambridge University Press.

Bohlen, Celestine. 2001. 'Think tank: In new war on terrorism, words are weapons, too'. *New York Times*, 29 Sept. www.nytimes.com/2001/09/29/arts/think-tank-in-new-war-on-terrorism-words-are-weapons-too.html. Accessed 23 Oct., 2011.

Boli, John. 1987. 'World polity sources of expanding state authority and organization, 1870–1970'. Pp. 71–91 in *Institutional Structure: Constituting State, Society and the Individual*, edited by G.M. Thomas, J.W. Meyer, F.O. Ramirez, and J. Boli. Newbury Park, Calif.: Sage.

Boli, John, and George M. Thomas. 1997. 'World culture in the world polity: A century of international non-governmental organization'. *American Sociological Review* 62 (2): 171–90.

Boli-Bennett, John and John W. Meyer. 1978. 'The ideology of childhood and the state: Rules distinguishing children in national constitutions, 1870–1970'. *American Sociological Review* 43 (6): 797–812.

Bonacich, Edna. 1972. 'A theory of ethnic antagonism: The split labor market'. *American Sociological Review* 37 (5): 547–59.

Boswell, Terry, and Christopher Chase-Dunn. 1996. 'The Future of the World-System'. *International Journal of Sociology and Social Policy* 16 (7/8): 148–79.

Boswell, Terry, and Christopher Chase-Dunn. 2000. *The Spiral of Capitalism and Socialism: Toward Global Democracy*. Boulder, Colo.: Lynne Rienner.

Boudreau, Vincent. 1996. 'Northern theory, southern protest: Opportunity structure analysis in cross-national perspective'. *Mobilization* 1 (2): 175–89.

Bourdieu, Pierre. [1986] 2001. 'The forms of capital'. Pp. 96–111 in *The Sociology of Economic Life*. 2nd edn., edited by M.S. Granovetter and R. Swedberg. Boulder, Colo.: Westview Press.

Bourdieu, Pierre. 1984. *Distinction: A Social Critique of the Judgement of Taste*. Cambridge, Mass.: Harvard University Press.

Bowden, Gary. 1989. 'Labour unions in the public mind: The Canadian case'.

Canadian Review of Sociology and Anthropology 26 (5): 723–42.

Bowden, Gary. 1990. 'From sociology to theology: A reply to Lipset'. *Canadian Review of Sociology and Anthropology* 27 (4): 536–9.

Brady, David, Jason Beckfield, and Martin Seeleib-Kaiser. 2005. 'Economic globalization and the welfare state in affluent democracies, 1975–2001'. *American Sociological Review* 70 (6): 921–48.

Bramham, Daphne. 2009. 'Olympics Bill Tops $6 Billion—So Far'. *Vancouver Sun*, 23 Jan. http://www.vancouversun.com/Sports/Olympics+bill+tops+billion/1207886/story.html. Accessed 24 Oct., 2011.

Braverman, Harry. 1974. *Labor and Monopoly Capital: The Degradation of Work in the Twentieth Century*. New York: Monthly Review Press.

Breton, Raymond. 1964. 'Institutional completeness of ethnic communities and the personal relations of immigrants'. *American Journal of Sociology* 70 (2): 193–205.

Breton, Raymond. 1998. 'Ethnicity and race in social organization: Recent developments in Canadian society'. Pp. 60–115 in *The Vertical Mosaic Revisited*, edited by R. Helmes-Hayes and J. Curtis. Toronto: University of Toronto Press.

Breton, Raymond. 2003. 'Social Capital and the Civic Participation of Immigrants and Members of Ethno-Cultural Groups'. Paper presented at the *Conference on The Opportunities and Challenges of Diversity: A Role for Social Capital?* Montreal, November.

Brinton, Mary C., and Victor Nee (eds). 1998. *The New Institutionalism in Sociology*. New York: Russell Sage.

Brubaker, Rogers. 1994. 'Nationhood and the national question in the Soviet Union and post-Soviet Eurasia: An institutionalist account'. *Theory and Society* 23 (1): 47–78.

Brubaker, Rogers. 1996. *Nationalism Reframed: Nationhood and the National Question in the New Europe*. New York: Cambridge University Press.

Brubaker, Rogers. 1998. 'Myths and misconceptions in the study of nationalism'. Pp. 272–305 in *The State of the Nation: Ernest Gellner and the Theory of Nationalism*, edited by J. Hall. New York: Cambridge University Press.

Brubaker, Rogers, Mara Loveman, and Peter Stamatov. 2004. 'Ethnicity as cognition'. *Theory and Society* 33 (1): 31–64.

Bruce, Steve. 2000. *Sociology: A Very Short Introduction*. New York: Oxford University Press.

Brym, Robert J. 1980. *Intellectuals and Politics*. London: George Allen and Unwin.

Brym, Robert J., and Bader Araj. 2006. 'Suicide bombing as strategy and interaction: The case of the Second Intifada'. *Social Forces* 84 (4): 1969–86.

Brym, Robert J., and Bader Araj. 2008. 'Palestinian suicide bombing revisited: A critique of the outbidding thesis'. *Political Science Quarterly* 123 (3): 485–500.

Brym, Robert J., and Bonnie J. Fox. 1989. *From Culture to Power: The Sociology of English Canada*. Toronto.: Oxford University Press.

Brym, Robert J., Michael W. Gillespie, and Rhonda L. Lenton. 1989. 'Class power, class mobilization, and class voting: The Canadian case'. *Canadian Journal of Sociology* 14 (1): 25–44.

Brym, Robert J., and Rhonda L. Lenton. 2001. *Love Online: A Report on Digital Dating in Canada*. Toronto: MSN.CA.

Brym, Robert J., and Barbara Neis. 1978. 'Regional factors in the formation of the Fishermen's Protective Union of Newfoundland'. *Canadian Journal of Sociology* 3 (4): 391–407.

Brym, Robert J., and R. James Sacouman. 1979. *Underdevelopment and Social Movements in Atlantic Canada*. Toronto: New Hogtown Press.

Brym, Robert J., and Celine Saint-Pierre. 1997. 'Sociology around the world (Part 2): Canada: Canadian sociology'. *Contemporary Sociology* 26 (5): 543–6.

Burawoy, Michael. 2004. 'Public sociologies: Contradictions, dilemmas, and possibilities'. *Social Forces* 82 (4): 1603–18.

Businessweek. See *Bloomberg Businessweek*

Butler, Judith. 1990. *Gender Trouble: Feminism and the Subversion of Identity*. New York: Routledge.

Calhoun, Craig. 1993. '"New social movements" of the early nineteenth century'. *Social Science History* 17 (3): 385–427.

Camfield, David. 2008. 'The working-class movement in Canada: An overview'. In *Group Politics and Social Movements in Canada*, edited by M. Smith. Peterborough, Ont.: Broadview Press.

Canada. Indian and Northern Affairs Canada. 1996. *Report of the Royal Commission on Aboriginal Peoples* (Vol. 1, Part 2). http://www.collectionscanada.gc.ca/webarchives/20071124124337/http://www.ainc-inac.gc.

ca/ch/rcap/sg/sgm9_e.html. Accessed 6 Aug., 2011.

Canadian Civil Liberties Association. 2011. 'G8 and G20'. http://ccla.org/our-work/focus-areas/g8-and-g20/. Accessed 8 Aug., 2011.

Caranci, Beata, and Pascal Gauthier. 2010. *Career Interrupted—The Economic Impact of Motherhood*. TD Bank Financial Group Special Report, 12 Oct. http://www.td.com/economics/special/bc1010_career_interrupted.pdf. Last accessed 30 Oct., 2010.

Carroll, William K. 1986. *Corporate Power and Canadian Capitalism*. Vancouver: University of British Columbia Press.

Carroll, William K. 2004. *Corporate Power in a Globalizing World: A Study in Elite Social Organization*. Don Mills, Ont.: Oxford University Press.

Carroll, William K. 2007. 'From Canadian corporate elite to transnational capitalist class: Transitions in the organization of corporate power'. *Canadian Review of Sociology and Anthropology* 44 (1): 265–88.

Carroll, William K. 2008. 'The corporate elite and the transformation of finance capital: A view from Canada'. *Sociological Review* 56 (S1): 44–63.

Carroll, William K., and James Beaton. 2000. 'Globalization, neo-liberalism and the changing face of corporate hegemony in higher education'. *Studies in Political Economy* 62: 71–98.

Carroll, William K., and Robert A. Hackett 2006. 'Democratic media activism through the lens of social movement theory'. *Media, Culture and Society* 28 (1): 83–104.

Carroll, William K., and William Little. 2001 'Neoliberal transformation and antiglobalization politics in Canada: Transition, consolidation, resistance'. *International Journal of Political Economy* 31 (3): 33–66.

Carroll, William K., and R.S. Ratner. 1996a. 'Master Frames and counter-hegemony: Political sensibilities in contemporary social movements'. *Canadian Review of Sociology and Anthropology* 33 (4): 407–35.

Carroll, William K., and R.S. Ratner. 1996b. 'Master framing and cross-movement networking in contemporary societies'. *Sociological Quarterly* 37 (4): 601–25.

Carroll, William K., and R.S. Ratner. 2001. 'Sustaining oppositional culture in "postsocialist" times: A comparative study of three social movement organizations'. *Sociology* 35 (3): 605–29.

Castells, Manuel. 1996. *The Rise of the Network Society*, vol. 1 of *The Information Age: Economy, Society and Culture*. Malden, Mass.: Blackwell.

Castells, Manuel. 2000. *End of Millennium*, vol. 3 of *The Information Age: Economy, Society and Culture*. Malden, Mass: Blackwell.

Castells, Manuel. 2004. *The Power of Identity*, vol. 2 of *The Information Age: Economy, Society and Culture*. 2nd edn. Malden, Mass.: Blackwell.

Castells, Manuel. 2007. 'Communication, Power and Counter-power in the Network Society.' *International Journal of Communication* 1: 238–66.

Castells, Manuel. 2009. *Communication Power*. New York: Oxford University Press.

CBC. 2008. 'Voter turnout drops to record low'. http://www.cbc.ca/news/canada/story/2008/10/15/voter-turnout.html. Accessed 21 Mar., 2011.

CBC. 2010a. 'Remembering the Winnipeg General Strike'. *CBC Digital Archives*. http://archives.cbc.ca/version_print.asp?page=1&IDLan=1&IDClip=4239&IDDossier=3217&IDCat=&IDCatPa=. Accessed 20 Feb., 2011.

CBC. 2010b. 'City balks at urban chickens proposal'. *CBC News*, 9 Nov. http://www.cbc.ca/news/canada/windsor/story/2010/11/09/windsor-backyard-chicken-bylaw-scrapped.html. Accessed 15 Aug., 2011.

CBC. 2010c. 'Toronto Humane Society charges dropped'. *CBC News*, 16 Aug. http://www.cbc.ca/canada/toronto/story/2010/08/16/humane-society-charges-dropped589.html. Accessed 27 Sept., 2010.

Chase-Dunn, Christopher, and Terry Boswell. 1999. 'Postcommunism and the global commonwealth'. *Humboldt Journal of Social Relations* 24 (1–2): 195–219.

Chomsky, Noam, and David Barsamian. 2003. 'Imperial ambition'. *Monthly Review* 55 (1): 11–19.

Clark, Samuel. 1995. *State and Status: The Rise of the State and Aristocratic Power in Western Europe*. Montreal: McGill-Queen's University Press.

Clark, S.D. 1942. *Social Development of Canada*. Toronto: University of Toronto Press.

Clark, S.D. 1948. *Church and Sect in Canada*. Toronto: University of Toronto Press.

Clark, S.D. 1959. *Movements of Political Protest in Canada, 1640–1840*. Toronto: University of Toronto Press.

Clemens, Elisabeth S., and James M. Cook. 1999. 'Politics and institutionalism: Explaining durability and change'. *Annual Review of Sociology* 25: 441–66.

Clément, Dominique. 2008a. 'The October Crisis of 1970: Human rights abuses under the War Measures Act'. *Journal of Canadian Studies* 42 (2): 160–86.

Clément, Dominique. 2008b. *Canada's Rights Revolution: Social Movements and Social Change, 1937–82*. Vancouver: University of British Columbia Press.

Clement, Wallace. 1975. *The Canadian Corporate Elite: An Analysis of Economic Power*. Toronto: McClelland and Stewart.

Clement, Wallace. 1977. *Continental Corporate Power: Economic Elite Linkages Between Canada and the United States*. Toronto: McClelland and Stewart.

Clement, Wallace. 2001. 'Canadian political economy's legacy for sociology'. *Canadian Journal of Sociology* 26 (3): 405–20.

Clement, Wallace, and Glen Williams (eds). 1989. *The New Canadian Political Economy*. Kingston: McGill-Queen's Press.

Cmiel, Kenneth. 2004. 'The recent history of human rights'. *American Historical Review* 109 (1): 117–35.

Coates, Ken. 2000. *The Marshall Decision and Native Rights*. Montreal: McGill-Queen's University Press.

Coleman, James S. 1988. 'Social capital in the creation of human capital'. *American Journal of Sociology* 94: S95–S120.

Colomer, Josep. 2008. 'The European Union: A federal, democratic empire?' Pp. 280–306 in *Comparative European Politics*. 3rd edn., edited by J.M. Colomer. New York: Routledge.

Conley, Jim. 2010. 'Book Review: Fighting traffic: The dawn of the motor age in the American city'. *Canadian Review of Sociology* 47 (2): 203–5.

Conley, Jim, and Arlene Tigar McLaren (eds). 2009. *Car Troubles: Critical Studies of Auto-mobility and Auto-Mobility*. Burlington, Vt.: Ashgate.

Cooney, Mark. 1997. 'From warre to tyranny: Lethal conflict and the state'. *American Sociological Review* 62 (2): 316–38.

Cormier, Jeffrey. 2004. *The Canadianization Movement: Emergence, Survival, and Success*. Toronto: University of Toronto Press.

Cormier, Jeffrey, and D.B. Tindall. 2005. 'Wood frames: Framing the forests in British Columbia. *Sociological Focus* 38 (1): 1–24.

Cottrell, Barbara, and Madine VanderPlaat. 2011. 'My Kids Want to Eat Pork: Parent–Teen Conflicts in Immigrant Families'. Pp. 267–96 in *Immigrant Women in Atlantic Canada: Feminist Perspectives*, edited by E. Tastsoglou and P. Jaya. Toronto: CSPI/Women's Press.

Couton, Philippe, and Stéphanie Gaudet. 2008. 'Rethinking social participation: The case of immigrants in Canada'. *Journal of International Migration and Integration* 9 (1): 21–44.

Creese, Gilliam, Arlene Tigar McLaren, and Jane Pulkingham. 2009. 'Rethinking Burawoy: Reflections from Canadian feminist sociology'. *Canadian Journal of Sociology* 34 (3): 601–22.

Crick, Bernard, and Alex Porter. 1978. *Political Education and Political Literacy: The report and papers of, and the evidence submitted to, the working party of the Hansard Society's Programme for Political Education*. London: Longman.

CRTC (Canadian Radio-Television and Tele-communications Commission).

della Porta, Donatella, Massimiliano Andretta, Lorenzo Mosca, and Herbert Reiter. 2006. *Globalization from Below: Transnational Activists and Protest Networks*. Minneapolis: University of Minnesota Press.

Diani, Mario. 2000. 'Social movement networks virtual and real'. *Information, Communication and Society* (3): 386–401.

Diani, Mario, and Doug McAdam (eds). 2003. *Social Movements and Networks: Relational Approaches to Collective Action*. New York: Oxford University Press.

Dickens, Charles. 1971. *A Christmas Carol: The Original Manuscript*. Don Mills, Ont.: General.

Dimaggio, Paul, and Walter W. Powell. 1983. 'The iron cage revisited: Institutional iso-morphism and collective rationality in organizational fields'. *American Sociological Review* 48 (2): 147–60.

Dowler, Ken. 2004. 'Dual realities? Criminality, victimization, and the presen-tation of race on local television news'. *Journal of Crime and Justice* 27 (2): 79–99.

Dowler, Ken, Thomas Fleming, and Stephen L. Muzzatti. 2006. 'Constructing crime: Media, crime, and popular culture'. *Canadian Journal of Criminology and Criminal Justice* 48 (6): 837–50.

Dunleavy, Patrick, and Brendan O'Leary. 1987. *Theories of the State: The Politics of Liberal Democracy*. New York: Meredith Press.

Edwards, Bob, Michael W. Foley, and Mario Diani (eds). 2001. *Beyond Tocqueville: Civil Society and the Social Capital Debate in Comparative Perspective*. Hanover, N.H.: University Press of New England.

Edwards, Bob, and John D. McCarthy. 2004. 'Resources and social movement mobilization'. Pp. 116–52 in *The Blackwell Companion to Social Movements*, edited by D. Snow, S. Soule, and H. Kriesi. Malden, Mass.: Blackwell.

Edwards, Peter. 2003. *One Dead Indian: The Premier, the Police, and the Ipperwash Crisis*. Toronto: McClelland and Stewart.

Eisinger, Peter K. 1973. 'The conditions of protest behavior in American cities'. *American Political Science Review* 67 (1): 11–28.

Elias, Norbert. 1998. 'The civilizing of parents'. Pp. 189–211 in *The Norbert Elias Reader: A Biographical Selection*, edited by J. Goudsblom and S. Mennell. Malden, Mass.: Blackwell.

Elias, Norbert. [1939] 2000. *The Civilizing Process*. Malden, Mass.: Blackwell.

Engels, Friedrich. [1881] 1972. *The Origin of the Family, Private Property, and the State*, edited by E.B. Leacock. New York: International.

Ericson, Richard V., Patricia M. Baranek, and Janet B.L. Chan. 1987. *Visualizing Deviance: A Study of News Organization*. Toronto: University of Toronto Press.

Ericson, Richard V., Patricia Baranek, and Janet Chan. 1991. *Representing Order: Crime, Law and Justice in the News Media*. Toronto: University of Toronto Press.

Esping-Andersen, Gøsta. 1989. 'The three political economies of welfare states'. *Canadian Review of Sociology and Anthropology* 26 (1): 10–36.

Esping-Andersen, Gøsta. 1990. *The Three Worlds of Welfare Capitalism*. New Jersey: Princeton University Press.

Evans, Peter B., Dietrich Reuschemeyer, and Theda Skocpol (eds). 1985. *Bringing the State Back In*. Cambridge, UK: Cambridge University Press.

Fanon, Frantz. 1967. *Black Skin, White Masks*. New York: Grove Press.

Featherstone, Liza. 1999. 'The burger international'. *Labour/Le Travail* 43 (Spring): 301–6.

Fine, Ben. 2001. *Social Capital versus Social Theory: Political Economy and Social Science at the Turn of the Millennium*. London: Routledge.

Fleming, Michael. 2003. 'Moore's hot-potato "911" docu loses an icon'. *Variety*, 8 May. www.variety.com/article/VR1117885862?refCatId=1742. Accessed 24 Oct., 2011.

Fleras, Augie, and Jean Lock Kunz. 2001. *Media and Minorities: Representing diversity in a Multicultural Canada*. Toronto: Thompson Educational.

Fleras, Augie, and Jean Leonard Elliott. 2003. *Unequal Relations: An Introduction to Race and Ethnic Dynamics in Canada*. 4th edn. Don Mills, Ont.: Prentice Hall.

Fleury, Dominique, and Myriam Fortin. 2006. *When Working Is Not Enough to Escape Poverty: An Analysis of Canada's Working Poor*. Cat. SP-630-06-06E. Ottawa: Human Resources and Social Development Canada.

Foucault, Michel. 1991. 'Governmentality'. Pp. 87–104 in *The Foucault Effect: Studies in governmentality*, edited by G. Burchell, C. Gordon, and P. Miller. Chicago: University of Chicago Press.

Foucault, Michel. 2002. *The Order of Things: An Archaeology of the Human Sciences*. New York: Routledge.

Frank, Andre Gunder. 1967. *Capitalism and Underdevelopment in Latin America: Historical Studies of Chile and Brazil*. New York: Monthly Review Press.

Frank, David John, and John W. Meyer. 2002. 'The profusion of individual roles and identities in the postwar period'. *Sociological Theory* 20 (1): 86–105.

Frank, Thomas. 2004. *What's the Matter with Kansas? How Conservatives Won the Heart of America*. New York: Henry Holt.

Fredericton City Chickens. 2011. http://frederictoncitychickens.com/arguments-against-chickens.html. Accessed 25 Apr., 2011.

Fukuyama, Francis. 1992. *The End of History and the Last Man*. New York: Free Press.

Galabuzi, Grace-Edward. 2006. *Canada's Economic Apartheid: The Social Exclusion of Racialized Groups in the New Century*. Toronto: Canadian Scholars' Press.

Gale, Fredric G. 1994. *Political Literacy: Rhetoric, Ideology, and the Possibility of Justice*. Albany, NY: SUNY.

Gamson, William, and David Meyer. 1996. 'Framing political opportunity'. Pp. 275–90 in *Comparative Perspectives on Social Movements*, edited by D. McAdam, J.D. McCarthy, and M. Zald. New York: Cambridge University Press.

Gannon, Maire, Karen Mihorean, Karen Beattie, Andrea Taylor-Butts, and Rebecca Kong. 2005. *Criminal Justice Indicators*. Cat. 85–227–XIE. Ottawa: Statistics Canada.

Gans, Herbert J. 1974. *Popular Culture and High Culture: An Evaluation of Taste*. New York: Basic Books.

Gellner, Ernest. 1983. *Nations and National-ism*. Oxford: Blackwell.

Gellner, Ernest. [1964] 1994. 'Nationalism and modernization'. Pp. 55–63 in *Nationalism,* edited by J. Hutchinson and A.D. Smith. Oxford: Oxford University Press.

Gellner, Ernest. [1983] 2006. *Nations and Nationalism*. Oxford: Blackwell.

Gerbner, George. 1998. 'Stories of violence and the public interest'. Pp. 135–46 in *The Media in Question: Popular Culture and Public Interests*, edited by K. Brants, J. Hermes, and L. van Zoonen. London: Sage.

Gibbon, John Murray. 1938. *Canadian Mosaic: The Making of a Northern Nation*. Toronto: McClelland and Stewart.

Giddens, Anthony. 1991. *Modernity and Self-Identity: Self and Society in the Late Modern Age*. Stanford, Calif.: Stanford University Press.

Gikow, Louise. 2009. *Sesame Street: A Celebration of Forty Years of Life on the Street*. New York: Black Dog and Leventhal.

Goffman, Erving. 1959. *The Presentation of Self in Everyday Life*. Garden City, NY: Doubleday.

Goldberg, Avi, and Axel van den Berg. 2009. 'What do public sociologists do? A critique of Burawoy'. *Canadian Journal of Sociology* 34 (3): 765–802.

Goldstone, Jack A., and Charles Tilly. 2001. 'Threat (and opportunity): Popular action and state response in the dynamics of contentious action'. Pp. 179–94 in *Silence and Voice in the Study of Contentious Politics*, edited by R.R. Aminzade, J.A. Goldstone, D. McAdam, E.J. Perry, W.H. Sewell Jr., S. Tarrow, and C. Tilly. New York: Cambridge University Press.

Goodwin Jeff, and James M. Jasper. 1999. 'Caught in a winding, snarling vine: The structural bias of political process theory'. *Sociological Forum* 14 (1): 27–54.

Gordon, Milton M. 1978. *Human Nature, Class and Ethnicity*. New York: Oxford University Press.

Gorges, Michael J. 2001. 'New institutionalist explanations for institutional change: A note of caution'. *Politics* 21 (2): 137–45.

Gough, Ian. 1979. *The Political Economy of the Welfare State*. London: Macmillan.

Grabb, Edward G. 1981. 'Class, conformity and political powerlessness'. *Canadian Review of Sociology and Anthropology* 18 (3): 362–69.

Grabb, Edward G. 2007. *Theories of Social Inequality* 5th edn. Toronto: Thompson/Nelson.

Gramsci, Antonio. 1971. *Selections from the Prison Notebooks of Antonio Gramsci*, edited by Q. Hoare and G. Nowell Smith. New York: International.

Grand Council of the Crees. 1998. *Never without Consent*. Toronto: *James Bay Crees' Stand against Forcible Inclusion into an Independent Quebec*. ECW Press.

Granovetter, Mark S. 1973. 'The Strength of Weak Ties.' *American Journal of Sociology* 78 (6): 1360–80.

Granovetter, Mark S. 1974. *Getting a Job: A Study of Contacts and Careers*. Cambridge, Mass.: Harvard University Press.

Gusfield, Joseph R. 1963. *Symbolic Crusade: Status Politics and the American Temperance Movement*. Urbana, Ill.: University of Illinois Press.

Habermas, Jurgen. 1989. *The Structural Transformation of the Public Sphere: An Inquiry into a Category of Bourgeois Society*. Cambridge, Mass.: MIT Press.

Hackett, Robert A., and William K. Carroll. 2006. *Remaking Media: The Struggle to Democratize Public Communication*. New York: Routledge.

Hadden, Jennifer, and Sidney Tarrow. 2007. 'Spillover or spillout? The global justice movement in the United States after 9/11'. *Mobilization* 12 (4): 359–76.

Hagan, John, and Ruth D. Peterson (eds). 1995. *Crime and Inequality*. Stanford, Calif.: Stanford University Press.

Haig-Brown, Celia. 1988. *Resistance and renewal: Surviving the Indian Residential School*. Vancouver: Arsenal Pulp Press.

Hall, John A. 1993. 'Nationalisms: Classified and explained'. *Daedelus* 122 (3): 1–28.

Hall, John A. (ed). 1998. *The State of the Nation: Ernest Gellner and the Theory of Nationalism*. New York: Cambridge University Press.

Hall, John A. 2006. 'Danish capitalism in comparative perspective'. Pp. 441–52 in *National Identities and Varieties of Capitalism*, edited by J.L. Campbell, J.A. Hall, and O.K. Pedersen. Montreal: McGill-Queens University Press.

Hall, John A. 2010. *Ernest Gellner: An Intellectual Biography*. London: Verso.

Hall, John A., and I.C. Jarvie (eds). 1992. *Transition to Modernity: Essays on Power, Wealth and Belief*. New York: Cambridge University Press.

Hall, John A., and Ralph Schroeder (eds). 2006. *An Anatomy of Power: The Social Theory of Michael Mann*. New York: Cambridge University Press.

Hall, Stuart. [1980] 2006. 'Encoding/decoding'. Pp. 163–73 in *Media and Cultural Studies: Key Works* (rev. edn), edited by M.G. Durham and D.M. Kellner. Malden, Mass.: Blackwell.

Haluza-DeLay, Randolph. 2008. 'A theory of practice for social movements: Environmentalism and ecological habitus'. *Mobilization* 13 (2): 205–18.

Haluza-DeLay, Randolph, and Debra J. Davidson. 2008. 'The environment and a globalizing sociology'. *Canadian Journal of Sociology* 33 (3): 631–56.

Hanisch, Carol. [1969] 1970. 'The personal is political'. In *Notes from the Second Year: Women's Liberation in 1970*, edited by S. Firestone and A. Koedt. New York: New York Radical Feminists.

Harary, Frank. 1966. 'Merton revisited: A new classification for deviant behavior'. *American Sociological Review* 31 (5): 693–97.

Haraway, Donna J. 1985. 'A manifesto for cyborgs: Science, technology and socialist feminism in the 1980s'. *Socialist Review* 80: 65–107.

Haraway, Donna J. 1991. *Simians, Cyborgs, and Women: The Reinvention of Nature*. New York: Routledge.

Haraway, Donna J. 2008. *When Species Meet*. Minneapolis, Minn.: University of Minnesota Press.

Haraway, Donna J. Interview with Nicholas Gane. 2006. 'When we have never been human, what is to be done? Interview with Donna Haraway'. *Theory, Culture and Society* 23 (7–8): 135–58.

Hardt, Michael, and Antonio Negri. 2001. *Empire*. Cambridge, Mass.: Harvard University Press.

Harrison, Trevor, and Harvey Krahn. 1995. 'Populism and the rise of the reform party in Alberta'. *Canadian Review of Sociology and Anthropology* 32 (2): 127–50.

Hartz, Louis. 1964. *The Founding of New Societies: Studies in the History of the United States, Latin America, Canada, and Australia*. New York: Harcourt, Brace and World.

Haste, Jerome C. 2003. 'What Do We Mean by Literacy Now?' *Voices from the Middle* 10 (3): 8–12.

Hechter, Michael. 2000. *Containing Nationalism*. New York: Oxford University Press.

Helford, Elyce Rae. 2000. 'Feminism, queer studies, and the sexual politics of *Xena: Warrior Princess*', Pp. 135–62 in *Fantasy Girls: Gender in the New Universe of Science Fiction and Fantasy*, edited by E.R. Helford. Lanham, Md.: Rowman and Littlefield.

Helmes-Hayes, Rick. 2002. 'John Porter: Canada's most famous sociologist (and his links to American sociology)'. *The American Sociologist* 33 (1): 79–104.

Helmes-Hayes, Rick. 2009. *Measuring the Mosaic: An Intellectual Biography of John Porter*. Toronto: University of Toronto Press.

Helmes-Hayes, Rick, and James Curtis (eds). 1998. *The Vertical Mosaic Revisited*. Toronto: University of Toronto Press.

Helmes-Hayes, Rick, and Neil McLaughlin. 2009. 'Public sociology in Canada: Debates, research and historical context'. *Canadian Journal of Sociology* 34 (3): 573–600.

Henry, Frances, and Carol Tator. 2002. *Discourses of Domination: Racial Bias in the Canadian English-Language Press*. Toronto: University of Toronto Press.

Herman, Edward, and Noam Chomsky. 1988. *Manufacturing Consent: The Political Economy of the Mass Media*. New York: Pantheon.

Hira, Anil, and Ron Hira. 2000. 'The new institutionalism: Contradictory notions of change'. *American Journal of Economics and Sociology* 59 (2): 267–82.

Hochschild, Arlie. [1983] 2003. *The Managed Heart: Commercialization of Human Feeling*. Berkeley: University of California Press.

hooks, bell. 1981. *Ain't I a Woman: Black Women and Feminism*. Boston: South End Press.

hooks, bell. 1984. *Feminist Theory: From Margin to Center*. Boston: South End Press.

Horkheimer, Max, and Theodor W. Adorno. 2006. 'The culture industry: Enlightenment as mass deception'. Pp. 41–72 in *Media and Cultural Studies: Key Works* (rev. edn), edited by M.G. Durham and D.M. Kellner. Malden, Mass.: Blackwell.

Howard, Rhoda E. 1991. 'The national question in Canada: Quebec'. *Human Rights Quarterly* 13 (3): 412–19.

Howard-Hassmann, Rhoda E. 2000. 'Canadians discuss freedom of speech: Individual rights versus group protection'. *International Journal on Minority and Group Rights* 7 (2): 109–38.

Huffington Post. 2010. 'Vancouver's "Poverty Olympics" protest millions spent on Winter Games'. 10 April. http://www.huffingtonpost.com/2010/02/08/vancouvers-poverty-olympi_n_453593.html. Accessed 25 June, 2010.

Huffington Post. 2011. 'SlutWalks sweep the nation'. 20 April. http://www.huffingtonpost.com/2011/04/20/slut-walk-united-states-city_n_851725.html. Accessed 27 Oct., 2011.

Infosphere, The. 2011. 'Hermes Conrad'. *The Infosphere, The Futurama Wiki.* http://theinfosphere.org/Hermes_Conrad. Accessed 8 Aug., 2011.

Inglehart, Ronald. 1990. *Culture Shift in Advanced Industrial Society.* Princeton: Princeton University Press.

Ingram, Paul, and Karen Clay. 2000. 'The choice-within-constraints: New institutionalism and implications for sociology'. *Annual Review of Sociology* 26: 525–46.

Inkeles, Alex. 1960. 'Industrial man: The relation of status to experience, perception and value'. *American Journal of Sociology* 66 (1): 1–31.

Inkeles, Alex. 1975. 'Becoming modern: Individual change in six developing countries'. *ethos* 3 (2): 323–42.

Innis, Harold. 1940. *The Cod Fisheries: The History of an International Economy.* Carnegie Endowment for International Peace, Division of Economics and History. Toronto: Ryerson Press.

Innis, Harold. 1956. 'The Wheat Economy'. Pp. 273–9 in *Essays in Canadian Economic History*, edited by M.Q. Innis. Toronto: University of Toronto Press. http://www.questia.com/PM.qst?a=o&d=30543904. Accessed 2 Sept., 2011.

Innis, Harold. [1930] 1956. *The Fur Trade in Canada: An Introduction to Canadian Economic History.* Toronto: University of Toronto Press.

James, Carl E. 2003. 'Schooling, basketball and US scholarship aspirations of Canadian student athletes'. *Race, Ethnicity and Education* 6 (2): 123–44.

Janks, Hilary. 2010. *Literacy and Power.* London: Routledge.

Jenkins, Henry. 1988. '*Star Trek* rerun, reread, rewritten: Fan writing as textual poaching. *Critical Studies in Mass Communication* 5 (2): 85–107.

Jenkins, Jonathan. 2011. 'McGuinty rejects G20 public inquiry'. *Toronto Sun*, 28 Feb. http://www.torontosun.com/news/torontoandgta/2011/02/28/17437861.html. Accessed 26 Apr., 2011.

Jenson, Jane, and Martin Papillon. 2000. 'Challenging the citizenship regime: The James Bay Cree and transnational action'. *Politics and Society* 28 (2): 245–64.

Jenson, Jane, and Susan D. Phillips. 1996. 'Regime shift: New citizenship practices in Canada'. *International Journal of Canadian Studies* 14 (Fall): 111–35.

Jenson, Jane, and Susan Phillips. 2001. 'Redesigning the Canadian citizenship regime: Remaking the institutions of representation'. Pp. 69–89 in *Citizenship, Markets, and the State*, edited by C. Crouch, K. Eder, and D. Tambini. New York: Oxford University Press.

Jenson, Jane, and Denis Saint-Martin. 2003. 'New routes to social cohesion? Citizenship and the social investment state'. *Canadian Journal of Sociology* 28 (1): 77–99.

Keck, Margaret E., and Kathryn Sikkink. 1998. *Activists beyond Borders: Advocacy Networks in International Politics.* Ithaca, NY: Cornell University Press.

Kerr, Clark, Frederick H. Harbison, John T. Dunlop, and Charles A. Myers. 1960. 'Industrialism and industrial man'. *International Labor Review* 82 (3): 236–50.

Khasnabish, Alex. 2008. *Zapatismo beyond Borders: New Imaginations of Political Possibility.* Toronto: University of Toronto Press.

Kierkus, Christopher A., and Douglas Baer. 2002. 'A social control explanation of the relationship between family structure and delinquent behaviour'. *Canadian Journal of Criminology* 44 (4): 425–58.

King, Anthony D. 1995. 'The time and spaces of modernity (or who needs postmodernism?)' Pp. 108–23 in *Global Modernities*, edited by M. Featherstone, S. Lash, and R. Robertson. Thousand Oaks, Calif.: Sage.

Kitschelt, Herbert P. 1986. 'Political opportunity structures and political protest: Antinuclear movements in four democracies'. *British Journal of Political Science* 16: 57–85.

Klandermans, Bert, and Suzanne Staggenborg (eds). 2002. *Methods of Social Movement Research.* Minneapolis: University of Minnesota Press.

Klein, Naomi. 2000. *No Logo: Taking Aim at the Brand Bullies.* Toronto: Vintage.

Korpi, Walter. 1983. *The Democratic Class Struggle.* New York: Routledge and Kegan Paul.

Korpi, Walter. 1985. 'Power resources approach vs. action and conflict: On causal and intentional explanations in the study of power'. *Sociological Theory* 3 (2): 31–45.

Korpi, Walter. 1989. 'Power, politics, and state autonomy in the development of social citizenship: Social rights during sickness in eighteen OECD countries since 1930'. *American Sociological Review* 54 (3): 309–28.

Kuhn, Thomas S. 1962. *The Structure of Scientific Revolutions.* Chicago: University of Chicago Press.

Kymlicka, Will. 1995. *Multicultural Citizenship: A Liberal Theory of Minority Rights*. New York: Oxford University Press.

Kymlicka, Will. 1998. *Finding Our Way: Rethinking Ethnocultural Relations in Canada*. Don Mills, Ont.: Oxford University Press.

Kymlicka, Will. 2003. 'Multicultural states and intercultural citizens'. *Theory and Research in Education* 1 (2): 147–69.

Lambertus, Sandra. 2004. *Wartime Images, Peacetime Wounds: The Media and the Gustafsen Lake Standoff*. Toronto: University of Toronto Press.

Langford, Tom, and J. Rick Ponting. 1992. 'Canadians' responses to aboriginal issues: The roles of prejudice, perceived group conflict and economic conservatism'. *Canadian Review of Sociology and Anthropology* 29 (2): 140–66.

Langtry, Mrs. 1884. 'Slumming in this town: A fashionable London mania reaches New York'. *New York Times*, 14 Sept. http://query.nytimes.com/mem/archive-free/pdf?res= 9A04E3D91338E033A25757C1A96F 9C94659FD7CF. Accessed 25 Apr., 2011.

LaSalle, LuAnn. 2010. 'Bell Canada parent BCE says winter Olympics helped push ahead deal to buy CTV'. Canadian Press. *680 News*, 10 Sept. http://www.680news.com/news/national/article/99763-bell-canada-parent-bce-buys-ctv-television-network-for-1-3-billion. Accessed 4 April, 2011.

Latour, Bruno. 2007. *Reassembling the Social: An Introduction to Actor-Network-Theory*. New York: Oxford University Press.

Laxer, Gordon. 1985. 'Foreign ownership and myths about Canadian development. *Canadian Review of Sociology and Anthropology*. 22 (3): 311–45.

Laxer, Gordon. 1989. *Open for Business: The Roots of Foreign Ownership in Canada*. Don Mills, Ont.: Oxford University Press.

LeBon, Gustave. [1895] 1995. *The Crowd*. New Brunswick, N.J.: Transaction.

Lewis, Justin, and Shut Jhally. 1998. 'The Struggle over Media Literacy'. *Journal of Communication* 48 (1): 109–20.

Lewis, Neil A. 1996. 'Black English is not a second language, Jackson says'. *New York Times*, 23 Dec. http://www.nytimes.com/1996/12/23/us/black-english-is-not-a-second-language-jackson-says.html. Accessed 5 May, 2011.

Lipset, Seymour M. 1963. 'The value patterns of democracy: A case study in comparative analysis'. *American Sociological Review* 28 (4): 515–31.

Lipset, Seymour M. 1964. 'Canada and the United States—A comparative view'. *Canadian Review of Sociology and Anthropology* 1 (4): 173–85.

Lipset, Seymour M. 1986. 'Historical traditions and national characteristics: A comparative analysis of Canada and the United States'. *Canadian Journal of Sociology* 11 (2): 113–55.

Lipset, Seymour M. 1990. *Continental Divide: The Values and Institutions of the United States and Canada*. New York: Routledge.

Lipset, Seymour Martin, and Reinhard Bendi. 1959. *Social Mobility in Industrial Society*. Berkeley: University of California Press.

Livingstone, Sonia. 2007. 'Engaging with Media—A Matter of Literacy?' Conference paper: *Transforming Audiences: Identity/ Creativity/ Everyday Life*, 6–7 Sept., University of Westminster, London.

Long, A. David. 1992. 'Culture, ideology, and militancy: The movement of Native Indians in Canada, 1969–1991'. Pp. 118–34 in *Organizing Dissent: Contemporary Social Movements in Theory and Practice*, edited by W.K. Carroll. Toronto: Garamond Press.

Lowe, Graham, and Sandra Rastin. 2000. 'Organizing the next generation: Influences on young workers' willingness to join unions in Canada'. *British Journal of Industrial Relations* 38 (2): 203–22.

Luxton, Meg. 1980. *More Than a Labour of Love: Three Generations of Women's Work in the Home*. Toronto: Women's Educational Press.

MacDougall, Graham. 1997. 'Caring—A masculine perspective'. *Journal of Advanced Nursing* 25: 809–13.

Manitobia. 2011. 'Strike 1919!'. *Manitobia: Digital Resources on Manitoba History*. http://manitobia.ca/cocoon/launch/en/themes/strike/5. Accessed 20 Feb., 2011.

Mann, Michael. 1984. 'The autonomous power of the state'. *Archives européennes de sociologie* 25 (4): 185–213.

Mann, Michael. 1986. *The Sources of Social Power*, Vol. 1. Cambridge, UK: Cambridge University Press.

Mann, Michael. 1993. *The Sources of Social Power*, Vol.2. Cambridge, UK: Cambridge University Press.

Mann, Michael. 1999. 'The dark side of democracy: The modern tradition of ethnic and political cleansing'. *New Left Review* 235: 18–45.

Mann, Michael. 2004. *Fascists*. Cambridge, UK: Cambridge University Press.

Mann, Michael. 2005. *The Dark Side of Democracy: Explaining Ethnic Cleansing.* Cambridge, UK: Cambridge University Press.

Manuel, Arthur. 2010. 'Arthur Manuel: Vancouver Olympics can't hide Canada's dismal record on indigenous peoples'. *Staight.com:Vancouver's online source,* 25 Jan. http://www.straight.com/article-282036/vancouver/arthur-manuel-vancouver-olympics-cant-hide-canadas-dismal-record-indigenous-peoples. Accessed 25 June, 2010.

Marchak, Patricia M. 1983. *Green Gold: The Forest Industry in British Columbia;* Vancouver: University of British Columbia Press.

Marchak, Patricia M. 1996. 'The future of the university . . . and now a word from our sponsor'. *Queen's Quarterly* 103 (3): 653–55.

Marchak, Patricia M. 1999. *God's Assassins: State Terrorism in Argentina in the 1970s.* Montreal: McGill-Queen's University Press.

Marchak, Patricia M., Neil Guppy, and John L. McMullan (eds.). 1987. *Uncommon Property: The Fishing and Fish-Processing Industries in British Columbia.* Vancouver: University of British Columbia Press.

Marx, Karl. 1977. *Critique of Hegel's 'Philosophy of Right'.* Cambridge, UK: Cambridge University Press.

Marx, Karl, and Friedrich Engels. 1970. *The German Ideology,* edited by C.J. Arthur. New York: International.

Marx, Karl, and Friedrich Engels. 1985 [1888]. *The Communist Manifesto.* New York: Penguin.

Massing, Michael. 2008. 'The Volunteer Army: Who Fights and Why?' *New York Review of Books,* 3 April.

Matthews, Ralph. 1981. 'Two alternative explanations of the problem of regional dependency in Canada. *Canadian Public Policy* 7 (2): 268–83.

Matthews, Ralph. 1983. *The Creation of Regional Dependency.* Toronto: University of Toronto Press.

May, Kathryn. 2010. 'Depression among public servants Canada's biggest "public health crisis": Expert'. *Ottawa Citizen,* 11 Jan. http://www.mentalhealthroundtable.ca/jan_10/Depression%20among%20public%20servants%20Canada's%20biggest%20'public%20health%20crisis'_%20Expert.pdf. Accessed 28 Oct., 2011.

McAdam, Doug. 1982. *Political Process and the Development of Black Insurgency, 1930–1970.* Chicago: University of Chicago Press.

McAdam, Doug, John D. McCarthy, and Mayer N. Zald (eds). 1996. *Comparative Perspectives on Social Movements: Political Opportunities, Mobilizing Structures, and Cultural Framings.* New York: Cambridge University Press.

McAdam, Doug, Sidney Tarrow, and Charles Tilly. 2001. *Dynamics of Contention.* Cambridge: Cambridge University Press.

McCarthy, John D., and Mayer N. Zald. 1973. *The Trend of Social Movements in America: Professionalization and Resource Mobilization.* Morristown, NJ: General Learning Press.

McCarthy, John D., and Mayer N. Zald. 1977. 'Resource mobilization and social movements: A partial theory'. *American Journal of Sociology* 82 (6): 1212–41.

McCarthy, John D., and Mayer N. Zald. 2002. 'The resource mobilization research program: Progress, challenge and transformation'. Pp. 147–71 in *New Directions in Contemporary Sociological Theory,* edited by J. Berger and M. Zelditch Jr. Lanham, Md.: Rowman Littlefield.

McClelland, David C. 1961. *The Achieving Society.* Princeton, NJ: Van Nostrand.

McKenna, Barrie, and Bernard Marotte. 2011. 'Layton's leftist nationalism wins hearts and minds in Quebec'. *Globe and Mail,* 25 Apr. http://www.theglobeandmail.com/news/politics/laytons-leftist-nationalism-wins-hearts-and-minds-in-quebec/article1997288/. Accessed 26 Apr., 2011.

McLaughlin, Neil. 2005. 'Canada's impossible science: Historical and institutional origins of the coming crisis in Anglo-Canadian sociology'. *Canadian Journal of Sociology* 30 (1): 1–40.

McLaughlin, Neil, and Antony Puddephatt 2008. 'Three Empirical Traditions of Sociological Theory'. Pp. 12–37 in *Sociology: Canadian Perspectives,* edited by Lorne Tepperman and Patrizia Albanese. Don Mills, Ont.: Oxford University Press.

McLaughlin, Neil, and Kerry Turcotte. 2007. 'The trouble with Burawoy: An analytic synthetic alternative'. *Sociology* 41 (5): 813–28.

McLaughlin, Neil, Lisa Kowalchuck, and Kerry Turcotte. 2005. 'Why sociology does not need to be saved: Analytic reflections on public sociologies'. *The American Sociologist* 36 (3–4): 133–51.

McMichael, Philip. 2008. *Development and Social Change: A Global Perspective.* 4th edn. Thousand Oaks, Los Angeles: Pine Forge Press.

Media Awareness Network. 2011. *How marketers target kids*. Media Awareness Network: Marketing and Consumerism. http://www.media-awareness.ca/english/parents/marketing/marketers_target_kids.cfm. Accessed 29 Apr., 2011.

Melucci, Alberto. 1989. *Nomads of the Present: Social Movements and Individual Needs in Contemporary Society*. Philadelphia: Temple University Press.

Melucci, Alberto. 1996a. *Challenging Codes: Collective Action in the Information Age*. Cambridge, UK: Cambridge University Press.

Melucci, Alberto. 1996b. *The Playing Self: Person and Meaning in the Planetary Society*. Cambridge, UK: Cambridge University Press.

Merton, Robert K. 1949. *Social Theory and Social Structure*. Glencoe, Ill., Free Press.

Merton, Robert K. 1968. 'The Matthew Effect in science: The reward and communication systems of science are considered'. *Science* 159 (3810): 56–63.

Meyer, David S. 2004. 'Protest and political opportunities'. *Annual Review of Sociology* 30: 125–45.

Meyer, David S., and Deborah C. Minkoff. 2004. 'Conceptualizing political opportunity'. *Social Forces* 82 (4): 1457–92.

Meyer, David S., and Suzanne Staggenborg. 1996. 'Movements, countermovements, and the structure of political opportunity'. *American Journal of Sociology* 101 (6): 1628–60.

Meyer, John W. 2000. 'Globalization: Sources and effects on national states and societies.' *International Sociology* 15 (2): 233–48.

Meyer, John W., John Boli, George M. Thomas, and Francisco O. Ramirez. 1997. 'World society and the nation state'. *American Journal of Sociology* 103 (1): 144–81.

Meyer, John, and F. Ramirez. 2000. 'The world institutionalization of education'. Pp. 111–131 in *Discourse Formation in Comparative Education*, edited by J. Schriewer. New York: Peter Lang.

Meyer, John, Francisco O. Ramirez, and Yasemin Nuhoglu Soysal. 1992. 'World expansion of mass education, 1870–1980'. *Sociology of Education* 65 (2) 128–49.

Meyerson, Debra E., and Joyce K. Fletcher 2000. 'A modest manifesto for shattering the glass ceiling'. *Harvard Business Review* 78 (1): 126–36.

Miliband, Ralph. 1969. *The State in Capitalist Society*. London: Weidenfeld and Nicolson.

Miller, James R. 1989. *Skyscrapers Hide the Heavens: A History of Indian-White Relations in Canada*. Toronto: University of Toronto Press.

Mills, C. Wright. 1956. *The Power Elite*. New York: Oxford University Press.

Mills, C. Wright. 1959. *The Sociological Imagination*. New York: Oxford University Press.

Moore Jr., Barrington. 1966. *Social Origins of Dictatorship and Democracy: Lord and Peasant in the Making of the Modern World*. Boston: Beacon Press.

Murphy, Christopher. 2007. ' "Securitizing" Canadian policing: A new policing paradigm for the post 9/11 security state?' *Canadian Journal of Sociology and Anthropology* 32 (4): 449–75.

Murphy, Raymond. 2004. 'Disaster or sustainability: The dance of human agents with nature's actants'. *Canadian Review of Sociology and Anthropology* 41 (3): 249–66.

Murphy, Raymond. 2009. *Leadership in Disaster: Learning for a Future with Global Climate Change*. Montreal: McGill-Queen's University Press.

Mutua, Makau. 2001. 'Savages, victims, and saviors: The metaphor of human rights'. *Harvard International Law Journal* 42 (1): 201–46.

Mutua, Makau. 2002. *Human Rights: A Political and Cultural Critique*. Philadelphia: University of Pennsylvania Press.

Nagel, Joane, and Susan Olzak. 1982. 'Ethnic mobilization in new and old states: An extension of the competition model'. *Social Problems* 30 (2): 127–43.

Nakhaie, M. Reza. 1992. 'Class and voting consistency in Canada: Analyses bearing on the mobilization thesis'. *Canadian Journal of Sociology* 17 (3): 275–99.

Nakhaie, M. Reza. 2000. 'Social origins and educational attainment in Canada: 1985 and 1994'. *Review of Radical Political Economics* 32 (4): 577–609.

Nakhaie, M. Reza. 2004. 'Who controls Canadian universities? Ethnoracial origins of Canadian university administrators and faculty's perception of mistreatment'. *Canadian Ethnic Studies* 36 (1): 92–110.

Nakhaie, M. Reza, and James Curtis. 1998. 'Effects of class positions of parents on educational attainment of daughters and sons'. *Canadian Review of Sociology and Anthropology* 35 (4): 483–515.

Ng, Roxana. 1984. 'Sex, ethnicity, or class? Some methodological considerations'. *Studies in Sexual Politics* 1: 14–45.

Ng, Roxana. 1988. *The Politics of Community Services: Immigrant Women, Class, and the State*. Toronto: Garamond Press.

Niezen, Ronald. 2000. 'Recognizing indigenism: Canadian unity and the international movement of indigenous peoples'. *Comparative Studies in Society and History* 42 (1): 119–48.

Noble, Trevor. 2000. *Social Theory and Social Change*. New York: Palgrave.

Norton, Peter D. 2008. *Fighting Traffic: The Dawn of the Motor Age in the American City*. Cambridge, Mass.: MIT Press.

Nye Jr., Joseph S. 2002. *The Paradox of American Power: Why the World's Only Superpower Can't Go It Alone*. New York: Oxford University Press.

Nye Jr., Joseph S. 2003. 'US power and strategy after Iraq'. *Foreign Affairs* 82 (4): 60–73.

Oakley, Ann. 2000. *Experiments in Knowing: Gender and Method in the Social Sciences*. New York: New Press.

Offe, Claus. 1984. *Contradictions of the Welfare State*. Cambridge, Mass.: MIT Press.

Olsen, Dennis. 1977. 'The state elites'. Pp. 199–224 in *The Canadian State: Political Economy and Political Power*, edited by L. Panitch. Toronto: University of Toronto Press.

Olsen, Dennis. 1980. *The State Elite*. Toronto: McClelland and Stewart.

Olzak, Susan. 1983. 'Contemporary ethnic mobilization'. *Annual Review of Sociology* 9: 355–74.

Ontario. 2010. Ombudsman. Press release. 'Ombudsman finds G20 regulation of "dubious legality"; Citizens unfairly trapped by secret expansion of police powers'. 7 Dec. http://www.ombudsman.on.ca/en/media/press-releases/2010/ombudsman-finds-g20-regulation-of-'dubious-legality'.aspx. Accessed 26 Apr., 2011.

Pablo, Carlito. 2010. 'Police bring out heavy-duty weapons for Vancouver Olympics protest on day two'. *Straight.com*. 13 Feb. http://www.straight.com/article-289547/vancouver/police-bring-out-heavyduty-weapons-vancouver-olympic-protest-day-two. Accessed 25 June, 2010.

Pasma, Chandra. 2010. 'Bearing the brunt: How the 2008–2009 recession created poverty for Canadian families'. *Citizens for Public Justice*. http://www.cpj.ca/files/docs/Bearing_the_Brunt_-_Summary.pdf. Accessed 23 Apr., 2011.

Patterson, Graham. 2007. 'Alan Greenspan claims Iraq war was really for oil'. *Sunday Times*, 16 Sept. http://www.timesonline.co.uk/tol/news/world/article2461214.ece. Accessed 9 Aug., 2011.

Peters, B. Guy. 1999. *Institutional Theory in Political Science: The 'New Institutionalism'*. London: Pinter.

Peters, John. 2002. *A Fine Balance: Canadian Unions Confront Globalization*. Ottawa: Canadian Centre for Policy Alternatives.

Peterson, Anna. 2008. Review of *When Species Meet*, by Donna J. Haraway. *Journal of Agricultural and Environmental Ethics* 21 (6): 609–11.

Piven, Franci Fox, and Richard A. Cloward. 1971. *Regulating the Poor: The Functions of Public Welfare*. New York: Pantheon.

Polletta, Francesca, and James M. Jasper. 2001. 'Collective identity and social movements'. *Annual Review of Sociology* 27: 283–305.

Ponting. J. Rick. 2000. 'Public opinion on Canadian aboriginal issues, 1976–98: Persistence, change and cohort analysis'. *Canadian Ethnic Studies* 32 (3): 44–75.

Porter, John. 1965. *The Vertical Mosaic: An Analysis of Social Class and Power in Canada*. Toronto: University of Toronto Press.

Porter, Marion R., John Porter, and Bernard R. Blishen. 1979. *Does Money Matter? Prospects for Higher Education in Ontario*. Toronto: Macmillan of Canada.

Portes, Alejandro. 1998. 'Social capital: Its origins and applications in modern sociology.' *Annual Review of Sociology* 24: 1–24.

Portes, Alejandro. 2000. 'The two meanings of social capital'. *Sociological Forum* 15 (1): 1–12.

Poulantzas, Nicos. 1973. *Political Power and Social Classes*. London: New Left Books and Sheed and Ward.

Putnam, Robert D. 2000. *Bowling Alone: The Collapse and Revival of American Community*. New York: Simon and Schuster.

Putnam, Robert D. 2007. 'E pluribus unum: Diversity and community in the twenty-first century'. *Scandinavian Political Studies* 30 (2): 137–74.

Ramirez, Francisco O., Yasemin Soysal, and Suzanne Shanahan. 1997. 'The changing logic of political citizenship: Cross-national acquisition of women's suffrage rights, 1890 to 1990'. *American Sociological Review* 62 (5): 735–45.

Ramos, Howard. 2000. 'National recognition without a state: Cree nationalism within Canada. *Nationalism and Ethnic Politics* 6 (2): 95–115.

Ramos, Howard. 2006. 'What causes Canadian Aboriginal protest? Examining resources, opportunities and identity, 1951–2000'. *Canadian Journal of Sociology* 31 (2): 211–34.

Ramos, Howard. 2007. 'Special plus and special negative: The conflict between perceptions and applications of "special status" in Canada'. Pp. 131–50 in *Race, Racialization, and Antiracism in Canada and Beyond*, edited by G. Fuji Johnson and R. Enomoto. Toronto: University of Toronto Press.

Ramos, Howard. 2008a. 'Aboriginal protest'. Pp. 55–70 in *Social Movements*, by Suzanne Staggenborg. Don Mills, Ont.: Oxford University Press.

Ramos, Howard. 2008b. 'Opportunity for whom? Political opportunity and critical events in Canadian Aboriginal mobilization, 1951–2000'. *Social Forces* 87 (2): 795–823.

Ramos, Howard, and Rima Wilkes. 2010. 'Oka matters 20 years later'. *Halifax Chronicle Herald*, 23 Sept.

Ramsey, Mike. 2008. 'GM, Chrysler win union concessions to bolster aid bid' (Update 3). *Bloomberg*, 3 Dec. http://www.bloomberg.com/apps/news?pid=newsarchive&refer=home&sid=aSm249vkuvUY. Accessed 9 Aug., 2011.

Ravensbergen, Frances, and Madine VanderPlaat. 2009. 'Barriers to citizen participation: The missing voices of people living with low income'. *Community Development Journal* 45 (4): 389–403.

Reiter, Dan, and Allan C. Stam. 2002. *Democracies at War*. Princeton: Princeton University Press.

Renan, Ernest. [1882] 1990. 'What is a nation?' Pp. 8–22 in *Nation and Narration*, edited by H.K. Bhabha. London: Routledge.

Reynolds Lewis, Katherine. 2011. 'Unpaid jobs: The new normal?' *Fortune*, 25 Mar. http://management.fortune.cnn.com/2011/03/25/unpaid-jobs-the-new-normal/. Accessed 31 Aug., 2011.

Roberts, Martin, Dee Cook, Martin Roche and Suki Desai. 2001. 'Just noise? Newspaper crime reporting and fear of crime'. *Criminal Justice Matters* 43 (1): 12–13.

Robertson, Jordan. 2010. 'Apple admits using child labor: 15-year-olds worked in factories'. *Huffington Post*, 28 Feb. http://www.huffingtonpost.com/2010/02/28/apple-child-labor-confess_n_479871.html. Accessed 23 Apr., 2011.

Robertson, Roland. 1995. 'Glocalization: Time-space and Homogeneity-Heterogeneity'. Pp. 25–44 in *Global Modernities*, edited by M. Featherstone, S. Lash, and R. Robertson. Thousand Oaks, Calif.: Sage.

Robidoux, Michael A. 2006. 'The nonsense of Native American sport imagery: Reclaiming a past that never was'. *International Review for the Sociology of Sport* 41 (2): 201–19.

Runciman, W.G. (ed.), and Eric Matthews (trans.). 1978. *Max Weber: Selections in Translation*. New York: Cambridge University Press.

Ruse, Michael. 1985. *Sociobiology: Sense or Nonsense?* 2nd edn. Boston, Mass: D. Reidel.

Rutenberg, Jim. 2004. 'Disney is blocking distribution of film that criticizes Bush'. *New York Times*, 5 May. http://www.nytimes.com/2004/05/05/us/disney-is-blocking-distribution-of-film-that-criticizes-bush.html?pagewanted=all&src=pm. Accessed 27 Oct., 2011.

Ryerson, Stanley B. 1963. *The Founding of Canada: Beginnings to 1815*. Toronto: Progress Books.

Sacouman, R. James. 1979. 'Underdevelopment and the structural origins of Antigonish Movement co-operatives in eastern Nova Scotia.' Pp. 109–26 in *Underdevelopment and Social Movements in Atlantic Canada*, edited by R.J. Brym and R.J. Sacouman. Toronto: New Hogtown Press.

Sacouman, R. James. 1980. 'Semi-proletarianization and rural underdevelopment in the Maritimes'. *Canadian Review of Sociology and Anthropology* 17 (3): 232–45.

Sacouman, R. James. 1981. 'The "Peripheral" Maritimes and Canada-wide Marxist political economy'. *Studies in Political Economy* 6: 135–50.

Sahlins, Marshall. 1978. *Culture and Practical Reason*. Chicago: University of Chicago Press.

Said, Edward. 1978. *Orientalism*. New York: Pantheon Books.

Sardar, Ziauddin, and Borin Van Loon. 1999. *Introducing Cultural Studies*. New York: Totem.

Satzewich, Vic, and Nikolaos Liodakis. 2007. *'Race' and Ethnicity in Canada: A Critical Introduction*. Don Mills, Ont.: Oxford University Press.

Schwalbe, Michael. 2004. *The Sociologically Examined Life: Pieces of the Conversation*. Boston: McGraw-Hill.

Scott, James C. 1998. *Seeing Like a State: How Certain Schemes to Improve the Human Condition have Failed*. New Haven: Yale University Press.

Searles, Ruth, and J. Allen Williams Jr. 1962. 'Negro college students' participation in sit-ins'. *Social Forces* 40 (3): 215–20.

Sennett, Richard. 1977. *The Fall of Public Man*. Cambridge, UK: Cambridge University Press.

Sinclair, Peter R. 1975. 'Class structure and populist protest: The case of Western Canada'. *Canadian Journal of Sociology* 1 (1): 1–17.

Skocpol, Theda. 1979. *States and Social Revolutions: A Comparative Analysis of France, Russia, and China*. New York: Cambridge University Press.

Skocpol, Theda. 1995. *Protecting Soldiers and Mothers: The Political Origins of Social Policy in the United States*. Cambridge, Mass.: Harvard University Press.

Skocpol, Theda. 2004. *Diminished Democracy: From Membership to Management in American Civic Life*. Norman, Okla.: University of Oklahoma Press.

Smith, Dorothy. 1973. *Women, the Family and Corporate Capitalism*. Toronto: New Press.

Sorenson, John. 2010. *About Canada: Animal Rights*. Black Point, NS: Fernwood.

Spivak, Gayatri Chakravorty. 1988. 'Can the subaltern speak?' Pp. 271–313 in *Marxism and the Interpretation of Culture*, edited by C. Nelson and L. Grossberg. Urbana, Ill.: University of Illinois Press.

Staggenborg, Suzanne. 1994. *The Pro-Choice Movement: Organization and Activism in the Abortion Conflict*. New York: Oxford University Press.

Staggenborg, Suzanne. 2008. *Social Movements*. Don Mills, Ont.: Oxford University Press.

Stanbridge, Karen. 1994. 'The French-Canadian bourgeois debate: History and the ideology of colonialism'. *International Journal of Comparative Race and Ethnic Studies* 1 (1): 127–33.

Stanbridge, Karen. 1997. 'England, France and their North American colonies: An analysis of absolutist state power in Europe and the New World'. *Journal of Historical Sociology* 10 (1): 27–55.

Stanbridge, Karen. 2002. 'Master frames, political opportunities and self-determination: The Åland Islands in the post-WWI period'. *Sociological Quarterly* 43 (4): 527–52.

Stanbridge, Karen. 2003a. *Toleration and State Institutions: British Policy Toward Catholics in Eighteenth-Century Ireland and Quebec*. Lanham, Md.: Lexington Books.

Stanbridge, Karen. 2003b. 'Quebec and the Irish Catholic Relief Act of 1778: An institutional approach'. *Journal of Historical Sociology* 16 (3): 375–404.

Stanbridge, Karen. 2005. 'Nationalism, international factors, and the 'Irish Question' in the era of the First World War'. *Nations and Nationalism*, 11 (1): 21–42.

Stanbridge, Karen. 2007. 'Framing children in the Newfoundland Confederation debate, 1948'. *Canadian Journal of Sociology* 32 (2): 177–201.

Stanbridge, Karen. 2008. 'Childhood as cognition, or taking Philippe Ariès at his word'. *Kasvatus & Aika* (Childhood and history) 4. http://www.kasvatus-ja-aika.fi/site/?lan=1&page_id=158.

Stanbridge, Karen. 2011. 'Do nationalists have navels? Where is childhood in mainstream nationalism theory?' Pp. 39–59 in *Against Orthodoxy: Studies in Nationalism*, edited by T.W. Harrison and S. Drakulic. Vancouver: University of British Columbia Press.

Stanbridge, Karen, and J. Scott Kenney. 2009. 'Emotions and the campaign for victims' rights in Canada'. *Canadian Journal of Criminology and Criminal Justice* 51 (4): 473–509.

Stanford, Jim. 2009. 'What's your hourly labour cost? On average, our auto workers are paid $35 an hour, not $75.' *CCPA Monitor* 16(2).

Statistics Canada. 2006a. 'Women in Canada'. *The Daily*, 7 Mar. http://www.statcan.gc.ca/daily-quotidien/060307/dq060307a-eng.htm. Accessed 4 Aug., 2011.

Statistics Canada. 2006b. 'General Social Survey: Paid and Unpaid Work.' *The Daily*, 19 July. http://www.statcan.gc.ca/daily-quotidien/060719/dq060719b-eng.htm. Accessed 4 Aug., 2011.

Statistics Canada. 2010. 'Canadian Internet use survey'. *The Daily*, 10 May. http://www.statcan.gc.ca/daily-quotidien/100510/dq100510a-eng.htm. Accessed 9 Aug., 2011.

Statistics Canada. 2011. 'Labour Forces Characteristics by Sex and Age Group'. *Summary Tables*. CANSIM, table 282–0002. http://www40.statcan.ca/l01/cst01/labor05-eng.htm. Accessed 4 Aug., 2011.

Steinmetz, George. 2005. 'Return to empire: The new U.S. imperialism in comparative historical perspective'. *Sociological Theory* 23 (4): 339–67.

Steinmo, Sven, Kathleen Thelen, and Frank Longstreth (eds). 1992. *Structuring Politics: Historical Institutionalism in Comparative Analysis*. New York: Cambridge University Press.

Stoddart, Mark C.J. 2011. 'Grizzlies and gondolas: Animals and the meaning of skiing landscapes in British Columbia, Canada'. *Nature and Culture* 6 (1): 41–63.

Stoddart, Mark C.J. Forthcoming. *Making Meaning out of Mountains: The Political Ecology of Skiing.* Vancouver: University of British Columbia Press.

Street, Brian V. 1995. *Social Literacies: Critical Approaches to Literacy in Development, Ethnography and Education.* London: Longman.

Tabuchi, Hiroko. 2009. 'In Japan, machines for work and play are idle.' *New York Times.* 12 July. http://www.nytimes.com/2009/07/13/technology/13robot.html. Accessed 9 Aug., 2011.

Tarrow, Sidney. 1988. 'National politics and collective action: Recent theory and research in Western Europe and the United States'. *Annual Review of Sociology* 14: 421–40.

Tarrow, Sidney. 1989. *Democracy and Disorder: Protest and Politics in Italy, 1965–1975.* Oxford: Clarendon Press.

Tarrow, Sidney. 1998. *Power in Movement: Social Movements and Contentious Politics.* New York: Cambridge University Press.

Tarrow, Sidney. 2005. *The New Transnational Activism.* New York: Cambridge University Press.

Tarrow, Sidney, and Charles Tilly. 2006. *Contentious Politics.* Boulder, Colo.: Paradigm.

Taylor, Charles. 1992. *Multiculturalism and 'the Politics of Recognition': An Essay.* Princeton: Princeton University Press.

Theberge, Nancy. 2000. *Higher Goals: Women's Ice Hockey and the Politics of Gender.* Albany: State University of New York Press.

Theberge, Nancy. 2008. '"It's part of the game": 'Physicality and the production of gender in women's hockey'. Pp. 121–130 in *The Gendered Society Reader* (Canadian edn), edited by Michael S. Kimmel, Amy Aronson, and Amy Kaler. Don Mills, Ont.: Oxford University Press.

Tilly, Charles. 1964. *The Vendée.* Cambridge, Mass.: Harvard University Press.

Tilly, Charles. 1978. *From Mobilization to Revolution.* Reading, Mass.: Addison/Wesley.

Tilly, Charles. 1986. *The Contentious French.* Cambridge, Mass: Harvard University Press.

Tilly. Charles. 1995. *Popular Contention in Great Britain, 1758–1834.* Cambridge, Mass.: Harvard University Press.

Tilly, Charles. 2004. *Social Movements, 1768–2004.* Boulder, Colo.: Paradigm.

Tilly, Charles. 2006. *Why? What Happens When People Give Reasons . . . And Why.* Princeton, NJ: Princeton University Press.

Tilly, Charles 2007. *Democracy.* New York: Cambridge University Press.

Tilly, Charles. 2008. *Contentious Performances.* New York: Cambridge University Press.

Tindall, David B. 2002. 'Social networks, identification, and participation in an environmental movement: Low-medium cost activism within the British Columbia wilderness preservation movement'. *Canadian Review of Sociology and Anthropology* 39 (4): 413–52.

Tindall, David B. 2003. 'Social values and the contingent nature of public opinion and attitudes about forests'. *Forestry Chronicle* 79 (3): 692–705.

Touraine, Alain. 2003. 'Sociology without Societies'. *Current Sociology* 51 (2): 123–31.

Turmel, André. 2008. *A Historical Sociology of Childhood: Developmental Thinking, Categorization, and Graphic Visualization.* New York: Cambridge University Press.

United Nations. 2005. *History of the United Nations* E.04.1.7. United Nations Publications. http://www.un.org/aboutun/unhistory/. Accessed 31 Aug., 2011.

United Nations. 2010a. *Cyber School Bus: Briefing Papers for Students.* http://www.un.org/cyberschoolbus/briefing/globalization/gbprogress.htm. Accessed 9 Aug., 2011.

United Nations. 2010b. *Membership of Principal United Nations Organs in 2010.*

United Nations. 2010c. *We Can End Poverty 2015: Millennium Goals.* http://www.un.org/millenniumgoals/pdf/MDG_FS_1_EN.pdf. Accessed 28 Oct., 2011.

Urmetzer, Peter. 2005. *Globalization Unplugged: Sovereignty and the Canadian State in the Twenty-First Century.* Toronto: University of Toronto Press.

Urry, John. 2000. *Sociology beyond Societies: Mobilities for the Twenty-First Century.* London: Routledge .

Urry, John. 2002. *The Tourist Gaze.* Thousand Oaks, Calif.: Sage.

Urry, John. 2007. *Mobilities.* London: Polity Press.

Ursel, Jane. 1986. 'The state and the maintenance of patriarchy: A case study of family, labour and welfare legislation in Canada'. Pp. 150–91 in *Family, Economy, and the State,* edited by J. Dickinson and B. Russell. Toronto: Garamond.

Valderrama, Fernando. 1995. *A History of UNESCO.* Paris: UNESCO Publishing.

Vallières, Pierre. 1967. *Nègres blancs d'Amérique.* Montreal: Parti pris.

Van Dyke, Nella, and Sarah A. Soule. 2002. 'Structural social change and the mobilizing effect of threat: Explaining levels of patriot and militia organizing in the United States'. *Social Problems.* 49 (4): 497–520.

VanderPlaat, Madine, Howard Ramos, and Yoko Yoshida. 2009. *A Preliminary Investigation of the Contributions of Sponsored Parents and Grandparents in Canada.* Atlantic Metropolis Centre Working Paper No. 25.: Atlantic Metropolis Centre.

Veenstra, Garry. 2007. 'Who the heck is Don Bradman? Sport culture and social class in British Columbia, Canada'. *Canadian Review of Sociology and Anthropology* 44 (3): 319–43.

Wallerstein, Immanuel. 1974. *The Modern World-System, Vol. 1: Capitalist Agriculture and the Origins of the European World-Economy in the Sixteenth Century.* New York: Academic Press.

Wanner, Richard A. 2005. 'Twentieth-Century Trends in Occupational Attainment in Canada'. *Canadian Journal of Sociology* 30 (4): 441–69.

Warren, Jean-Philippe. 2009. 'Quebec: A sociological overview regional chapter'. In *Sociology: The Points of the Compass*, edited by R.J. Brym and J. Lie. Toronto: Nelson.

Waring, Marilyn. 1990. *If Women Counted: A New Feminist Economics.* San Franciso: HarperCollins.

Waters, Malcolm. 1995. *Globalization: Key Ideas.* London: Routledge.

Watkins, Mel. 2007. 'Staples redux'. *Studies in Political Economy* 79 (Spring): 213–26.

Watkins, Melville H. 1963. 'A staple theory of economic growth'. *Canadian Journal of Economics and Political Science* 29 (2): 141–58.

Watson, Alexander John. 2006. *Marginal Man: The Dark Vision of Harold Innis.* Toronto: University of Toronto Press.

Watson, James L. (ed.). 1997. *Golden Arches East: McDonald's in East Asia.* Stanford, Calif.: Stanford University Press.

Weber, Max. 1946. *From Max Weber: Essays in Sociology.* Translated by H.H. Gerth, and C.W. Mills. New York: Oxford University Press.

Weber, Max. 1968. *Economy and Society*, Vol. 1, edited by G. Roth and C. Wittich. Berkley, Calif.: University of California Press.

Weber, Max. [1920] 1997. *The Theory of Social and Economic Organization.* Edited with an Introduction by Talcott Parsons. New York: Free Press.

Weiner, Eric. 2008. 'Slum visits: Tourism or voyeurism?' *New York Times*, 12 Mar. http://www.nytimes.com/2008/03/12/travel/12iht-14heads.10986274.html. Accessed 25 Apr., 2011.

White, D. Steven, Angappa Gunasekaran, Timothy Shea, and Godwin Ariguzo. 2011. 'Mapping the global digital divide'. *International Journal of Business Information Systems.* http://ssrn.com/abstract=1436167. Accessed 31 Aug., 2011.

Wilkes, Rima. 2004. 'First Nation Politics: Deprivation, Resources and Participation in Collective Action'. *Sociological Inquiry* 74 (4): 570–89.

Wilkes, Rima. 2006. 'The protest actions of indigenous peoples: A Canadian-US comparison of social movement emergence'. *American Behavioral Scientist* 50 (4): 510–25.

Wilkes, Rima, and Danielle Ricard. 2005. 'How does newspaper coverage of collective action vary? Protest by indigenous people in Canada'. *Social Science Journal* 44 (2): 231–51.

Wright, Erik Olin. 1985. *Classes.* London: Verso.

Wright, Erik Olin. 1989. 'The comparative project on class structure and class consciousness: An overview'. *Acta Sociologica* 32 (1): 3–22.

Wright, Erik Olin. 1998. *The Debate on Classes.* London: Verso.

York, Geoffrey, and Loreen Pindera. 1991. *People of the Pines: The Warriors and the Legacy of Oka.* Boston: Little, Brown.

Index